To the Arab Youth

The Arab
Military Option

THE ARAB MILITARY OPTION

General Saad El-Shazly

AMERICAN MIDEAST RESEARCH • San Francisco

ST. PHILIP'S COLLEGE LIBRARY

© Copyright 1986, American Mideast Research,
All Rights Reserved.

First Edition

American Mideast Publishing
3315 Sacramento Street, Suite 511
San Francisco, California 94118

Also by General El-Shazly in English:
THE CROSSING OF THE SUEZ

THE ARAB MILITARY OPTION: $26.

THE CROSSING OF THE SUEZ: $20.

Single copies can be mail ordered for the list price plus $2. for postage and handling
from the above address. Check should be made payable to American Mideast Research.
Quantity discounts available. Write to the above address for information, or contact
your local bookstore or distributor.

Library of Congress Cataloging-in-Publication Data

Shazly, Saad El.
  The Arab military option.

  Bibliography: p.
  Includes index.
    1. Jewish-Arab relations—1973– . 2. Near East-
Politics and government—1945– . 3. Arab countries
—Military policy. I. Title.
DS119.7.S3819   1986   956′.048   85-30653

ISBN 0-9604562-1-X

Contents

Tables

The source for all military tables is General Saad El Shazly unless otherwise indicated.

Introduction

"The military option" is a phrase new in Arab language and Arab thinking. Until Anwar Sadat's journey to Jerusalem on 19 November 1977, the Arabs talked of only one way to recapture their lands occupied by Israel. That was war. Yet war was not seen as the military option: it was perceived as the only option; there was no other. Sadat overturned that conviction. The peace talks he initiated with the Israeli Prime Minister Menachem Begin led, under the auspices of the United States, to the initial signing of the Camp David agreement by those three parties on 17 September 1978. In the face of intense criticism throughout the Arab world, Sadat, by the terms of that agreement, explicitly rejected war as an option in resolving the disputes between Egypt and Israel. Sadat gave as his reason the cost of war: the Egyptian economy, he said, could no longer bear such a burden.

Desperate to prevent the final signing of the Camp David agreement—and concerned to undercut Sadat's claim that the deterioration of the Egyptian economy was the main cause of this peace agreement with Israel—the Arab summit met in Baghdad on 3 November 1978. The leaders decided that if Egypt rejected the Camp David accords, the rest of the Arab world would support Egypt's economy to the tune of 50 billion dollars over a period of ten years. Sadat refused the offer, demonstrating to many that the state of Egypt's economy was not in fact the main reason behind his move towards Israel.

Shortly after the final signing of the Camp David agreement, 18 Arab countries severed diplomatic relations with Egypt. This, in April 1979, marks the high point in Arab rejection of any but the military option as a means of settling their dispute with Israel. Resolve did not last. Israel's invasion of Lebanon in June 1982 demonstrated once again the Arabs' military and political weaknesses, and the corridors of several Arab capitals began to rustle with seductive whispers. The Arabs, it was murmured, had no apparent option but to reach the best settlement they could with Israel by negotiation.

Duly, in September 1982, the Arab summit met in Morocco and agreed upon an eight-point peace plan. It came to be known as the Fez Plan—and 19 Arab countries, together with the PLO, approved it. (Libya refused to attend the Fez summit, on the grounds that the Fez Plan did not meet minimum Arab demands. Egypt did not attend because, after Sadat's peace treaty with Israel, Egypt's membership in the Arab League had been suspended.)

Since the great majority of Arab leaders supported it, the Fez Plan had without question the status of the official Arab plan for a peaceful settlement with Israel. It differed markedly from the Reagan Plan, the European Plan, the so-called Egyptian-French Plan—all the other "plans" for peace in the region. It is important to make those points, in view of what was to happen.

The Fez summit appointed a committee of seven members to explain the Fez Plan to the outside world in general and, in particular, to those countries with permanent membership in the U.N. Security Council. But when this committee toured Europe and America, some of its members were quoted as having praised the Reagan Plan rather more than the Fez Plan they were supposed to be advocating. There are two possible explanations for this. One is that the Western media deliberately distorted what those Arab leaders were saying. The other is that some Arab countries approved the Fez Plan merely as a facade behind which they could covertly support the Reagan Plan. The latter is, in my view, the more plausible theory.

The architects of the Egypt-Israel peace treaty hoped that Egypt would, by the power of its example, persuade other Arab countries to follow in concluding similar treaties with Israel. But, initially at least, the Arabs were adamant; and President Sadat, signatory to the treaty, was assassinated on 6 October 1981. The advocates of the Camp David approach tried to capitalise even on this, to create a climate of sympathy within which Sadat's successor, Hosni Mubarak, could invite other Arab countries to re-establish diplomatic and economic links with Egypt—while Egypt, of course, continued to honour its treaty with Israel. For Mubarak was as insistent as his predecessor that Egypt would stand by the Camp David treaty; that the Arabs should reach a similar agreement with Israel by negotiation; and that for the Arabs the military option was now impossible.

Officially, these ideas were rejected by virtually all the Arab world. But the meeting of the PLO leader Yassir Arafat with Mubarak in

Cairo on 22 December 1983 showed, like a weather vane, the changing direction of the winds now blowing across the Middle East. In his criticisms of Camp David, Arafat had been the most extreme of any Arab leader. The Egyptian regime was guilty of treason, he said; and when Sadat was assassinated, no group cheered more loudly than the PLO. Nor did Arafat change his mind when Mubarak took over: the suspension of Egypt from the Arab League must stand, he said, so long as Egypt bound itself to the Camp David treaty. All changed when Arafat met Mubarak. Within days Arafat was saying that Egypt should, after all, be allowed to return to the Arab League without pre-conditions. Mubarak, he explained, had not been responsible for the Camp David treaty. In short, everything Arafat said after his meeting with Mubarak flatly contradicted his statements before the visit. Nor was Arafat's shift confined to words. When the Moslem summit met in Casablanca in January 1984— Egypt had been suspended from the Moslem conference too—the meeting adopted a resolution to restore Egypt's membership. It passed thanks to Arafat's enthusiastic support.

This shift in Arafat's attitude has had far-reaching consequences. Several Arab or Moslem regimes had privately wanted to support, even join, the Camp David process but had seen no way of publicly declaring this. Now they could pose the classic question: "Why should we be more royalist than the king?" The PLO had been the most bitter foe of the Egyptian regime because of its treaty with Israel. Now Arafat was shaking hands with Egypt without insisting that the treaty be denounced. Why should other Arabs hold out? Talk of the political option had steadily grown. Some even say, and write, that the military option is now impossible.

The object of this book is to demonstrate that the military option is possible. The military data in this book are drawn from public sources, in particular from the following publications: *The Military Balance, Strategic Survey, Survival and Adelphi Papers* (all published by the International Institute for Strategic Studies in London); the Jane's volumes, *All the World's Aircraft, Fighting Ships, Armour and Artillery,* and *Weapons Systems* (all published in London); and the publications of the Stockholm International Peace Research Institute. The conclusions I draw from a study of these data are my own responsibility. (A word about method. In assessing relative force levels, I have eliminated from the calculations much old or obsolete equipment; and I have re-classified some new equipment in the light of its characteristics and my judgment of its capability to meet the demands of modern war. For example, I have eliminated from the force levels all combat aircraft more than 30 years old; all combat aircraft of limited capabilities, such as the Magister and the MiG-15; and all light tanks such as the AMX-13 and T-76. Modern combat aircraft I have grouped into front-line and second-line forces according to their speed.)

In demonstrating that the Arab military option is possible, I do not contend that it is necessarily the preferable option—nor that it is the only option. But I do insist that it must never be excluded as a possible option, and that the Arabs must work to give it reality. If the Fez Plan for political resolution of the dispute with Israel is to get anywhere, the military option must march beside it. The Arabs must understand that it is idle to believe they can persuade Israel to give up in negotiation what they cannot compel Israel to cede in battle.

General Saad El-Shazly

The Arab
Military Option

1

Israel

The Israeli Mind

Power Politics and the Jewish State

Israel is unique. It was created to serve the ends of one empire; it survives as the creature of another. Many nations have histories distorted by the imperial experience; Israel alone has a history which is nothing but the imperial experience. Externally, the forces which created and now sustain it have been those of empire—first the British Empire, now the American. Internally, the history of Israel has been that of an imperial drive by a settler people to dispossess and expel the native inhabitants of a conquered land. Israeli thinking today is shaped and suffused by that history. All empires are racist: racism is inseparable from the imperial mission: the mythos of a superior people fulfilling some higher purpose by conquering another people and land. When, as in the case of the Jews and Israel, the people are God's chosen people—an exclusive group defined by consanguinity—colonising a "Promised Land," the racist element is dominant. When, on 10 November 1975, the United Nations General Assembly adopted Resolution 3379 declaring Zionism a form of racism, it was significant how anxious Western nations were to condemn it without analysis. (The resolution was supported by 72 nations, opposed by 35, with 32 abstentions. The USA, Canada, and Western Europe were among those opposing the resolution. The Eastern Bloc, most Third World countries, and the Arab nations supported the resolution.) The history of Israel explains the thinking of modern Israelis; both history and thinking warrant the epithet "racist."

The founder of the Zionist movement to establish a Jewish homeland was Theodor Herzl. Herzl's thinking, as laid out in his book *The Jewish State* and described in numerous biographies, can

be summarised like this:
- Jews throughout the world are one nation. They must reject assimilation into other nations.
- A Jewish state must be created, as the focus and refuge of this Jewish nation.

Where this Jewish state should be established was not of great importance to Herzl. He thought first of Palestine, but his approaches were rejected by the Sultan of the Ottoman Empire, which then ruled the area. So, pragmatically, Herzl turned to Britain, which offered him Uganda. Herzl and several of his colleagues in the Zionist movement were quite ready to accept this: only violent opposition at the 1903 Zionist Congress, particularly from Russian Jews, dissuaded Herzl.

Palestine was Herzl's first choice as a potential Jewish state partly for its biblical connotations, but mainly because Herzl realised that such a plan would suit British imperial strategy in the area, a strategy going back more than 60 years. Ever since the resurgence of modern Egypt under Mohammed Ali in 1820–1840, the British had been alarmed lest Egyptian expansion eastward round the Mediterranean coast lead to the creation of an independent Arab empire, which in turn would bring the collapse of the Ottoman empire and the ending of British influence in the area. The British solution was to create an alien buffer state between Egypt and its neighbours to the east—a buffer state in Palestine. And the alien people who would populate this European outpost against Arab independence were to be the Jews. As early as 11 August 1840, Lord Palmerston, British foreign secretary and later prime minister, wrote to the British ambassador to the High Porte in Istanbul instructing him to press for the creation of a Jewish state in Palestine. Many Jews wanted to return to Palestine, Palmerston wrote, and if their return were permitted by the Sultan then the resulting Jewish nation would stand as an obstacle in the path of any ambitions of Mohammed Ali's successors. A week later *The Times* reported that the creation of a Jewish state in their ancestral land was now the subject of serious official study.

The Ottoman Sultan proved immune to pressure and temptation alike: he would not agree to a Jewish state. But the British did not abandon the plan. When the Liberals came to power in 1874, Disraeli approached the Sultan again. Disraeli's project was to settle Jews in Palestine under cover of an agrarian investment company—which would have enjoyed a near-sovereign independence. This project, too, was rejected by the High Porte.

When Britian occupied Egypt in 1882, the project for a Jewish state lost its immediate *raison d'être*. Even so, successive British governments kept it in mind. They consented, for example, to the establishment of Jewish settlements in the Sinai. (That project failed for two reasons. The High Porte, unhappy at the British presence in Egypt, tried to strip the Sinai from Egypt and place it under Ottoman administration in Syria. Control of the Sinai was only resolved in Egypt's favour in 1906. The other reason was that the Jews themselves disliked the Sinai desert; it reminded them of the wilderness years after their ancestors' exodus from Egypt 3000 years before.)

There can be no doubt, in other words, that the creation of a Jewish state in Palestine was a British project, devised to serve British imperial ends, some twenty years before Theodor Herzl was born and 56 years before he published his seminal work, *The Jewish State,* in Vienna in February 1896. And Herzl knew this. From the start, Herzl foresaw a marriage of convenience between his Zionist movement and the British Empire. (To the question whether Britian's offer of Uganda did not signal the end of that old imperial goal in the Middle East, my reply—based on some years experience with politicians —is that while Herzl may have taken it seriously, I do not think the British Government did. To my mind, it was one of those offers politicians make in the knowledge that it need never be fulfilled.)

That Britain never abandoned Palmerston's plan is demonstrated by the dramatic changes in Palestine after the British occupation of 1917. Jewish immigration to Palestine raised the Jewish population there from 65,671 in 1918 to 649,632 in 1948—a tenfold increase in one generation. And the British conceded some of the trappings of statehood: the Jews were allowed to form their own militia, and they enjoyed a good deal of independence in the running of their internal affairs. By the eve of that fateful date in the calendar of the Middle East, 15 May 1948, the Jews had been allowed to construct all the building blocks of a Jewish state: an organised community; an army; hundreds of settlements; scores of factories. In short, whatever doubts or hesitations may have been expressed by successive British governments in London, the reality on the ground was that the British occupation of Palestine was so run that the Jewish community there was able to develop—and then proclaim—an independent Jewish state.

It was independence of a peculiarly dependent kind, however. The turning point in the history of Israel was the historic shift in the alle-

ST. PHILIP'S COLLEGE LIBRARY.

giance of its leaders after World War Two. In Herzl's time, the British Empire was the most powerful in the world: he attached the Zionist movement to it. But after World War Two, the United States emerged as the dominant global superpower: the leaders of Israel promptly switched and sought protection now by allying Israel to the American cause. It was an easy transition. American strategy in the region, it soon emerged, was no different from the old British imperial design. America wanted a Jewish state in the heart of the region for precisely the same reason Palmerston had wanted it. The United States' support for Israel will be discussed in detail in the next chapter; what is relevant here is that it is *only* American support which enables Israel to survive. In the most literal sense, Israel, born of one empire, is now the creature of another. And the Jews in Israel—indeed, Jews all over the world—know this. They know that Israel is the product of power politics, and survives now to satisfy power politics. This is not in any sense to minimise the efforts of the Jews themselves first to create their state, then to maintain its survival. The point is that those efforts, however remarkable, could never have succeeded had the Jews of Israel not attached themselves—allied themselves and their nation's policies—to the most influential power of the time: Britain their ally in the creation of the state, America the ally to ensure its survival. The skill with which Israel's founders took such advantage of the shifts and accidents of history is impressive. The consequences within Israel have been disastrous.

A Chosen People in a Promised Land

Among nations as among plants, an ecology is to be seen. As plants adjust to each other to form a self-regulating environment, so in time do nations. The process of adjustment may be halted at times—as, for example, the power blocs dividing Europe have frozen the historical evolution there for a generation. But eventually the process reasserts itself. Not so in Israel. Great-power protection absolves Israel from the normal duties of prudent statecraft—above all, the need to establish a *modus vivendi* with one's neighbours. Because of its imperial role—its birth and being as an avowed outpost of European power in the heart of the Arab world—Israel cannot come to terms with its neighbours. The only relationship Israel can have with the Arabs is that of denial, conquest, and subjugation. That is why it is there.

To this alienation of function add the exclusivity conferred by the Jews' own view of the mission of Israel: the result is a potent brew. For Israel, like all nations, has needed to construct legends about its birth. Israel has three. The first is religious: Israel as the fulfillment of some divine promise. The second is the myth of the empty land: Palestine was a desert which the Jews won—by extension, "deserve" —because they made the desert bloom. The third legend is the vision of Israel as place of refuge for the survivors of Hitler's persecutions.

Divine Promise

The religious claim was never a dominant feature of the Zionist movement. Only after the creation of the State of Israel did it come to the fore—and then mainly for demographic reasons. The Zionist movement was largely the work of Ashkenazi Jews, from central Europe and eastwards. The Ashkenazi were the first to settle in Israel: the leaders were the ruling group; the Ashkenazi were the backbone of the early state. But into Isreal since then have come such thousands of Sephardi Jews—Jews from the Mediterranean basin and from the Middle and Far East—that the Sephardi are now the majority tribe. Tensions between the two groups, polarised as the haves-versus-the-have-nots, are now a determining factor in Israeli politics: the power base of the Likud party is to be found in the resentments of the Sephardi. With the rise of the Sephardi has come a surge in Ortho-dox and Ultra-Orthodox—which is to say, extremist—religious tendencies.

To these Believers, a Jewish state with Jerusalem as its capital is the fulfillment of a promise made by God. By definition, God's will is non-negotiable. The only argument is about the issue God seems to have left unaccountably hazy: the exact boundaries of this Promised Land. The least intransigent of the Orthodox believe the state should cover the whole of Palestine—as conveniently defined under the Brit-ish mandate of 1919–1948—plus Jordan, the southern parts of Syria, and the south of Lebanon up to and including the Litani River. At the other extreme are those who assert that God has something altogether more expansive in mind for Israel: a state stretching from the Nile in the west to the Euphrates in the east, and from the Turkish border in the north to a southern frontier at Elmadina in Saudi Arabia, the resting place of the Prophet Mohammed. In between come the compromisers, who restrict their ambitions to a Greater Israel incorporating Sinai, Lebanon, and Syrian territory as far east as Homs.

In another, more stable society, such ambitions could be dismissed as fantasy: nasty, verging on madness, but of no consequence. In Israel these dreams are dreamed by a politically significant fraction of the populace. The Divine Right to a land has swollen into a God-given claim to empire—with the other imperial ingredient, racial superiority, now openly asserted. We do not need to rely upon outside sources or commentators to demonstrate this: not the least of the virtues of *In The Land of Israel* is that its author, the writer Amos Oz, is a Jew and an Israeli citizen—and is therefore immune to the charge of anti-Semitism routinely flung at all who criticise Israel. Oz records his interviews with Jewish settlers on the West Bank of the Jordan. One couple comprised a husband of Yemeni origin, still holding a British passport, married to a woman of American origin, still holding an American passport. Hear what these new Israelis said.

Harriet, the wife: "In the Six-Day War and the Yom Kippur War too we should never have stopped. We should have gone on, brought them to total surrender. Smashed their capital cities. This is a religious war. A holy war against all of Islam. They must realise that this land belongs to the Jews and that they live under our sovereignty and do the dirty work for us. Isn't that the way it is in the Bible? Weren't they hewers of wood and carriers of water? Whenever we gave in to them we had trouble. That is the way it was in the Bible. King Saul lost his whole kingdom because he took pity on Amalek. The goyim are bound to be against us. It's their nature. Sometimes it's because of their religion, sometimes it's out of ideology, sometimes it's out of anti-semitism, but actually it's all God's will. It's them [the Arabs] or us."

Menachem, the husband: "I am much more extreme than Harriet, but I actually do see a good possibility of living with the Arabs in friendship—as soon as they realise they are here through our mercy and not by right. I talk Arabic really well; my family is from Aden. The Arab's not a war monger. He just has to know very clearly what his place is."

For most nations, international opinion would act as a restraint upon the freedom to fulfill such dreams. Not Israel, as Amos Oz's interview with the man he calls Mr Z indicates:

"Call it Judeo-Nazi, the way Professor Liebowitz did. Why not? Harry Truman killed half a million Japs with two sweet bombs. I want to be smarter, more clever and more efficient. I want Israel to be a member of this club. Maybe the world will finally begin to fear me instead of feeling sorry for me. Maybe they'll start quaking in fear of my whims instead of admiring my nobility. Let them quake. Let them call us a mad-dog nation. Let them realise that we're a wild country, deadly and dangerous to everyone around, awful, crazy, capable of suddenly going nuts because they murdered one of our kids—even one—and running wild and burning all the oil fields in the Middle East.

"Had our forefathers come here in time and wiped out six million Arabs, or only one million: what would have happened? Sure, the world would have written a couple of nasty pages about us in the history books; they would have called us all kinds of names; but we would have been a nation of 25 million people here today. Pretty respectable, don't you think? And our authors would write elegant novels, like Günter Grass and Heinrich Böll, about our collective guilt and collect a couple of Nobel prizes for literature and morality. Maybe the government would have paid the Arabs we didn't manage to kill some reparations from the oil revenues in Iraq. But the people of Israel would be sitting on its land. From the Suez canal all the way to the oilfields. And believe me, in spite of our crimes, all those bastards would be courting us, propositioning us and sucking up to us.

"One direct bonus of the war in Israel is that the gentiles now and always are sickened by the *zhids* [that is, Jewish "Uncle Toms" living outside Israel] and their consciences. Then the Jewish people will have only one option left: to come home and soon. If anyone raises a hand against us, we'll just take away half his land for good and burn the other half. Including the oil. Including the nuclear weapons. Until they have lost all desire to make trouble for us. And after that peace will reign in the land for forty years or more.

"Listen, even today I'm willing to volunteer to do the dirty work for the people of Israel: to kill as many Arabs as it takes, to deport, to expel, to burn, to see that they hate us, to put a torch to the ground under the feet of the *zhids* in the Diaspora, so they'll be forced to come running here whining. Even if I have to blow up a few synagogues here and there to get the job done. Then you can bring me before a Nuremberg Tribunal and hang me as a war criminal if you like. Then you can carefully launder your Jewish conscience in bleach and join the respectable club of civilised nations."

If Mr. Z does, as Amos Oz claims, exist and say such things, he is clearly a monster. For myself, I suspect Mr. Z is one of the more famous figures in the leadership of the Likud party. But what matters beyond the question of his identity—individual or collective—is that thoughts and attitudes very like Mr. Z's demonstrably infect Israeli political leaders such as Begin, Shamir and Sharon. "Is it possible," Oz asks in his remarkable book, "that Hitler not only killed the Jews but also infected them with his poison? Did that same venom in fact seep into some hearts, and does it continue to seep out from there?" To glimpse the answer, consider the careers of three leaders of the Likud bloc.

Menachem Begin

Begin is a terrorist. That is a statement about his personality as much as his career. It was Begin who led the infamous attack on the Arab village of Deir Yassin on 9 April 1948. It was Begin whom David Ben Gurion—one of Israel's founding fathers and its first prime minister—described, in a letter to a colleague in 1963, as a "Hitlerite type." The verdict was shared by others. On the occasion of Begin's first visit to the United States, a group of prominent American Jews—among them Albert Einstein—wrote a letter to the *New York Times* on 4 December 1948 in which they said: "It is inconceivable that those who oppose fascism around the world would support Mr. Begin if they knew the truth about his activities and the outlook of his political movement. He is the leader of a political party very close to the Nazi and fascist parties in its organisation, its methods, its political philosophy, and in the class it addresses. Its members are drawn from the old Irgun Zvai Leumi, a nationalist terrorist organisation of the extreme Right in Palestine. On 9 April 1948, Begin and his terrorist partisans attacked the village of Deir Yassin, a peaceful community which constituted no military objective, and killed almost its entire population. The facts about this incident should be known in this country. . . . Consequently, the signatories now ask all those involved not to support this last manifestation of fascism."

That was Begin the terrorist. Was Begin the prime minister from May 1977 to August 1983 so different? In his report to the Knesset on 28 December 1977, Begin outlined his proposals for the occupied West Bank and the Gaza Strip. Its main points were:

- The creation of an administrative council composed of 11 members elected by the inhabitants of the region;
- This council to administer education, religious affairs, finance, transportation, construction and housing, industry, commerce and tourism, agriculture, health, labour and social welfare, care of refugees, the department of justice, and the supervision of local police forces;
- Security and public order in the areas of Judea, Samaria (Israeli definition for the West Bank of Jordan), and Gaza to be the responsibility of the Israeli authorities;
- Residents of Israel to have the right to acquire land and settle in Judea, Samaria, and Gaza;
- Israel reasserts its claim to sovereignty over Judea, Samaria, and Gaza. But, recognising that other claims exist, it proposes that the issue be left open;
- These principles to be subject to review after five years.

Those were Begin's political proposals, and they will be examined in detail later. If those were his words, what were Begin's deeds? While Begin was its prime minister, Israel invaded southern Lebanon on 14 March 1978; annexed east Jerusalem on 14 May 1980; carried out an air-raid to destroy the Iraqi nuclear plant on 7 June 1981; annexed the Golan Heights on 14 December 1981; and invaded Lebanon once more on 7 June 1982. The Israeli forces in Lebanon killed about 30,000 people, left another 9000 crippled for life, and made about one million people homeless. All that was Begin's doing.

The bombardment of Beirut by Israel's army and air force moved even some Israelis to protest. Only a few, though: active membership of the Israeli anti-war protest movement is put at no more than 3000. When a group of military reservists calling themselves "Soldiers Against Silence" demonstrated outside the prime minister's office, only 100 or so turned up. Even so, their impact was disproportionate to their numbers because many of the protesters were combat soldiers who had taken part in the invasion of Lebanon. And "Soldiers Against Silence" had direct knowledge of facts the Israeli government was anxious to conceal. In a report by the group, published on 10 August 1982, an air force pilot, Major Boge Emir, testified that the

Air Force had been given orders to bomb populated areas of Beirut and other towns and villages in Lebanon in revenge for Israeli casualties. Who else could have given such orders but Begin?

Begin shares responsibility with his defence minister, General Ariel Sharon, for the massacres of Palestinians at the Sabra and Shatila camps in Beirut. He tried to wash his hands of the affair by saying: "Goyim killed goyim. How could anybody blame us for that?"—a remark which itself reveals a good deal about the man. But as a defence, it lacks substance. Nor was he cleared by the committee of inquiry he himself was finally forced to set up, the Kahane Commission, which blamed Christian Phalangist militia for the killings but also laid some blame upon Sharon for not intervening in time to stop the massacres.

The military fact is that there was complete coordination between the Israeli army in Lebanon and the Christian militias of both the Phalangists in Beirut and Major Saad Haddad in southern Lebanon. Shortly after the assassination of the Lebanese President Beshir Gemayel, there was a meeting of senior officers of the Israeli army and those militias. Soon afterwards, Israeli troops moved in west Beirut to isolate the two Palestinian refugee camps. On their heels came the Phalangist militia. At the same time, Israeli transport aircraft were ferrying units of Haddad's militia into Beirut from the south. As darkness fell, the two militias began the attack on the camps —which the Israeli troops had surrounded to prevent those within from fleeing to safety. All night Israeli artillery fired flares over the camps to aid the militia in their hunt. The attackers had also been supplied with bulldozers and other heavy equipment by the Israelis. As the terrible scenes in the camps unfolded, the local Israeli commander overlooked events from his command post on top of a seven-storey building used by the United Nations less than 200 yards from the entrance to Sabra camp. That the Israelis controlled the whole area was never in doubt: not until two days after the massacres did the Israeli commander permit journalists to visit the scene. The journalists discovered that the bulldozers obligingly lent to the militia by the Israelis had dug a mass grave for the victims of the massacre *outside* the west wall of Sabra camp just 200 paces from the Israeli command post. The final toll at the camps is still uncertain. General Sharon talked of 700–800 Palestinian dead; PLO leader Yassir Arafat gave a total of 3297; neutral sources put the figure at 1000 dead or missing.

The point about the massacres at Sabra and Shatila is that they were not an aberration; they were the logical culmination of Begin's career, the logical product of his attitude towards Arabs. Begin's earliest mentor was Vladimir Jobotinsky, who preached that Jews had the right, the duty, to use force to regain the Promised Land. The thinking of Jabotinsky lay behind the actions of Irgun Zvai Leumi, the terrorist organisation Begin led from 1937–1948. Irgun's aim was to expel the Arabs from Palestine; their weapon was terror—terror provoked by killings. The massacre at Deir Yassin was no accident, any more than the slaughter at Sabra and Shatila was an accident. The butchering of Deir Yassin was a warning to other Palestinians of the fate awaiting them if they stayed in the new State of Israel. The killings at Sabra and Shatila were a warning to Palestinians of the fate awaiting them if they stayed in Lebanon. There is a political, as well as an intellectual, line between the two events as well. After the establishment of the State of Israel, all nationalist terrorist organisations were dissolved. Begin promptly formed a political party called Herut: its members were the alumni of Irgun Zvai Leumi. In September 1973, Begin managed to bring all the right-wing parties in Israel together into a coalition with Herut, the coalition being called the Likud. He was its head; and it was as its head that Begin became prime minister after the 1977 election. In the intervening 30 years, Begin never changed his mind. He remained convinced of the need to purge the Jewish state of its Arab inhabitants, to make room for the Jews newly arriving in Israel. To achieve this, he was willing to use all means at his command. He made no secret of those views. Which is the final point: a man like Amos Oz's "Mr Z" might be dismissed as a solitary madman; but Begin—whose views are really little different from those of Mr Z—was elected by a substantial proportion of the people of Israel. We have to conclude that they share his views.

Yitzhak Shamir

Shamir too is a terrorist: a disciple of Jabotinsky and a member of Irgun Zvai Leumi. But in 1940, the Irgun split; Shamir sided with the radical faction which rejected Begin's leadership and broke away to form a new group, the Lohamei Herut Yisrael (Lehi) or Israeli Freedom Fighters—better known as the Stern Gang after their leader Abraham Stern.

In their pursuit of a Jewish state, the Stern Gang was willing to deal with the Devil himself, as papers unearthed by the German historian Klaus Polken in the archives of the Third Reich reveal. In 1941, Stern actually proposed an alliance with Nazi Germany. His ideas were transmitted to the German naval attache in Ankara, who was responsible for the Nazis' special missions in the Middle East. In a letter of 11 January 1941, the attaché reported Stern's proposals to Berlin:

• Mass evacuation of the Jews from Europe is the only solution to the Jewish problem. But such evacuation would only be possible after the establishment of the Jewish state within its historic borders. That was the objective of Lohamei Herut Yisrael.

• There are thus common interests between the new Order established in Europe by Germany, and the aspirations of the Jewish people as represented by Lehi.

• An alliance between the Jewish state and the German Reich could contribute in the future to the maintenance and strengthening of the position of Germany in the Middle East.

As a senior member of the Stern Gang, Shamir shares responsibility for that appallingly cynical proposition. In the matter of the killing in Cairo in November 1944 of Lord Moyne, British minister of state for the Middle East, however, Shamir's responsibility is direct and personal: it was he who masterminded the assassination. Shamir's group was also responsible for the murder of Count Folke Bernadotte of Sweden, a United Nations representative, in Jerusalem in September 1948—Bernadotte's supposed "crime" being his assumed responsibility for a plan to partition Palestine between Arabs and Jews. To escape the British, Shamir had to flee to France, returning from a comfortable exile only after the establishment of the Jewish state.

In the service of that state, Shamir has remained unrelentingly aggressive. From 1955 to 1965, he worked for Mossad, the Israeli intelligence agency. As speaker of the Israeli Parliament in 1979, he abstained in the vote on the Camp David Treaty with Egypt. It was noticeable, in fact, that after he became foreign minister in 1980, though he followed Prime Minister Begin on key policy questions, Shamir's own attitude was often tougher even than Begin's. On 2 September 1983, after Begin had announced his decision to retire, Shamir was elected his successor as head of the Herut party. When he was duly sworn in as Israel's seventh prime minister on 10 October

1983, his first pledge was to follow the course charted by Begin in Lebanon and on the occupied West Bank. The impasse that course inevitably led to is indicated by the fact that Shamir lasted less than a year. Then he became foreign minister in a "government of national unity" under Shimon Peres, who was sworn in as eighth prime minister on 14 September 1984.

What of the views that underpinned Shamir's rise? One French political scientist has concluded: "The career of Mr. Shamir has always been marked by racism. His views about the world and about international relations are captured in an article he wrote in *Yediot Aharanot* on 14 November 1975, after the United Nations had passed a resolution noting Zionism as a form of racism. Shamir wrote: 'It is unacceptable that nations composed of people who until recently were living in the treetops should consider themselves fit leaders of the world. How could primitive people be expected to come to sensible judgement.... At all events, this insult from the United Nations should convince us yet again that we are a unique nation, set apart from other nations.'"

The political thinking legitimised by such racisim was set out in the spring of 1982 in an article Shamir wrote as foreign minister. Titled *Israel's Role in a Changing Middle East,* the article wove the following seamless argument:

- Between 1920 and 1950 Palestine was effectively partitioned. Palestinian Arabs now have exclusive domain over Trans-Jordan, or eastern Palestine. Palestinian Jews are the majority power in Cis-Jordan, comprising Israel within the pre-1967 armistice lines plus its later conquests—an area Shamir computes as 23 percent of the original Palestine. Thus the re-introduction of the term Palestinian and its application exclusively to the Arabs of Cis-Jordan is a semantic device for laying claim to the entire area of western Palestine and so undermining the legitimacy of Israel.
- Israel has consistently made it clear that it considers it has a legitimate claim to sovereignty over Judea, Samaria, and Gaza. However, to keep open the door to a solution acceptable to all parties— as envisaged at Camp David—Israel has deliberately refrained from exercising what it considers to be its rights under this claim.
- Undoubtedly, though, this claim will be presented again at the end of the five-year interim period. For their part, therefore, the Arabs should refrain from pushing now for the adoption of measures or even principles—such as self-determination, an embryonic Parlia-

ment in the occupied territories, and the like—that would fall clearly beyond the parameters of Camp David.

- As for a territorial settlement, Israel will entertain no thought of a return to the pre-1967 armistice lines or anything approximating to them. On this point there is in Israel virtually unanimous agreement.

- The very act of granting the Palestine Liberation Organisation (PLO) a status—any status—in the political negotiations would be self-defeating. It would elevate the PLO's standing from terrorist organisation to that of recognised aspirant to a totally illusory political entity. Hence, association of the PLO with any aspect of the political process and the prospects for peace are mutually exclusive.

- There is a similarly broad national consensus in Israel that the Golan Heights should under no circumstances return to Syria.

- Israel believes that any peace plan with the Arabs should include the following elements:

  a) Negotiations between Israel and each of its neighbours aimed at agreement on a just and lasting peace, laid down in formal peace treaties which would provide for the establishment of normal diplomatic, economic, and good neighbourly relations.

  b) Recognition of the sovereignty and political independence of all existing states in the region, and of their right to live in peace within secure and recognised boundaries, free from threats or acts of force including terrorist activity.

  c) Autonomy for the Arab inhabitants of Judea, Samaria, and the Gaza district for a five-year period, as set out in the Camp David accords, and deferment of the final determination of the status of these areas until the end of this transitional period.

  d) Restoration of the full independence of Lebanon through the withdrawal from Lebanese territory of all Syrian and PLO forces.

  e) Negotiations among all states of the region aimed at declaring the region a nuclear-weapon-free zone.

From that background of thought, word, and deed, Shamir emerges as a virtual clone of Begin. It would be idle to expect any change in the attitudes of the Herut party or of the Likud coalition under Shamir's leadership. It would be equally foolish to expect significant change in the direction Israel is heading so long as Yitzhak

Shamir is at the helm. Under the pact signed on 13 September 1984 by Shamir, as leader of the Likud, and Shimon Peres, as leader of the Labour party, Peres is to head this "Government of National Unity" first, with Shamir as vice-premier and minister of foreign affairs. After 25 months, Shamir takes over at the top. All in all, Shamir's influence will dominate Israel's relations with its neighbours for some years to come. The prospect invites no optimism.

General Ariel "Arik" Sharon

General Sharon has one supreme virtue. His record is so appalling that his entire career may be taken as lethal reproof to those who talk glibly of a political settlement with Israel. Sharon held high office only for a short time—he was minister of defence from August 1981 until February 1983. His departure, characteristically truculent, was forced by international opinion in the wake of the Sabra and Shatila massacres. The (temporary) end of Sharon's career was of a piece with its beginning. For thirty years Sharon has dreamed of two things: Israel the Superpower, and the cleansing of Arabs from the Promised Land.

It was surely not by accident that in August 1953 Moshe Dayan selected the young Sharon to create and command a special army group, Unit 101. The aim of the unit was to attack Arab villages and kill as many as possible of their inhabitants, so as to frighten the rest of the Arab population of Israel into flight. (A doctrine familiar from the career of Menachem Begin.) Sharon's first raid was on a small Arab village called Qibya on the night of 14/15 October 1953. Unit 101 killed 66 people that night, three quarters of them women and children. United Nations observers who arrived at Qibya two hours after Unit 101 withdrew reported that the corpses had been perforated with bullets while inside their houses; and bullet marks found on the doors and window frames of demolished houses suggested that their inhabitants had been forced by gunfire to shelter indoors until their homes were blown up on top of them. Survivors of the massacre were insistent that throughout this night of horror Israeli soldiers had run amok in the village streets, firing their automatic weapons and throwing grenades through doors and windows indiscriminately. The casualty list supported their stories.

Qibya was only the first of Unit 101's battle honours under Sharon. Other attacks followed against civilian Arab targets in the occupied territories and even in neighbouring states. Unit 101's main hunting grounds were Gaza, the West Bank, and Syrian territory near Lake Tiberias.

So valiant a warrior could not fail to rise, especially since Sharon put this indifference to atrocity at the service of nationalist ambitions, an indifference so vaulting as to verge on the megalomaniac. These found their most succinct expression in a famous article he wrote in *Yediot Aharanot* on 26 July 1973. "Israel is now a military superpower," Sharon proclaimed. "All the forces of Western Europe combined are less than those we possess. In one week Israel could conquer the whole region between Khartoum, Baghdad and Algeria." On another occasion he announced pointedly that Saudi oilfields were within range of Israeli bombers. The irresponsibility of such comments alarmed even Israel's allies. When Sharon was appointed defence minister in Begin's second government after the 1981 elections, the sober *Newsweek* reported that his choice had embarrassed many moderates in Israel. Presciently, *Newsweek* went on to report that Sharon opposed the cease-fire then in force in Lebanon—and to prophesy that nobody else in Begin's government was strong enough to challenge Sharon. Less than ten months later, Israeli troops were invading Lebanon.

Sharon's ambitions stretch far beyond Lebanon, however. Addressing a strategic studies conference in Tel Aviv in December 1981, he announced: "Israel's strategic interests cannot be confined to the Arab countries. They must expand in the Eighties to include Turkey, Iran, Pakistan, Africa in general and its northern and middle tiers in particular." That a military commander in a small, bankrupt Middle Eastern state can proclaim such fantasies and still be taken seriously as a candidate for high office is true to the imperial logic of Zionism. Sharon himself seems to see this. In November 1982, in an interview with *Yediot Aharanot,* Sharon said: "The only card left in the hands of the Arabs is the oil card, with which they exert pressure—blackmail—on those countries anxious to buy their oil. The Israeli army could occupy Jordan in two days: it could then become a homeland for the Palestinian Arabs. Then our troops could move to the Gulf and occupy its oilfields—there would be no resistance—and in this way we could solve the Palestinian problem permanently." In other words, Zionism, having created the "Palestinian problem" by seizing one country, now dreams of "solving" it by seizing the entire region. The logic is impeccable, and quite mad.

In any normal society, of course, the massacres at Sabra and Shatila camps would have ended the career of the minister of defence whose army permitted such atrocities. But the Israeli committee of inquiry into the affair was highly political: it cast just enough blame upon Israeli army officers to mute international criticism while, in effect, absolving Israel of responsibility—a tricky assignment which the committee managed triumphantly by the invention of the concept of "indirect responsibility." Thus Sharon, adjudged only indirectly responsible for massacres which were, in reality, the logical culmination of a career founded upon similar killings thirty years before, stepped down from the defence post but remained in the government —and was even given a new job, minister of trade and industry, in the Government of National Unity formed in September 1984.

After 25 months, it will be the Likud's turn to take the prime minister's chair; Sharon is expected then to return to the ministry of defence. If he can oust Shamir, he could even become Prime Minister of Israel. At least that would confer the benefit of certainty: nobody could doubt that Israel, with Sharon at its head, would aspire to conquest over an area greater even than the biblical dreams of a land from the Nile to the Euphrates. We have been warned.

The Myth of the Empty Land

Of all the legends which nourish the self-esteem of Israel, none is more potent than that of the empty land: the saga of Jewish pioneers reclaiming a wilderness. Israel, the land won by honest toil—the picture is appealing. It is of course false. Certainly, the Israelis have reclaimed tracts of desert in the south (though nothing like the area reclaimed with far less fuss by Egypt). But for thousands of years Palestine has been a fertile and intensively cultivated land, which means an intensively settled land. The myth of the empty land thus forces the Jewish State to live two lies. The historical lie: the land of Palestine was won by conquest, not cultivation. The present lie: while Israelis assert their desire to live in harmony with their Arab neighbours, and point to the Arabs in Israel as supposed exemplars of this concord, the secret truth is that successive Israeli governments have had as their objectives the expulsion of the remaining Arabs from Israel, and the wholesale reorganisation of the states round Israel's borders to provide a new home for these. Israel can never acknowledge this strategy, of course—less out of regard for international opinion than because to do so would be to admit the myth of the empty land. But the strategy remains the secret thread running through all Israel's actions. The empty land was a lie: Israel's strategy is to make it true.

It follows that Israeli politics are different from those of most other democratic countries. Elsewhere the questions of security and foreign policy admit of shades of opinion: commonly, those of both hawks and doves. Israel has no doves. On this central fact of Israel's existence —the seizure of Arab land by Jews and the expulsion of Arabs which must logically follow—there are only hawks and super-hawks. To take the prime example of this: it suits the Israeli Labour Party right now to represent itself to the world as more moderate than the Likud. But Labour was in power for the first 29 years of Israel's existence, from 1948 to 1977. In that time, one generation, Israel launched four wars against its neighbours, occupied the West Bank and Gaza, the Sinai and the Golan Heights, and began the construction of Jewish settlements in these new territories. That Labour politicians should think to present this record as one of moderation is itself revealing. Nor, to anticipate another Israeli alibi, were the Labour leaders of those years merely responding to events: the myth of "embattled little Israel" is as vacuous as the myth of the empty land. From the start, Israel's leaders have followed a plan; they have not, to borrow Disraeli's famous phrase about the British, acquired their empire in a fit of absentmindedness.

Consider a meeting held on 16 May 1954 in the office of the then-prime minister of Israel, Moshe Sharett. Also present were the defence minister, David Ben-Gurion, and the chief of staff, Moshe Dayan. The meeting was to discuss the situation in Lebanon. We know what was said because Sharett kept a diary, which has since been published. Sharett recorded: "According to Dayan, the only thing that's necessary [in Lebanon] is to find an officer, even just a major. We should either win his heart or buy him with cash, and get him to agree to declare himself the saviour of the Maronite population. Then the Israeli army will enter Lebanon, occupy the necessary territory, and set up a Christian regime which would ally itself with Israel. The [Lebanese] territory from the Litani [river] southward would be annexed as a piece by Israel—and everything will be all right. If we were to accept the advice of the chief of staff, we would do it tomorrow, without awaiting a signal from Baghdad; but under the circumstances, the government of Iraq will do our will and occupy Syria."

Sharett disagreed, but not with the principle, only with the timing. He supported the idea of creating a Maronite Christian state in Lebanon, but urged that the time was not ripe because there was as yet no Maronite separatist movement in Lebanon. There was no point, he said, in trying to create from the outside a movement that did not exist inside: it was, as he put it, impossible to inject life into a corpse. But he assured his colleagues that were there such a separatist movement he would be in favour of aiding it, or any manifestation of unrest within the Maronite community that tended to strengthen its isolationist tendencies—even if there were no real chance of achieving the goal Israel sought.

But Ben Gurion was adamant: "Lebanon is the weakest link in the Arab League. It is time to bring about the creation of a Christian state on our borders. Without our initiative and our vigourous help this will not be done. It seems to me that this is the central duty, or at least one of the central duties, of our foreign policy. The creation of a Christian state will find support among wide circles in the Christian world, both Catholic and Protestant. This is an historic opportunity: missing it would be unpardonable. There is no challenge to the world powers in this. Everything should be done—in my opinion rapidly and at full steam."

Ben Gurion and his protege Dayan were premature. On timing, Sharett was right; but on strategy they prevailed. Twenty-four years after that discussion, Israel found its major, Saad Haddad, to play his allotted role as separatist Maronite leader and so provide the pretext Dayan had mapped for an Israeli invasion of Lebanon. In the Israeli invasions of Lebanon in 1978 and 1982, it was a Likud government which ordered the tanks to roll, but it was Labour which had drawn their route maps.

If Jabotinsky was the mentor of the Right in Israel, David Ben Gurion—the first prime minister of Israel and the dominating figure of its first 15 years—was the philosopher and guide to the present generation of Labour leaders, men like Shimon Peres and Yitzhak Rabin. But reconstructing Ben-Gurion's thinking from the memoirs and diaries now available, it becomes clear that his differences with the Right were nothing by comparison with the convictions they shared. That imperial disregard for the rights of anyone in the region except Jews; that breath-taking assumption of Israel's right to remake whole countries to suit its convenience; above all, that messianic assertion of Israel's divine right to do whatever it chooses—everything we now associate with, say, Begin or Sharon, speaks from the memoirs and diaries of early Israel in the confident tones of David Ben-Gurion.

Take the Suez Affair. When Ben-Gurion landed secretly outside Paris on 22 October 1956, it was, as all the world now knows, to put the finishing touches to an attack on Egypt, which Israel planned to launch one week later. Ben-Gurion had come to talk with the French Prime Minister Guy Mollet and his most senior colleagues, and with the British Foreign Secretary Selwyn Lloyd. With Ben-Gurion were Dayan and Peres. The interesting point now is not the conspiracy itself but the views with which Ben-Gurion regaled the French as they sat in the Villa Bonnier de la Chapelle at Sevres, waiting for Selwyn Lloyd to arrive. Dayan recorded them in his memoirs. "Jordan is not viable as an independent state and should be divided," Ben-Gurion said. "The area east of the Jordan river should be given to Iraq against her undertaking to receive and settle the Arab refugees in her midst. Western Jordan should become an autonomous region within Israel. Lebanon too should divest itself of some of its Moslem areas in order to guarantee for herself stability based on the Christian areas of the country. In such a Middle Eastern structure, Britian would exercise influence over Iraq—including eastern Jordan—and over the southern parts of the Arabian peninsula. France's sphere of influence would be Lebanon and possibly also Syria, with close relations with Israel. There should be guaranteed international status for the Suez canal; and the straits of Tiran should come under Israeli control." Evidently foreseeing some doubts about this grand design, Ben-Gurion added, according to Dayan: "Attempts should be made to persuade the United States and Britain to support these aims. The present situation is a suitable opportunity for a comprehensive consideration of the future of the Middle East with a view to reaching a joint policy for the United States, Britain, France, and Israel."

Note that revealing alignment of Israel with the imperial powers. Ben-Gurion had no doubts. Back in 1937, he drew a map of the future Israel inside what he considered its biblical boundaries. Palestine under the British mandate was the mere core of the land Ben-Gurion foresaw. His Israel included southern Lebanon up to the Litani River, southern Syria as far east as Homs, all of what we now call Jordan, and all of Sinai. He never changed his mind. In 1956, to applause from the Israeli Parliament, he declared Sinai to be Israel's on the basis that it had been part of the kingdom of David and Solomon.

Ben-Gurion openly asserted Israel's right to conquest. "We are creating a dynamic state, oriented towards expansion," he once said. "The United States' frontier kept moving for a century, until they had annihilated the Indians, occupied the territory, and possessed their land. Only when its troops reached the Pacific Ocean did the United States define its borders. Why should anyone ask us to maintain the status quo? We are entitled to create a dynamic state, oriented towards expansion."

The Labour Party was in power in Israel for the first 29 years of the state's existence: Ben-Gurion, 1948–December 1953; Sharett, December 1953–November 1955; Ben-Gurion, November 1955–June 1963; Eshkel, June 1963–February 1969; Meir, March 1969–April 1974; Rabin, April 1974–April 1977; Peres, April 1977–May 1977. After a spell in opposition from 1977 to September 1984, Labour shared power with the Likud bloc to form a coalition. Throughout those 29 years, Labour consistently followed the doctrines and policies of Ben-Gurion. Ben-Gurion himself split with Mapai, the Labour Party, in 1965, of course, to form a breakaway party called Rafi. But that had no strategic importance: Ben-Gurion and Labour remained two faces of the same coin. And to this day, Labour's leaders live off his intellectual legacy.

By any standards, Labour's record of actions against the Arabs is appalling. It was Labour which set up Sharon's Unit 101; Labour which authorised the massacre of Kafr Kasem; Labour which bulldozed 385 Arab villages; and Labour which set in place the legal structure that allows Israel first to terrorise the Arabs into leaving their land and then to confiscate the vacated land and homes on the grounds that they are no longer owned by anyone. It was Labour which built 370 Jewish settlements in the occupied territories. Sixty eight of these, housing 25,000 Jews, were built between 1967–1977. It was Labour which conceived the strategy of destroying Lebanon by encouraging Maronite separatist tendencies. (An Israeli journalist, Benny Morris, uncovered a letter dated 28 December 1950 from Gideon Rafael, counsellor to the Israeli delegation to the United Nations, to the Israeli foreign minister. The letter, along with other documents, proved there were secret contacts between Israel and the Phalangists even that early—and a secret subsidy of 3000 dollars from Israel to the Phalangists in the run-up to Lebanon's 1951 election.)

And at the root of Labour's strategy is the myth of the empty land. Ever since it was defined by Herzl, Zionism has ignored the fact of the Palestinian nation. Herzl's own book *The Jewish State* did not even mention the Palestinians; nor did the founding assemblies of the Zionist movement. Now the alleged non-existence of the Palestinian nation is the corner-stone of Labour's structure of thought. "There are no Palestinians," declared Mrs. Golda Meir in June 1969. "It is not as if there was a Palestinian nation and we came to kick them out and take their land. There was no such nation."

That is a lie, just as the empty land was a lie. Israel's strategy—Labour's strategy—is to make it true. Professor Benzion Dinur, who was a close friend of Ben-Gurion and Israel's first minister of education, wrote in 1954: "There is no place in our country for anyone but the Jews. We say to the Arabs, get out. Should they say no and resist, we must expel them by force." Thirteen years later, Josef Weitz, ex-director of the colonisation department—revealing title—of the Jewish Agency, wrote in precisely the same terms: "There is no place in this country for the two nations. The only solution is to expel the Arabs from west Israel west of the River Jordan and transfer them to the neighbouring countries."

In effect, there is no difference between the Labour Party and the Likud. To expect, as some Arabs profess, that a future Labour Government in Israel would be more moderate, more accommodating, than the Likud, is to ignore history and live in a world of dreamlike naïveté.

A Refuge for the Jews

The third legend which nourishes Israel is the notion of this Zionist state as a deserved refuge for those Jews who survived the Nazi persecutions in Europe. Israel is somehow "owed" to the Jews in recompense for Hitler's atrocities.

It was an American academic, Professor Dwight James Simpson, professor of political science at the State University in San Francisco, who most succinctly demolished that myth, in a lecture he gave in January 1984: "Of today's Jewish population of Israel, the over-whelming majority—between two-thirds and three-quarters—are in Tel Aviv, Jerusalem, Haifa, and elsewhere, having come *not* as victims from Hitler's Berlin, Munich, or Hamburg, but are in Israel for many other reasons and come not from German cities but from places such as Algiers, Johannesburg, Casablanca, Los Angeles, Baghdad, Buenos Aires, Miami, places where their forebears have lived for generations or even for hundreds of years.

"For instance, a small but not unimportant example is the large number of colonists who have been brought as settlers in the past five years to the newly created West Bank settlements. Very many of these people are quite young, are from the United States, and of these many are from California, mainly Los Angeles. As one walks through the market place of the Palestinian Arab city of Hebron, one can observe these Americans, residents of the nearby settlement of Kiryat Arba, carrying their sub-machine guns and speaking English to each other in a Californian accent. By no stretch of the imagination are these people—and indeed at least two thirds of Israel's Jewish population—actually the surviving victims of Hitler's atrocities.

"Even if one were to grant that there are European Jews who actually are personally the surviving victims of the Nazis and who therefore deserve a state of their own, why in the name of God, or of political justice, or even of simple common sense, should the Palestinian Arabs be thrown out of their homes to accommodate them? If you are in the business of giving other people's ancestral lands to victims of persecution, surely it is only reasonable to give the land of the offenders to those who have been offended. Empty out Bavaria, for example, for Jewish settlement and colonisation. Munich could function as the capital city of the new Jewish state. Absurd as this may sound, at least one could then argue that it was Germans who were being displaced or colonised, and that it was Germans who deserved this fate because they were in some sense responsible for Hitler and the Nazi atrocities."

The Israeli Armed Forces

A People's Army

With its limited manpower resources, Israel keeps only one-third of its armed forces in full-time regular service. The other two-thirds are reservists. Thus in 1983 Israel's armed forces totalled 500,000, but of these only 172,000 were classified as regulars. The reservists, however, can be mobilised in two to five days—so quickly and efficiently, in fact, that for the purposes of military calculation the reservists are best considered as regular troops on short leave from their duties.

Israel recruits these enormous forces from a Jewish population of 3.3 million—men being liable for military service up to the age of 54, childless women up to the age of 34. Very few recruits are drawn from Israel's Arab population of 800,000; most of these are actually forbidden to serve. (Three groups of Arabs are accepted into the Israeli armed forces. The Druze population of Israel, about 45,000 in number, are recruited on the same basis as Jews. Christian Arabs are accepted as volunteers. Caucasians, who migrated from the Caucasus in 1870 and are now thought to number about 2000 in Israel, are recruited in the normal way, even though they are Moslem. But Moslem Arabs, the great bulk of the Palestinian Arab population of Israel, are not allowed to serve in Israel's armed forces.)

These numbers demonstrate that the armed forces are the single most pervasive element and experience in Israeli society. That can be called a "people's army" of course. It can also be called a militarised society.

The Strength of the Armed Forces

This scale of military effort has been a feature of the Jewish State since its birth, as study of the Arab-Israeli wars demonstrates. On 15 May 1948, the Jewish population of Palestine was 649,632. Yet the new state was able to deploy in the field an army of 30,000, rising to 40,000 by December 1948—with another 60,000 troops defending Jewish settlements and rear areas. The size of this force becomes clear when it is contrasted with the fact that the total population of those

Arab states which took part in that first war with Israel—Egypt, Syria, Lebanon, Trans-Jordan, Iraq, Palestine—was more than sixty times that of the newborn Jewish state. Yet the Arabs deployed against Israel no more than 40,000 regular troops and another 5000 irregular volunteers. That is being generous; the most precise figures available for the Arab forces deployed in 1948 against Israel are:

REGULARS		
Egypt	5 infantry brigades	15,000
Iraq	2 infantry brigades	6000
Trans-Jordan	5 infantry battalions	5000
Syria	3 infantry battalions	3000
Lebanon	1 infantry battalion	1000
		30,000

Irregulars

Two groups of irregulars were deployed. One, under the command of Fawzi Kawkji and amounting to about 2000 volunteers, mainly Druze, was deployed in north Palestine. The second group of about 3000 volunteers, mainly Egyptian and under the command of Egyptian Lt. Col. Ahmed Abdelaziz, was deployed in the area south of Jerusalem.

In 1956, for its invasion of the Sinai, Israel deployed 60,000 troops with 400 tanks and 70 combat aircraft. The ground forces were organised in five infantry brigades, three armoured brigades, and one parachute brigade. By today's standards that might seem a modest army, but in 1956 it was quite sufficient for the task—sufficient, at any rate, in the light of the alliances Israel had prudently made beforehand. Egypt possessed two infantry divisions, one armoured division, and one parachute battalion. Only one of these infantry divisions was deployed in the Sinai; the other was west of the Canal Zone, while the armoured division and the parachute battalion were stationed in the Cairo area. The Egyptian air force, meanwhile, with 150 combat aircraft, was demonstrably superior to that of Israel. It followed that if Egypt were to deploy all its ground forces in the Sinai in the early stages of the battle it could match the Israeli invaders.

Israel declined to accept the risk of war on those terms. Instead, Israel decided to go to war only as part of a three-pronged assault upon Egypt—its partners in this brave enterprise being Britain and France. Under the terms of the secret pact between the three, Britain and France were to provide a force of four infantry divisions and 520 combat aircraft (400 fighters, 120 bombers). One hundred French fighter aircraft were to take responsibility for air-defence over the Sinai to provide an umbrella over the Israeli ground forces. The rest of the Anglo-French armada was to destroy the Egyptian air force and occupy the Canal Zone.

As a result, Israel could be confident that Egypt would not be able to send its second infantry division to reinforce its first in the Sinai; nor could the Egyptian air force pose a threat to the Israeli ground forces. The Israeli invasion of Sinai was a safe bet. In the event, of course, President Nasser took the political decision on 31 October 1956—48 hours after the Israeli invasion started—to evacuate all Egyptian forces from the Sinai to meet the Anglo-French assualt on the Canal Zone, and by the morning of 2 November, this Egyptian withdrawal was complete. The famous Israeli "victory" in the Sinai was in reality the triumph of an army painlessly occupying abandoned ground.

War and diplomacy are the means by which any country tries to achieve its international aims. Each supports the other. But the Sinai invasion of 1956 was a case where the military means was made possible only by diplomacy. But for the intervention of Britain and France, Egypt could have matched the invaders in the Sinai: the Israeli expedition would have been doomed. This interaction of the diplomatic and the military is a lesson the Arabs have been slow to learn.

By 1967, the population of Israel had grown to 2,225,000, of whom 1.8 millions were Jews. From this tiny population, however, Israel mobilised a field army of 275,000 troops equipped with 1200 tanks and 385 combat aircraft. The ground forces were organised in 28 brigades:

Type of Brigade	Deployed on Egyptian front	Deployed on Eastern front	Total
Armoured Bde	7	3	10
Mechanised Infantry Bde	4	2	6
Infantry Bde	3	7	10
Parachute Bde	1	1	2
Total	15	13	28

The front-line Arab countries by contrast totalled 40 million in population—Egypt 32m, Syria 5.8m, Jordan 2.2m—but were unable even jointly to deploy more than half the forces Israel mobilised. Egypt deployed 80,000 troops in the Sinai; Syria deployed 40,000; Jordan deployed 20,000. So in ground forces Israel had a clear edge over its three front-line adversaries. And in the air Israel had a crushing superiority both in numbers and quality of combat aircraft.

Two other factors added to Israel's superiority over its Arab neighbours. The first was Israel's central location. Israel operated on internal lines of communication, which meant that it could concentrate its fighting effort on one front at a time while holding the other with minimal forces. That is just what happened: only after achieving victory on the Egyptian front did Israel turn to the eastern front. The second factor enhancing Israel's superiority was its success in destroying the Arab air forces in the earliest stages of the war. From midday on the first day, the Arab ground forces were not only deprived of air support in their own actions but were relentlessly attacked by the Israeli air force with practically no response available from ground or air. Superior in the air and on the ground, the Israelis were able to cut the Arab forces to pieces and deal with them piecemeal—enjoying at times a tactical superiority on the battlefield of three-to-one and sometimes even five-to-one.

The year 1973 was the turning point in this bloody chronicle. For the first time since Israel's birth, Egypt and Syria were able in 1973 to deploy forces to match those of Israel in number and which were their equal in quality. In the air, however, the Israeli air force was superior to the Egyptian and Syrian air forces combined. For reasons I have narrated elsewhere, the Arab victory in that war was thrown away. Nevertheless, the lesson remains. In 1973 the Arabs fought Israel for the first time on roughly equal terms—and demonstrated that Israel is not invincible.

The pattern of these wars is clear. In war Israel mobilises about 15 per cent of its Jewish population (which means about 12.5 per cent of its entire population, including Arabs and other races). If we can forecast the future population trends in Israel, therefore, we can predict with some accuracy the scale of military effort the Arabs must match.

The Defence Budget

A defence budget is an index of a nation's concern for its security. It is not a good indicator of how strong its armed forces are. Providing the money is one thing; spending it sensibly is another. A defence budget has to include salaries, food, housing, fuel, medical care, equipment—many elements besides arms and their maintenance. The more spent on salaries and welfare, the less remains for arms and the other teeth of war. Increasing the percentage of a defence budget allocated to the buying of new weaponry and the maintenance of old is the first step in any programme to strengthen a nation's armed forces. The following table, showing the 1982–1983 defence budgets of various nations, demonstrates the point:

Country	Defence budget in billion $	% of GNP
U.S.A.	240.6	11.2
USSR	150	10.0
UK	25.2	5.0
France	21.9	4.0
West Germany	18.9	2.8
Japan	10.4	0.9
China	9.0	1.8
Israel	6.461	29.7

From which it is clear that the Israeli defence budget, though so large in relative terms as to distort the entire economy, is in absolute terms very much less than those of Britain, France, and West Germany. Yet Israel's ground forces and air force are stronger than their counterparts in any of those other countries. It is true that both Britain and France have strategic nuclear forces which consume perhaps 20–25 per cent of their defence budgets; even so, their budgets for conventional forces are about three times that of Israel. Yet their forces are smaller. The secret is that Israel saves billions of dollars by keeping the bulk of its armed forces in reserve. By saving those salaries, housing costs, and welfare expenditures, Israel is able to allot well over 50 per cent of its defence budget to the maintenance of its existing weapons and the purchase of new ones.

Ground Forces

The ground forces of Israel are generally rated third in the world, behind only those of the Soviet Union and the United States, in the mobility and offensive capabilities of their armour. Only 30 per cent of Israel's ground forces are kept as a standing army; the other 70 per cent are held as reserves. These reserves are called for training for one month a year, and all reserve fighting units can be mobilised within 48 hours.

In 1983, the Israeli ground forces deployed 450,000 troops, organised as follows:

33 armoured brigades	(each of three tank battalions and one mechanised infantry battalion)
10 mechanised brigades	(five of these parachute-trained)
12 territorial/border infantry brigades, with Nahal militia	
15 artillery brigades	(each of five battalions with three batteries apiece)

To grasp the scale of those forces, set them against the armies of other countries in 1983:

	Israel	West Germany	France	USA
Strength	450,000	335,000	311,000	159,065
Main battle tanks	3960	4254	1240	970
Light tanks	—	—	1110	271
Armoured fighting vehicles	8000	7636	5257	5931

But while Germany has more tanks than Israel, Israel has 33 armoured brigades while Germany has only 17. This is because Israel masses all its tanks into armoured brigades, while Germany distributes about a quarter of its tanks among the infantry, massing only three quarters of the force into armoured brigades. The Israeli method of organisation is fitted for offensive and counter-attack concepts; the German organisation is best suited for defence. That at any rate is the theory, though in my judgement the Israeli concept of massing all armour into brigades is the better, even for defence. This I take to be one of the operational lessons of the 1973 war. When Israeli tanks penetrated the Egyptian postions around Deversoir, the Egyptian army was almost bare of armoured reserves for counter-attack, yet more than 700 tanks were distributed and idle among infantry divisions.

In predicting the future shape of Israel's armed forces, manpower is the dominant factor. By 1993, demographers expect the population of Israel to reach 4,961,000, which on extrapolation of the historical pattern would give armed forces of 620,125. These troops would be distributed among the fighting services as follows:

Service	Strength	% of total
Ground forces	558,112	90.0
Navy	12,402	2.0
Air force	45,889	7.4
Miscellaneous	3,722	0.6
Total	620,125	100.00

This means that between 1983 and 1993 the probable increase in the strength of Israel's armed forces will be of the following order:

Service	Increase in strength by 1994	% increase
Ground forces	108,112	24.02
Air force	8,889	24.02
Navy	2,402	24.02
Miscellaneous	722	24.07
Total	120,125	24.02

With ground forces of 558,112 troops by 1993, Israel would be in a position to deploy 5040 tanks and 12,000 armoured fighting vehicles, organised into 21 armoured divisions (each of two armoured brigades and one mechanised infantry brigade). Israel's ground forces would then be:

42 armoured brigades
21 mechanised infantry brigades
6 territorial brigades

This build-up will not, of course, happen overnight. Even by the late 1980s, the same demographic data suggest, Israel will be able to deploy ground forces significantly bigger than today's. By 1988, Israel could be deploying 4533 tanks and 10,000 armoured fighting vehicles, organised in 62 brigades:

   37 armoured brigades
   16 mechanised infantry brigades
   9 territorial brigades
A formidable challenge. (For more details, see tables 27–29.)

Israel's Air Force

Like its ground forces, Israel's air force is rated the third most powerful in the world, inferior only to those of the two superpowers. Israel pays such attention to its air force for three principal reasons. First, a modern air force gives far more "bang per man"—destructive capability per combatant—than ground or naval forces. In manpower terms (and manpower, remember, is the limiting factor for Israel) an air force is extremely cost-effective. Second, Israel can exploit its technological superiority over its Arab neighbours to strengthen and enlarge its air force faster than they can. Ground forces, by contrast, need less advanced technology, so there the Arabs have the chance to match Israel. Third, its air force provides Israel with the long arm it needs to enforce its imperial will over the region as a whole.

The secret of Israel's ability, as a small country, to sustain such a massive air force is this: Israel leads the world in its ratio of "teeth-to-tail." It has kept to an absolute minimum in its air force the numbers of technical and administrative personnel per combat aircraft. The following table demonstrates this:

Country	Combat aircraft 1983	Air force strength	Men per aircraft
Israel	830	37,000	44.6
UK	620	89,827	144.9
West Germany	551	105,900	192.2
France	522	89,800	172.0
Egypt (with air defence forces)	282	112,000	397.2
Egypt (without air defence forces)		27,000	95.7

These figures need to be interpreted with caution. In all the countries except Egypt, air defence units—missile forces—are included in the air force strengths. In Egypt, the figures are separable because air defence is an independent service with a strength of 85,000, while the air force proper has a strength of 27,000. The greater emphasis a country places on air defence, the worse that tail-to-teeth ratio will appear—because air defence personnel swell overall numbers while making no contribution to the back-up needed by modern combat aircraft. Even so, the figures are an indication of how efficiently Israel runs its air force.

And that is the achievement which underpins Israel's entire defence effort. Because, unlike Israel's ground forces, Israel's air force relies on regular troops: only 25 per cent of the air force strength is held in reserve, to be mobilised in a crisis. In practice, Israel's air force is the only one of its armed services in a constant state of readiness; and its first mission in war is to buy enough time for Israel's ground forces to mobilise. Thus Israel can remain on constant alert with minimum standing forces. But this is only possible so long as the air force lays a modest burden on Israel's manpower resources—hence the crucial importance of the man-per-aircraft ratio.

By 1993, it can be expected that Israel's air force will increase by 24 per cent in personnel and by about 26–27 per cent in combat aircraft strength:

Year	Personnel	Combat aircraft
1983	37,000	830
1988	41,716	948
1993	45,889	1052

And this increase in quantity will be matched by an upgrading of quality too. (For more details, see table 30.)

The Israeli Navy

Israel's navy comes a poor third in its priorities, well below the air force and ground forces. It is the smallest service, with the smallest share of the defence budget. Israel within its pre-1967 borders has a coastline of about 175 kilometres; add the coast of Gaza, which has been under Israeli control since 1967, and the coastline grows to about 225 kms. Logically, Israel—with its short coast, its central position, and its command of all enemy targets, including naval ones, from the air—has paid relatively little attention to its navy.

The most formative influence on Israeli thinking about its navy was the sinking of the Israeli destroyer *Eilat* on 21 October 1967. Egyptian fast-attack craft of the Komar class fired two surface-to-surface missiles at the *Eilat* and sank it in a few minutes. According to official Israeli figures, 47 of *Eilat's* crew were killed and 90 injured out of a total complement of 199. To Israel, with its limited manpower, such losses in one blow were simply unacceptable, a catastrophe. Immediately, Israel adopted the concept of small fast-attack craft.

Israel's were in fact designed by a West German firm of naval architects, *Lürssen Werfte;* though for political reasons—mainly to disguise the budding relationship between Israel and West Germany —the designs were handed to a French company, *Ch de Normandie,* to build. The French constructed twelve of these craft for Israel: six of type SAAR-2, delivered in 1969; the other six of type SAAR-3, handed over in 1970. All twelve were fitted with Israel's own *Gabriel* surface-to-surface missile. Subsequently, Israel developed this design into type SAAR-4, and began to build the craft in its own Haifa shipyards. The first SAAR-4, named *Reshef,* was launched in February 1973; and since then Israel has built about two SAAR-4 boats a year. (For more details see table 18.)

In 1973, the strength of the Israeli navy was 5000, organised into the following main units:

3   submarines
1   fast-attack craft (missile carrying) SAAR-4: *Reshef*
12 SAAR-2 and SAAR-3 FAC(M)

By 1983 the navy had grown to 10,000 in strength, with the following units:

3   submarines
24 FAC(M)

By 1988, the navy is predicted to be 11,276 in strength, with the following units:

5   submarines
2   corvette
34 FAC(M)
10 LCAC

By 1993, the navy is predicted to be 12,402 in strength, with the following units:

6   submarines
4   corvette
44 FAC(M)
20 LCAC

Even in the navy, therefore, the most neglected of Israel's armed forces, the same pattern is visible—that of inexorable build-up in quantity and quality.

Israel's Arms Industry

Economic and Political Benefits

Israel's arms industry had its beginnings as early as 1933, when Palestine was still under the British mandate; and its earliest task was to fulfill the territory's own military needs. Since the October 1973 war, however, the Israeli arms industry has grown rapidly until it is now a vital element in the Israeli economy; while foreign arms sales have become a significant Israeli diplomatic weapon.

Before the 1973 war, Israeli arms sales abroad were in the region of $60 million a year. By 1979, that total had shot up to $600 million; and by 1981, it had reached $1300 million. Despite the world recession in 1982–83, and the loss of two of its most important clients, Iran and Nicaragua, Israel still stood to make $1000 million worth of arms sales in 1983 (the last year for which figures are available).

Little of this would be possible without American help. Israel now manufactures advanced weaponry of almost every kind: combat aircraft, fighting vessels, main battle tanks, a whole alphabet of missiles —AAMs, ASMs, SSMs and SAMs—plus radar, radios, computers, and a range of the most sophisticated electronic equipment. Israel also has a thriving trade in guns and ammunition of several calibres. Yet across the whole range of Israeli hardware, American help in developing this arms industry has been decisive. The US provides Israel with the three ingredients essential to a flourishing arms industry: funds for research and development; technological know-how; and a market.

The relationship is open. By way of example, Caspar Weinberger, the US secretary of defence, announced on 17 October 1984, at the end of a visit to Israel, that the Reagan administration had decided to grant Israel access to the most advanced US technology which it needed to produce its own ultra-modern *Lavi* jet fighter. Weinberger also said that Washington would consider an Israeli request that the US buy the Israeli-made 120mm mortar for the US army. Weinberger did not specify how many mortars might be purchased; but the Washington correspondent of the Tel Aviv daily *Maariv* reported that he wanted 4400 of these mortars, plus five million shells, to replace the 107mm mortar currently in use. Other Israeli papers talked of a one-billion-dollar deal—"the arms deal of the century" they called it. Less speculatively, the US has since 1979 bought about $150 million worth of military equipment from Israel: small arms ammunition, tank and aircraft parts, aircraft fuel tanks, and walkie-talkie radios.

Subsidy goes further. US military credits are in general given to a country to help it finance purchases of American-made military equipment—reasonably enough, since the US taxpayer is putting up the money. But Israel is different. Israel hopes to have its *Lavi* fighter in operation in the 1990s, but it lacks the cash to build it. On 12 November 1983, after fierce lobbying by Israel and its supporters, the US Senate and House of Representatives approved legislation that would allow Israel to use US military credits to finance the construction of the *Lavi* in Israel.

On some reckonings, the arms industry is now the backbone of the Israeli economy. It has been estimated that one third of the entire Israeli labour force now works on armaments; and the billion-dollar-a-year arms trade is about the only thing saving the country from utter bankruptcy. The list of Israeli clients indicates the political, as well as economic, importance of the industry. Top customer, reportedly, is South Africa, followed by Argentina. Other countries which reportedly bought arms from Israel in the five years to late-1983 include Bolivia, Colombia, Ecuador, El Salvador, Ethiopia, Guatemala, Honduras, Indonesia, Kenya, Malaysia, Mexico, Nicaragua, Peru, Singapore, and Taiwan. Israel seeks more than money from its arms sales—though it apparently bargains toughly for payment in hard currency. Israel has a political price too: in return for arms, military advisors, even training facilities, Israel wants recognition. The restoration of diplomatic relations between Israel and Liberia, and the decision of El Salvador to open an embassy in Jerusalem, are just two examples of the price paid for Israeli weapons.

Israel's Aircraft Industries

The core of the Israeli arms industry is the firm IAI. Established in 1953, it now employs more than 20,000 people. It is licensed by the aviation authorities of Britain and the US as a repair and maintenance organisation for civil and military aircraft; and in fact it inspects, repairs, and overhauls more than 30 types of aircraft (among them the Boeing 707, 727, 747, and 767; the Lockheed C-130; and the F-4, F-5, and F-16 fighters), 28 types of civil and military aircraft engines, and some 8000 assorted components, accessories, and systems. As a manufacturer, IAI makes the *Kfir* fighter, the *Arava* short-take-off transport, the *Westwind* executive aircraft and its Seascan maritime surveillance version, and the *Scout* remotely piloted reconnaissance aircraft. In addition, IAI manufactures a vast range of spares and assemblies for the Israeli air force; and as a subcontractor to several US and European aircraft manufacturers it produces major aircraft structures, flight control surfaces, cargo loading systems, and spares.

One of IAI's subsidiaries, Elta Electronic Industries, specialises in the design, development, and production of sophisticated electronic equipment, such as air, ground, and shipborne communications, and radars, transceivers, and navigational aids, general communications equipment, automatic test systems and—as a civilian spin-off—medical devices such as cardiac resuscitation units.

Other divisions of IAI produce a variety of missiles, including the air-to-surface and surface-to-surface versions of the *Gabriel;* the 240mm and 290mm multiple rocket launchers; and the *Barak* surface-to-air missile.

Israeli Ordnance Corps (IOC)

IOC plant at Tel-a-Shumer near Tel Aviv manufactures the *Merkava* main battle tank. The first batch of 40 was delivered to the Israeli army in 1979, and the *Merkava-3* is now coming off the assembly line at a rate of 40–50 tanks a year. (For more details see tables 16 and 29.) Tel-a-Shumer also makes equipment for clearing passages through minefields for tanks.

Israeli Military Industries (IMI)

IMI at Tel Aviv manufactures a wide range of ammunition (75mm, 105mm, 155mm among the calibres). IMI also makes a medium-range battlefield missile, the MAR-290, on behalf of a so-far-unnamed NATO country. Reportedly, the MAR-290 is also deployed by Israel's ground forces as a mobile, heavy-warhead artillery rocket.

Ramta Structures and Systems

This is an IAI subsidiary at Beersheba. It manufactures the light armoured reconnaissance vehicles, the RAM V-1 and RBY Mk 1, and a 20mm twin-barrelled anti-aircraft gun. It also designed and built the world's smallest missile craft, the *Dvora* class, which is mainly for export.

Soltam

Based at Haifa, Soltam has developed a 155mm self-propelled gun/howitzer. The L-33 marque of this type of weapon was basically a Sherman tank-chassis fitted with a diesel engine: it entered service in 1973 just in time to see action that October. The L-33 production line is now closed down and the considerably more sophisticated M-72 has begun to appear. Soltam also manufactures a towed 155mm gun/howitzer. The earlier version of this, the M-68, entered service in 1970; the later model, the M-71, came in 1975.

Haifa Shipyards

Haifa developed the German-designed French-built SAAR fast-attack craft, and on 19 February 1973, launched the *Reshef,* first of a new 450-ton SAAR-4 class. Nine of these were built for South Africa; five were sent to Chile. On 11 July 1980, the *Alia,* first of a new 488-ton SAAR-5 class boat, was launched. This is big enough to carry an anti-submarine helicopter. It has since been reported that Haifa is now sufficiently confident of its naval design expertise to be working on a 1000-ton vessel of corvette type. Haifa also builds tank and general purpose landing craft.

High Technology Industries

Israel is poor in natural resources. With its agriculture developed close to capacity, and with an arms industry which—though buoyant —is essentially dependent upon government support, industrially based high-technology civilian industries remain the only route to economic security for Israel. For that reason, Israel created in 1970 the Office of the Chief Scientist to encourage the growth of what is commonly called science-based research and development. Today about one-third of Israel's industrial exports are science-based. The trade is worth about $1.3 billion annually, and the goal is to increase this to $5 billion a year by 1990. So far, about 600 Israeli companies are active in scientific R & D, with about a hundred new companies appearing each year. Given Israel's relatively well-educated population—about 10,000 scientists and 20,000 engineers in a population of three million—the ground is clearly fertile for growth. Israel has three industrial priorities in the high-technology field: electronics, chemicals, and biotechnology.

The production of two of those three industries was an important factor in Israel's past victories over the Arabs, so Israel's industrial ambitions have obvious military significance. More generally, if Israel is to achieve its ambition to enforce its will over the whole region, it must remain qualitatively superior to its Arab neighbours in men and equipment. The Arabs, by contrast, have to close or at least narrow the gap between themselves and Israel in the modern technologies. The Arabs have the capacity: the issue is one of will. As Dr. Zahlan, professor of Physics at the American University of Beirut, pointed out in 1980, there are 30,000 Arab graduates at doctorate level, half of them specialists in physics and engineering, and the number is growing by about ten per cent a year. The Arabs do not lack the brains to develop their countries; what is missing is an Arab leadership that will accept this challenge. It is hardly surprising that so many of the Arabs' best brains emigrate in despair to countries where their skills will be used to the fullest. This is a subject to which I will return.

Israel and the Bomb

When Did Israel Get the Bomb?

On 1 December 1974, the president of Israel, Ephraim Katzir, announced to a startled group of science writers: "It has always been our intention to develop a nuclear potential. We now have that potential." It was the first official confirmation of what the world in general, and Egypt in particular, already knew. Back in 1969, I recall, I and some other generals were at a meeting with President Nasser to discuss military problems. Someone remarked that Israel was on its way to getting an atomic bomb, had indeed got close to achieving one, and that this posed a need for Egypt to build its own nuclear deterrent. "You must not worry about that," Nasser replied. "If Israel gets the Bomb, Egypt will immediately get it too." Nasser did not explain this, and further questions were not invited; but it was clear to all of us that he was indicating he had a promise of nuclear assistance from a friendly country if Israel ever became a nuclear power. I have sometimes suspected that an Israeli awareness of this pledge to Nasser accounted for the calculated ambiguity of Israeli official statements about its nuclear status.

Certainly, Israel has all the ingredients needed to become a nuclear power. It has sources of explosives. It has a scientific and technical community sophisticiated enough to engineer fissionable material into useable weapons. And it has the means to deliver them. The heart of the Israeli nuclear programme is its two reactors. One, provided by the United States and constructed at Nahal Soreq, must undoubtedly have helped Israel to train its scientists and technicians and develop its technology; but its small size, only five megawatts, rules it out as a source of weapons-grade explosive. But the second reactor, provided by France and constructed at Dimona in the early 1960s, is a different proposition. It has a 24-megawatt capacity, and can be run to produce 5.8 kilos of plutonium a year. A bomb with an explosive power equivalent to about 20,000 tons—20 kilotons—of TNT needs roughly 8.5 kilos of plutonium. So Dimona can give Israel enough plutonium for two bombs every three years. It is therefore likely that Israel had twelve bombs by the end of 1983; assuming its reactor started production in early 1966, it could have 15 bombs by 1988.

That is a minimum technical estimate: it assumes Israel has received no plutonium or enriched uranium from sources other than Dimona. But three stories of recent years about the disappearance of uranium, enriched uranium, and plutonium from other Western countries strongly suggest that Israel may in fact have acquired the means to build a considerably bigger nuclear arsenal.

The first consignment to disappear was a cargo of 200 tons of uranium from aboard a West-German freighter bound from Antwerp to Genoa. The cargo disappeared, and so did the ship. It was reported lost at sea. A year later the vessel reappeared, with a new name and a new crew, but without its cargo. Strangely, none of the authorities supposed to monitor the trade in uranium investigated the affair, or took legal action of any kind. The case remained a mystery until a Norwegian lawyer and sometime public prosecutor, Haaken Wiker, revealed its solution on 8 May 1977. He said that an Israeli intelligence agent, Dan Aerbl, who had been sentenced by a Norwegian court to five years imprisonment for his part in the killing of an Arab named Ahmed Bouchiki, had told Norwegian police during questioning in 1973 that he, Aerbl, had taken part in the operation to divert 200 tons of uranium to Israel in 1968. (Aerbl was later pardoned and sent back to Israel after just twelve months in jail.)

The second mysterious disappearance of nuclear material came to light only two months after Haaken Wiker's revelations. In July 1977, Britain's Atomic Energy Authority admitted that more than 100 kilos of plutonium, enough to make a dozen atomic bombs, had disappeared from British research centres since 1970.

Barely a week later, on 30 July 1977, came news of a third mysterious loss. It was reported that 66.6 kilos of enriched uranium had disappeared from a small, privately owned processing plant at Apollo in western Pennsylvania in the US—and that this had been hushed-up by US Atomic Energy Commission officials since September 1964, when the loss was discovered. In fact, a total of roughly double that quantity of uranium had disappeared from the Nuclear Material & Equipment Corporation plant at Apollo, but only 66.6 kilos of this had been in the highly enriched form directly useable in nuclear weapons. An analyst with the US Nuclear Regulatory Commission was quoted as saying that he believed the lost uranium had been diverted to a foreign country. The analyst wrote a letter to President Carter outlining his suspicions; he was transferred to another job. The loss provoked a congressional inquiry, and after some prevarication, the US government admitted to Congress that nuclear plants in America were unable to trace no less than 3400 lbs. of plutonium and 5037 lbs. of enriched uranium. Federal officials insisted there was no evidence of theft. The fact remains that the missing material was enough to make 288 atomic bombs, each with a 20-kiloton yield.

In all, the plutonium and enriched uranium lost just from British and American nuclear plants—and ignoring any losses from France— was enough to make 300 bombs. Assume that only ten per cent of that lost material was diverted to Israel: it would still add another 30 bombs to Israel's nuclear arsenal. To add to the controversy over Israel's nuclear capabilities, a Washington research institute, the Center for Strategic and International Studies (CSIS)—which is part of Georgetown University but has close ties to the Pentagon—announced in December 1984 its conclusion that Israel possesses about 100 nuclear warheads. CSIS did not specify the size of these; but if they were, say, ten kilotons each, then in terms of destructive capability, the center's estimate would be close to my own assessment of an Israeli stockpile of 45 warheads, each averaging a 20 kiloton yield.

Project Jericho

Nuclear weapons have to be delivered. The best delivery means yet known is the ballistic missile: swift, accurate, unstoppable. Israel's chosen delivery means is the missile code-named *Jericho*. The programme is based on a French design, the MD-620—MD standing for Marcel Dassault, the French aircraft and missile manufacturer. It is believed that the missile is fired from a mobile ramp and has a design range of 450 kms. Test firings are said to have taken place as early as 1968. In a television interview in mid-1975, Marcel Dassault confirmed that he had developed, built, and supplied battlefield missiles to Israel before the arms embargo which President de Gaulle imposed in 1967.

Aside from *Jericho,* Israel has several types of aircraft which have the capacity to carry nuclear weapons; and there is good evidence that Israel has acquired and fitted the necessary equipment—special bomb-racks, different bomb-sights—for a nuclear mission. But Israel possesses a plentitude of land-based delivery systems, all of American manufacture. There is:

Lance: a battlefield missile capable of carrying a 50 kiloton explosive device for 120 kms.

SRAM: a battlefield missile capable of carrying a 200 kiloton weapon for 60-160 kms.

155mm howitzer: capable of firing a 0.5-2 kiloton shell about 20 kilometres.

203mm howitzer: capable of firing a 0.5-2 kiloton shell about 21 kilometres.

The design of some of these warheads, particularly for the howitzer shells, would be taxing for Israeli scientists and engineers—especially in the absence of a test programme to verify design concepts. It is unlikely, therefore, that Israel has attained the sort of explosive yields I have specified above. More plausibly, the Israeli nuclear arsenal consists of relatively crude and, in terms of fallout, "dirty" weapons. But that the arsenal exists no prudent Arab leader can reasonably doubt.

Nuclear Proliferation

This judgment can only be reinforced by Israel's adamant refusal to accede to the Non-Proliferation Treaty. The Treaty on the Non-Proliferation of Nuclear Weapons was signed simultaneously in London, Moscow, and Washington on 1 July 1968; it came into force on 5 March 1970. The treaty lays prohibitions upon both nuclear and non-nuclear states. It prohibits nuclear-weapons states from transferring nuclear weapons or devices, or control over them, to any recipient whatever. It also prohibits the inducement, encouragement, or assistance of any non-nuclear state in the manufacture or acquisition of nuclear weapons. And it prohibits non-nuclear states from acquiring, by transfer or manufacture or any other means, nuclear weapons or devices. Non-nuclear states also undertake to conclude with the International Atomic Energy Agency a "safeguards agreement," allowing inspection of civil nuclear facilities to prevent the diversion of fissionable material into military projects. Finally, the parties to the treaty agree to certain general provisions. They undertake that the benefits of the peaceful applications of nuclear energy, including nuclear explosions, will be made available to non-nuclear states through the supply of equipment, nuclear material, and scientific and technical information. The nuclear states also promise to pursue in good faith negotiations on effective measures to end the nuclear arms race, and to bring about nuclear disarmament, and, finally, a treaty on general and complete disarmament.

Up to the end of 1983, the treaty had been signed by 121 countries; but only 76 of those had taken the further step of concluding a safeguards agreement. Thirteen Arab countries had signed the treaty: Egypt, Iraq, Jordan, Kuwait, Lebanon, Libya, Morocco, Somalia, Sudan, Syria, Tunisia, the Yemen Arab Republic, and the People's Democratic Republic of Yemen. But only seven of these had signed a safeguards agreement: Egypt, Iraq, Jordan, Lebanon, Libya, Morocco, and Sudan.

Israel has not signed the treaty. At the peace negotiations at Camp David in August 1978, Egypt proposed to Israel that both countries renounce nuclear weapons. The Israelis rejected this, on the grounds that even after a peace treaty had been concluded with Egypt, Israel would face continuing military threat from Syria, Iraq, and other Arab countries, and would need to retain even the most terrible military options. As a pretext, that is threadbare. The three Arab countries with the potential to acquire nuclear weapons are Iraq, Syria, and Libya. All three had signed the treaty long before the Camp David talks.

Egypt ratified the treaty in 1981, two years after the Camp David agreement—when it was clear, in other words, that Israel would not follow suit. The intransigence of Israel on this issue must be of concern—is intended by Israel to be of concern—to all Arab countries, whether or not they signed the Non-Proliferation Treaty.

Western Double Standards

The United States and France supplied Israel with nuclear reactors, nuclear technology, plutonium, and enriched uranium—all the ingredients Israel needed to produce nuclear weapons. The same countries supplied Israel with delivery systems: aircraft, missiles. Israel was even helped to build her own nuclear missile. Yet those same countries now enforce strict controls on the technology even for the peaceful uses of atomic energy in Arab countries. All this despite the fact that Israel has not signed the Non-Proliferation Treaty, while the Arab states on which these restrictions are enforced have signed not only the treaty but also a safeguards agreement allowing inspection by the International Atomic Energy Authority. The restrictions these countries place on the transfer of peaceful nuclear technology are themselves a breach of the treaty. The real scandal, however, is that the two countries which helped Israel to become a nuclear power have colluded with Israel in the destruction of the Arab world's embryonic nuclear industry. The first victim of this technological imperialism was Iraq.

It was at 4:00 pm on the afternoon of Sunday 7 June 1981 when eight Israeli F-16s, each loaded with two 2000 lb. bombs, took off from an airfield in the Sinai. Riding herd to protect them were another six F-15s. The code-name of the mission was *Babylon*. Its objective: the destruction of the Osirak nuclear reactor on the outskirts of Baghdad. It took three hours; by 7:00 pm the 14 aircraft landed once more in Israel, their mission accomplished. The reactor was totally destroyed. As a military man I cannot ignore the skill with which the raid was carried out. I must also point out that the success of *Operation Babylon* was the logical outcome of years of nuclear collaboration between Israel and the West on the one hand, and years of betrayal of the Arabs on the other.

The destruction of the Osirak reactor was, on any terms, a flagrant violation of international order and security. Here was a country which had refused even to sign the Non-Proliferation Treaty attacking a nation which had signed not only the treaty but the safeguards agreement which gave the treaty teeth. Yet the international community proved unable or unwilling to take action against the aggressor. Nine days after the raid, President Reagan solemnly declared that it had been an act of self-defence. In the Security Council of the United Nations, the US warned it would veto any resolution condemning Israel or seeking to impose political or economic sanctions upon it. To get anything at all, the rest of the Security Council was forced to adopt the mildest of resolutions condemning the raid upon the reactor but neglecting even to mention the country which had carried it out. This amputated resolution was carried unanimously on 19 June 1981.

The truth was, the United States could not condemn Israel—for the good reason that the US had been an accomplice in the raid. Of course, Washington denied all prior knowledge of the strike; but who believed that? Israel itself destroyed that alibi. The Israeli government was clearly prepared to take no more than the most face-saving quotient of criticism from America. Swiftly, the Israeli prime minister Begin began to threaten, none too subtly, that he would reveal the American role. On 15 June, he declared publicly that Washington had supplied Israel with the technical information it needed on the reactor. On 18 June, he revealed that Israel had sent two experts to the US in October 1980 to discuss the effects that might follow from the destruction of a nuclear reactor with 2000 lb. bombs. Meekly, America fell into line—blackmailed by its own client state. Nor could the US give adequate answers to questions as to why it had not, allegedly, learned of the impending raid from its reconnaissance satellites—or, more embarrassingly, from the AWACS early-warning aircraft which it was operating in Saudi Arabia. For it was later revealed that Israel had built a dummy reactor resembling the Osirak plant deep in the Negev desert to train the Israeli pilots for six months before their mission. It was frankly inconceivable that the United States had not detected what was afoot. On 6 November 1981, President Saddam Hussein of Iraq publicly accused the US of involvement in the raid, and of concealing from the Saudis information the US had gleaned from the AWACS aircraft operating from Saudi territory.

France's attitude was no less hypocritical than America's. In an interview published on 19 June 1981, President Mitterand said: "There was a secret clause in the French-Iraqi nuclear arrangements giving France the right through 1989 to inspect the nuclear installations in Iraq. . . . I have very warm feelings about the historic achievements of Israel and about its culture. I know the magnitude of its sacrifices. I admire the abilities of its people and I want to guarantee its existence. The Israeli attack will not change my opinion on the fundamentals. I remain true to my opinions. We condemn the raid, not Israel. We criticise the action of its leaders. We do not request sanctions against its people." Mitterand, in short, chided Begin for failing to place total confidence in the president of France. How could Begin even dream that France would supply Iraq with a weapon that could threaten Israel? No doubt Begin would have something to say about the naïveté of that; the Arabs are entitled to challenge its hypocrisy. Why did France not bother to impose upon Israel the same conditions when it provided the Dimona reactor as it imposed upon Iraq as part of the Osirak contract? When Israel refuses to sign the Non-Proliferation Treaty while Iraq has accepted it in full, what can possibly justify that discrimination? For what good reason, moreover, did France help Israel to construct the *Jericho,* a missile designed from the start to be a nuclear delivery system? President Mitterand's concern for Israel's security is touching; but the Arabs are entitled to be concerned for theirs—and to ask France some hard questions. For President Mitterand's remarks make abundantly clear the fact that France's present policy of currying favour in the Arab world through the supply of arms to Iraq and a few other countries is a sham. France, it is clear, will give no help to the Arabs that could remotely constitute a challenge to Israel.

The implications of Israel's attack upon the Osirak reactor are, of course, profound. For the air strike was the climax of two years of sustained effort by Israel to sabotage the project. In April 1979, unknown saboteurs—even at the time, some reports identified them as Israeli—tried to blow up the core of the Osirak reactor while it lay in a warehouse at La-Seyne-sur-Mer in France awaiting shipment to Iraq. A year later, Yahia el-Meshed, the Egyptian-born director of Iraq's nuclear programme, was found bludgeoned to death in a Paris hotel room. A few weeks later, a French prostitute named Marie-Claude Magal—rumoured to have been a witness to the death of Meshed—was killed by a hit-and-run driver in Paris. The next month, bombs wrecked the Rome offices of SNIA Techint, the Italian nuclear company working in Iraq. The same day there was an unsuccessful attempt to assassinate a French scientist working on the Osirak project. The old principle of *cui bono* tells us where to look for the culprits in all this.

Israel's concern at the possibility of an Arab country acquiring nuclear weapons is understandable. But if Israel really did want to live in harmony with its neighbours, its logical response to this concern would be to press for a nuclear-free Middle East—which in turn would mean its accepting the Non-Proliferation Treaty and agreeing to its safeguards. What is unacceptable is Israel's apparent determination to remain the only nuclear power in the region. It is also foolish: in the long run, Israel must surely see that the Arabs will respond to the nuclear threat hanging over them by seeking their own deterrent.

Israel's Weaknesses

The Giant Robot

Israel appears more powerful than it is. Israel has enormous and impressive armed forces. Its industry produces a good proportion of the equipment those armed forces need; and its weapons sales make it the fifth biggest arms exporter in the world. It commands much advanced technology. But in contrast to this display of external power, Israel is internally very weak.

It has a relatively tiny population. It is poor in natural resources. It is particularly short of water. Most fundamentally, its economy is unbalanced beyond all hope of recovery: the prime reason for this being that Israel's Jewish citizens appear to regard it as their birthright to consume vastly more than they produce. The upshot is that Israel's foreign debt now stands at $22.5 billion, the highest debt per head of population of any country in the world. By any normal measure, Israel is bankrupt: it survives, the remittance man of the Middle East, on handouts from the United States. The closer we examine Israel, in fact, the more we see that it resembles nothing so much as a giant robot: looming over its surroundings, crushing all in its path, outwardly invincible; but inside hollow, its actions and even its survival wholly dependent on the impulses and commands of others.

Energy

Israelis joke that when God asked Moses where he wished to lead His people, Moses intended to say Canada but, because of a stutter, could only mumble Canaan—so dooming the Jewish people to a land possibly rich in milk and honey but notably short of other resources. Oil is Israel's biggest single import, costing the country around $2250 million a year. To cut this bill, Israel has ambitious plans to diversify its energy sources. By the year 2000, Israel wants to use oil for only 30 per cent of its energy needs, with solar energy, coal-fired plants, and nuclear and hydro-electric generators filling the gap. These plans reveal a good deal about Israel's designs for the region.

The Dead Sea is at the heart of those plans. A $20 million solar energy programme plans to exploit a peculiarity of the mineral soup filling the great lake: its surface layers act as insulation, trapping heat from the sun in its lower depths, which in consequence are as hot as 200 degrees Fahrenheit. The Israelis plan to tap this heat-bank by lowering into it a network of pipes through which they will pump a special liquid called Feron; converted into steam by this trapped heat, the Feron will return to the surface to power turbines developed by the Israeli firm Ormat. Already, Ormat has installed a 150 kilowatt generator for a local tourist hotel. Now, in a series of pilot projects, it is building up a 62-acre pond which is planned to give five megawatts of electricity.

But the most ambitious project is to produce hydro-electricity by digging a canal from the Mediterranean to the Dead Sea. In this too, Israel is following the designs of its Zionist founders. As long ago as 1902, Herzl noted that the level of the Dead Sea is 395 metres below that of the Mediterranean. A canal between the two would enable a power station to take advantage of this natural fall. For many years such plans were ignored in Israel: the Israeli leaders assumed that they would always be able to command oil supplies from the region. The oil crisis which followed the October 1973 war destroyed that illusion, and revealed Israel's vulnerablility. Golda Meir's government asked Professor Yuval Ne'eman—a super-hawk and the father of Israel's atomic bomb—to study the problem. Ne'eman reported in 1980; and the Begin government accepted his proposals.

Ne'eman's plan for the Dead Sea comprises three smaller projects. Project One is to construct a 110 km canal linking it with the Mediterranean: a hydro electric plant at the Dead Sea end will produce about 1500 megawatts. (The High Dam at Aswan was planned to give 2100 megawatts, but currently produces only about 1000 megawatts.) Project Two is to build a nuclear power plant at the Mediterranean entrance to the canal, harnessing the canal's current to cool the reactor. Project Three is to expand the Ormat idea and turn the entire surface of the Dead Sea into solar ponds. Together, Ne'eman has calculated, these three projects will produce 3000 megawatts—enough electricity to make Israel self-sufficient in energy.

Israel has dismissed as of no consequence the fact that the canal would run through the occupied West Bank; so its construction would violate the Geneva Convention with regard to the treatment of occupied territories. The truth, of course, is that the canal will seal Israel's possession of land which it has no intention of giving up anyway. Israel is also indifferent to the damage the whole project will do to Jordan, and in particular to its potassium-extraction plant on the eastern shore of the Dead Sea. (Mindful of those considerations, the United Nations General Assembly voted against the project on 16 December 1983. The voting was 141 to two, the two being Israel and the United States.)

Water

Israel is short of water. Its total exploitable resources amount to less than 2000 million cubic metres of water a year, and already Israel is consuming about 95 per cent of that. Agriculture accounts for 80 per cent of Israel's water needs; industry a mere five per cent. The future of Israel, no less, depends upon its finding more water.

There is nothing new in this. The Zionist plans to give Israel that water go back for decades before the state was born. When Chaim Weizman argued for the creation of a Jewish state at the 1919 Geneva peace conference, the map he produced included the Litani River of southern Lebanon within the borders of his projected state. Ben-Gurion's 1937 map was more expanisve still: he included both the Litani and the Jordan and all their feeder tributaries. The state as it emerged, of course, included none of these; but in 1967 the Israeli prime minister Levi Eshkol made clear Israel's determination to remedy that: "More than half a billion cubic metres of the Litani River's waters are allowed to flow wastefully into the sea every year. Thirsty Israel cannot stand unconcerned while that water is thrown away into the sea."

The logic is clear. Israel cannot resolve its water problems by re-cycling. Already Israel purifies for agricultural use some 30 million cubic metres of water from its sewage. This could be increased, but only to about 300 million cubic metres of re-useable water a year, still far below Israel's needs. Without internal resources, Israel must look to the Litani and Jordan rivers. It is now clear that the waters of the Litani were one of the main targets, perhaps even the primary tar-get, of Israel's invasion of Lebanon in 1982. Foreign journalists ac-companying the invading army reported that on the heels of the tanks came Israeli engineers, building pumping stations and pipelines to draw water south to Israel. In its propaganda, of course, Israel declared that the sole purpose of this invasion was to destroy the PLO and to secure Israel's northern region; withdrawal was promised as soon as those usefully hazy missions were accomplished. But armies hunting guerrillas do not take water engineers along with them; plans and materials for a major water extraction project are not assembled overnight; and pumping-stations and pipelines, once built, have continuously to be guarded. Thus the tapping of the Litani makes a lie of every Israeli public statement about its invasion of Lebanon.

Already Israel is reportedly drawing off 400 million cubic metres of the Litani each year. But the river's entire annual flow is no more than 700 million cubic metres; even if it were feasible to tap all that, it would satisfy Israel's needs for only the next 10–15 years. The Jordan has to be its next target. Through its invasion of the Jordan's west bank, Israel secured access to the river in 1967; now it takes 800 million cubic metres of water from it each year. The Jordan's total annual flow is only 1,450 million cubic metres. Inevitably, Israel has looked to further exploit the rivers which feed the Jordan; and under international agreements going back years, it has the right to some water from the Jordan's main feeder, the Yarmuk. But it is now reaching the limits of what it can lawfully extract. In 1984, the *Jerusalem Post* reported: "Israel's water commissioner Zemah Yishai said on April 3 that Israel would begin this summer to take all the water from the Yarmuk river to which it is entitled under agreements with Jordan. By the end of 1985 Israel will be able to draw 60–70 million cubic metres a year. The water commission has also decided to draw water from the Sea of Galilee, lowering its autumn level by one metre to 213 metres below sea level, so as to be able to take in additional Yarmuk water and rain water."

By the end of this century, Israel will be thirsty once more. It will be able to quench that thirst only by seizing control of all the headwaters of the River Jordan, which lie in Jordanian, Syrian, and Lebanese territory. The Israeli Defence Ministry has without doubt already drawn up plans for the invasion.

Population

The founders of the Jewish state had a simple concept: it should become the homeland of Jews now scattered across the world. Without Jewish immigration, in fact, Israel has no future. So one of the new state's first laws, passed in 1950, was the Law of Return: every Jew who arrives in Israel is automatically an Israeli citizen. But now the tide of immigrants, like the flow of Israel's water, is ebbing.

In the first place, the reservoir of world Jewry is limited in size. The Israeli government estimated in 1983 that the global Jewish population was about 14.25 million, distributed as follows:

3.3 million:	Israel
6.0 million:	United States of America
2.75 million	USSR and Eastern Bloc
1.375 million:	Western Europe, Australasia
550,000:	Latin America
300,000:	Canada
250,000:	Africa and Asia

Fanatically religious Jews reject these figures, on the grounds that many here counted as Jews were in fact born to non-Jewish women and so—because Jewish descent is matrilineal—are not "true" Jews. Such strict reckoning cuts the world Jewish population to perhaps 13 million. And it is, seemingly, declining. The Institute of Jewish Studies at the Hebrew University of Jerusalem has calculated that by the year 2000 the world Jewish population will be 11.8–12.9 million. The Institute's study attributes the fall predicted over the next two decades to several reasons: a low birthrate among Jewish families, and mixed marriages between Jews and non-Jews. The Institute further reckons that by the end of the century, 36 per cent of the world's Jews will be living in Israel—giving the country a Jewish population by the year 2000 of 4.25–4.65 million.

To the Arabs these arguments about Jewishness are a matter of supreme indifference. What concerns the Arabs are not Jews but Zionists; and here the Arabs follow the definition usefully provided by David Ben-Gurion: "A Zionist is a Jew who plans to become an Israeli." To the Arabs, in other words, any Jew who lives in Israel is a Zionist. So while Arab demographers reckon that by the end of the century the world Jewish population might in fact reach 16 million, the question important to Arabs is how many of those will be living in Israel—and the answer seems unlikely to be anything approaching 36 per cent. The truth is, immigration to Israel has lost its appeal.

This is not surprising. The great waves of immigrants to Palestine in the past comprised Jews escaping from persecution or poverty, plus those of particularly strong religious convictions. But now, 36 years after the establishment of Israel, most Jews falling into those categories have already arrived. And circumstances have changed dramatically in the world at large. With the destruction of Nazism and its allied regimes, anti-semitism has waned—at any rate, anti-semitism as government policy. Most Jews in the world outside Israel live peaceful and prosperous lives, commonly with a measure—and in some cases a good deal—of economic and political power within their societies. The incentive to uproot themselves has withered, especially when what awaits them is an Israel with inflation running at around 200 per cent a year (inflation reached a high of 445 per cent during 1984 and 180 per cent during the first ten months of 1985) —an Israel locked in a seemingly endless spiral of violence and repression. With mounting desperation, the Israeli leadership looks for immigrants from the last great Jewish community which still professes to be oppressed: the 2.75 million Jews living in the Soviet Union and the Eastern Bloc. Oppressed they may be; eager to come to Israel many are not. In 1982, one Savik Shuster, a Jew born in the Soviet Union but now living in Canada, reported the findings of a study he had made into the lives of Soviet Jews in Israel. Mr. Shuster found that between 1968 and 1982 about 160,000 Jews emigrated from the Soviet Union, but only half of them settled in Israel. Many of these, he found from the scores of interviews he did, were now disillusioned with Israel and wished to return to the Soviet Union. The Soviets would not accept them. "I would crawl back on my knees," Shuster quotes one of these would-be-returnees as saying. Shuster's study was too anecdotal to quantify this disillusion (though the mere fact of it raises questions about the degree of alleged persecution in the Soviet Union). But there is solid evidence of Israel's deepening loss of appeal even to Soviet Jews. In August 1984, Chaim Aron, head of the Jewish Agency—the organisation responsible for Jewish immigration to Israel—reported that 80–90 per cent of the Jews leaving the Soviet Union on visas to Israel never in fact arrived: they went to the United States instead.

There is equally compelling evidence of general disillusion inside Israel. Since 1980, immigration to Israel has been outnumbered by emigration from it. According to the Arab League, which has kept such figures since Israel's birth, the population flow over the years has been as follows:

Year	Immigration to Israel	Emigration from Israel	Net flow
1948–1973	1,542,178	241,074	1,301,104
1974	32,200	16,400	15,800
1975	20,600	20,200	400
1976	19,954	13,300	6,654
1977	24,000	15,000	9,000
1978	35,000	12,000	23,000
1979	38,000	28,000	10,000
1980	27,254	31,000	-3,746
1981	12,000	21,000	-9,000
1982	13,300	14,587	-1,287
1983	16,500	6,500	10,000

In 1984, the raw statistics seemed to show a check in this trend: there was a net inflow. Though 17,000 Jews emigrated from Israel, 19,236 immigrated there. But those immigrants included 12,000 Ethiopians, of the tribe known as the Falasha, who profess Judaism and who were in consequence secretly airlifted to Israel. In 1985, it is predicted that the trend will reassert itself, with an outflow of probably 30,000 emigrants greatly outnumbering new arrivals.

To halt this trend, the United States Congress passed in April 1980 the Refugee Act, laying down that Jews settled in Israel will no longer be considered refugees and as such eligible for entry into the United States. It is ironic that the same American legislators who complain so loudly about the Soviet Union's supposed reluctance to let out its Jews should with this measure be conspiring with the Israeli leadership to make it harder for Jews to leave Israel. The predictable outcome was of course just what Chaim Aron has since reported: Soviet Jews now head straight for the United States rather than risk being trapped in Israel on the way.

In the light of these trends, the best Arab estimate is that, barring unforeseen and extraordinary developments, the Jewish population of Israel will be about 3.63 million by 1993, and about 3.88 million by the year 2000. The Arab estimates, that is, are about half a million less than those of the Institute of Jewish Studies in Jerusalem. But of course the exact size of Israel's future population—be it three, four, or five million—is of less consequence than the sheer disparity of scale foreshadowed by any of those projections. Because, by the end of the century, the Arab world around Israel is forecast to have a population of at least 250 million. How can a tiny nation, however militarised, hope to dominate a world of that size? Ben-Gurion used to say: "Only an idiot or a genius could believe that Israel can conquer the Arabs." Yet every year Israel grows more imperial, less accommodating; while all the time the population balance in the region tilts inexorably against it. The dream of regional hegemony which inflames men like Begin and Sharon is a fantasy for the asylum. It offends against common sense, against logic, against everything we know from history. Britain, France, Holland, Portugal, Spain: all in their day held dominion over peoples and nations many times larger then they. But even they, with advantages in their time denied to Israel today, could not hold their empires. The history of Jerusalm provides a lesson closer to home: the Crusaders occupied Jerusalem for more than 80 years—but in the end the Arabs regained it. At the turn of this century, Lenin cautioned the world against awakening what he called "the sleeping giant", China. Israel's continued occupation of Arab lands is a permanent affront to the sleeping Arab giant. Those population projections—matching an Israel of perhaps four million people against an Arab world of 250 million—should make Israel and its supporters think hard of what will happen when the sleeping giant rises to his feet.

Arabs in the Occupied Lands

At the end of 1983, there were 2,025,000 Arabs living in the territories occupied by Israel. That figure excludes those Arabs under the boot of the invading Israeli army in south Lebanon, and is made up as follows:

700,000	Arabs in land occupied between 1948 and 1966
100,000	living in east Jerusalem
775,000	living on the West Bank of the River Jordan
450,000	living in Gaza

Counting the 350,000 Lebanese Arabs living south of that country's Awali River, and so overrun by the Israeli army in 1982, the total Arab population under Israeli occupation had grown by the end of 1983 to 2,375,000 people. They represent Israel's most intractable problem.

The Jewish victory in 1948 brought an Arab exodus from Palestine. Few Arabs wanted to live under the conqueror's rule in the new Israel, fewer still once the intended lesson of Deir Yassin had sunk home. For almost its first twenty years, Arabs constituted no more than 15 per cent of the population of Israel. That was as the Israeli leadership had planned. The founding fathers were true to their Zionist beliefs: Israel was to be a Jewish state, a state for Jews. No other voices welcome: Arabs out.

But the stunning Israeli victory of 1967 brought with the border changes an equally abrupt shift in the demography of Israel. Now the Arabs living under Israeli occupation were 40 per cent of the total population. No doubt Israel considered re-running 1948 and expelling these Arabs as it had expelled their fathers. There seem to have been two reasons why it did not take that course. One was the hope that the Arabs of the occupied West Bank, in particular, might provide a human bridge over which Israel could "normalise" relations with other Arab countries—on Israel's terms, naturally. An Israeli diplomat explained in a lecture in 1983: "Through the 'Open Bridges' policy [that is, relatively free traffic over the River Jordan] which Israel followed soon after the 1967 war, merchants from the West Bank were able to sell Israeli goods in Arab countries on the pretence that these were made by Palestinians in the West Bank and Gaza. At first the merchants were anxious to hide the fact that such goods were made in Israel; but later the restrictions eased and now Israeli goods can be seen on public sale in Arab markets." The second reason why Israel did not expel Arabs from the territories occupied in 1967 was that, unlike 1948, there were no waves of Jewish immigrants waiting to take the Arabs' place.

That remains Israel's dilemma. The Arabs are now an important factor in the Israeli economy. They provide the cheap and unskilled labour, freeing the Jews for work in the science-based industries on which Israel's future hangs—and of course for service in the country's massive armed forces. Israel has tried over the years to lessen its dependence on this Arab labour by deliberately seeking to confine it to seasonal agricultural work or to industries such as construction where, in time of recession, the Arab workers can be laid off first, so providing a cushion for Jewish workers' jobs. But this purposeful creation of an under-class only worsens Israel's problems in the long term, because nothing alters the fact that the Arabs in the occupied territories now constitute 38 per cent of Israel's total population. Yet they cannot, by definition, be integrated into Israeli society—for to do so would be to destroy the Jewish state.

So the Arabs living under Israeli occupation are treated as second-class citizens. Economically they are exploited. Politically their rights are curtailed. Socially they are set apart. And in Israel as in South Africa the philosophy of the rulers—that the state is founded on a basis of religious and racial exclusivity—means that the Arabs, like the South African Blacks, know matters can never fundamentally change for them. They are doomed to remain strangers in their own land. Not surprisingly, the Arabs in this humiliating position resent and oppose Israel more bitterly with each passing year. And how do the Israeli authorities respond to this opposition? With harsher repression: the state-organised repression by the security forces, backed increasingly by the "unofficial" activities of extremist Jewish settler groups whose mounting ferocity signals a clear conviction that the Israeli authorities are willing to look the other way. *Newsweek* reported as much on 16 January 1984: "Most Israeli experts are convinced that strong political pressure has prevented Shinbet—the Israeli FBI—from infiltrating right-wing Israeli circles. Begin himself is rumoured to have refused to authorise Shinbet to infiltrate the Gush Emunim, the militant settlers' group, after the car-bomb attack against the West Bank mayors. Abraham Ahituv, who headed Shinbet until three years ago, recently wrote an article in which he blamed the growing phenomenon of extremism on the sympathetic political environment."

Israel today is a society gestating into a second South Africa.

Jews-versus-Jews

What is Zionism? Elon Salmon, an Israeli-born writer now living in Britain, offered his answer to that question in an article in the *Economist* at the end of 1981: "For the founders of Zionism, Judaism without a living link with the land was devoid of meaning. Zionism sought to normalise the Jews and turn them into a nation like other nations. Persecution in Europe, culminating in the Nazi Holocaust, forced urgency on the Zionist programme, but it was never Zionism's *raison d'être*. Israel as a refuge state for persecuted Jews was and always has been a secondary aim in Zionism. The first aim was self-redemption in the ancient homeland."

Ben-Gurion's definition of Zionism was the pragmatic expression of that philosophy: "A Zionist is a Jew who plans to become an Israeli. A Jew who has no intention of doing so is not a Zionist no matter how enthusiastically he supports Israel." And this clear, operational definition of Zionism was accepted by most Israelis—until 1967. But after the 1967 war two developments diverted Zionism from its early ideals, seduced Israel from the path set for it by founding fathers like Ben-Gurion. The first was that Israel allowed its economy to become dependent on cheap Arab labour from the occupied territories. The Israelis discovered the delights of serfdom. The second outcome of the 1967 war was that Israel gradually became isolated in the world, a trend which accelerated after the 1973 war. (Israelis and their supporters commonly attribute this drift to the alleged "blackmail" of Arab oil. Economics surely played a part in it: the oil crisis of 1973 was the first, faltering demonstration of the Arabs' potential power; and as the world realised this, so it began to listen to the Arab viewpoint. That is the way of things. But the international disenchantment with Israel had begun in 1967, when the Arabs still had no economic levers worth the name; so "blackmail" cannot have been the cause. The simple fact is that sympathy initially given to "gallant little Israel," alone and supposedly embattled in 1948, is not so easily bestowed upon an arrogant military giant clearly bent upon occupying more Arab lands.) Whatever their cause, the effect of these two developments after 1967 was that, internally, Israel turned away from the austere ideals of the Kibbutzim and adopted instead the worldly, consumerist values of the West; while, internationally, it sought escape from its isolation through closer ties with the Jews of the Diaspora.

It is doubtful if more than a few old Israelis mourned or even noticed that shift in social values. But the turning towards the Diaspora was visible and, in its consequences, profound. For Israelis, it meant a shift of emphasis: from "Israeliness" as the root of their being, to "Jewishness." Thus Zionism, as Salmon put it, began to reverse its historic role: instead of Israelifying the Jews, now it was Judifying the Israelis.

But the Jews of the Diaspora—many of them, at any rate—were not content indefinitely to remain passive in this partnership. There is now a significant school of thought among the Diaspora which holds that organised world Jewry should have a greater say in how Israel conducts itself. Advocates of this view would say that Israel's future depends on its coming to terms with the Arabs. Fortress Israel has survived so far, but it is not a viable proposition in the long run. The odds of demography and economic power are stacked too heavily against it. To this bleak view of the future these critics in the Diaspora add doubts about the present. Israel, they say, has lost its soul, turning into a consumer society dependent on cheap labour at home and billions in aid from abroad. These critics look at the numbers of Israelis emigrating each year and they ask: what has gone wrong? The conclusion they tend to reach is that unless the aims and aspirations of early Zionism are revived, both the movement and its offspring Israel are heading for a crisis greater than any they have faced.

The Jews in Israel—at any rate, their leaders—vigorously dissent. The Jews of the Diaspora, they say, have an absolute duty to support Israel, economically with their donations, politically with their unswerving loyalty. In return, they say, Israel is responsible for the protection of Jews wherever they live. This concept of Israel as a sort of Jewish Superman, on call around the world, took flight in August 1982, when a Jewish-owned restaurant in Paris was machine-gunned, with six deaths and 22 seriously injured. Begin, then prime minister of Israel, reacted so hysterically he actually called on French Jews to stockpile arms to defend themselves, and pledged Israel's readiness to send men to France to help the Jews defend themselves against what he termed the "anti-Semitic movement" there. When France formally objected to Begin's outburst as being interference in France's domestic affairs, Begin replied: "The killing of Jews can never be con-sidered a domestic affair. It is the responsibility of Israel to protect Jews everywhere." The silence which greeted this in the Diaspora was deafening: Jews around the world seemed unaccountably unwilling to huddle under Mr. Begin's umbrella. The truth, as many in the Diaspora have divined, is that Israel is no longer a refuge from anti-Semitism; now Israel is a cause of anti-Semitism. By its actions, Israel is dooming itself to destruction; but in the process it is unleashing around the world waves of anger and criticism which are but a step from anti-Semitism. Small wonder that the response of many in the Diaspora of recent years has been to absent themselves, their voices, and their money, from a society seemingly so bent upon suicide.

The divisions provoked by Israel's policies are not merely between Jews in Israel and Jews abroad: a gulf is opening at home between first-class and second-class Jews. The first-class are the Ashkenazim, the Jews of Russian or east European background, whose forebears were the stalwarts of the Zionist movement and who came to Palestine in the great waves of immigration the Jews call the *aliyahs* around the turn of the century. The second-class citizens in Israel today are the Sephardim, the Oriental Jews—many from Arab lands. The discrimination against the Sephardim has deep roots. In his memoirs, Moshe Dayan quoted Ben-Gurion as frequently saying:

> Our main concern is immigration. We have to do everything possible to increase it and to attract immigrants from Western countries in particular. The strength of the Jewish people lies in quality not quantity; and only if we raise our quality will we be able to stand up to our numberless enemies.

Ben-Gurion was using code-words: for "quality" read Ashkenazim; for "quantity" read Sephardim. Another biographer of Ben-Gurion quotes him as calling the Oriental Jews "the scum of the earth." In theory, of course, all Jews are welcome in Israel. In practice, some are very much more welcome than others. In April 1984, a French journalist, Christian Hoche, published in *L'Express* his findings from a search through the archives of the Jewish Agency, the body officially responsible for immigration to Israel. He reported that in 1954, at a meeting in Jerusalem between the Jewish Agency and officials of the Israeli government, the president of the agency, Nahum Goldman, proposed halting the immigration of Moroccan Jews and, further, taking steps to repatriate Yemeni and Iraqi Jews to their countries of origin. A high official of the Israeli foreign ministry, Gideon Raphael, replied: "Nahum, for the sake of your prestige and for the sake of the high post you occupy, I ask that your proposal be wiped from the record." Goldman agreed. The discussion survives, however, in the agency's archives.

Discrimination against the Oriental Jews in Israel can even be quantified. A study published in January 1984 showed that of the 17 ministers in Yitzhak Shamir's government, only four were Sephardic. Of the 120 members of the Israeli Parliament, the Knesset, only 20 were Sephardic. (Interestingly, in view of Begin's apparent electoral appeal among the Oriental Jews, 13 of the Sephardic parliamentarians were Labour Party members and only seven were in the Likud.) Of the 33 members of the executive council of the Histadrut, the trade-union organisation, only nine were Sephardic. And throughout 139 publicly or Histadrut-owned enterprises in Israel, only nine directors were Sephardic. Yet Oriental Jews make up 56 per cent of the Jewish population of Israel.

The invaluable Amos Oz, himself an Ashkenazi, has given us the human face of this discrimination in long interviews with Oriental Jews in his book *In the Land of Israel.* Some of his interviewees lived in the village of Bet Shemesh, not far from an Ashkenazi settlement, Kibbutz Tzora. This is what Oz was told:

> You go tell your friends: until they let us come to Kibbutz Tzora when we want, to swim in their pool and play tennis and go out with their daughters; until they accept the children of Bet Shemesh in their school, or bring their kids to school here instead of dragging them a hundred kilometres by bus to some white school; until they stop being so snooty, they've got nothing to look for here.

> Take a look at Bet Shemesh and take a look down there at Kibbutz Tzora. Their daughters fuck around with the volunteers; their sons smoke dope, steal cars and come to Bet Shemesh to joyride at night; they disobey orders during the war, spread dirt about the government and the army, marry Swedish girls and leave the country. But so what, they are beautiful. They are the beautiful land of Israel. And we are the gangsters, hooligans, riffraff: the ugly face of Israel. Why don't you ask who dragged the Moroccans into prostitution and crime? Why don't you ask who taught the kids, while they were still in the transit camps, to make fun of their parents, to laugh at old people, to ridicule their religion and their leaders?

> You whites want us to do the dirty work. When you didn't have the Arabs, you needed our parents to do your cleaning and be your servants and your labourers. You brought our parents to be your Arabs. But now I'm a supervisor; and he's a contractor, self-employed; and that guy there has a transport business, also self-employed. If they give back the territories the Arabs will stop coming to work, and then you will put us back to work in the dead-end jobs. My daughter works in a bank now; and every evening an Arab comes in to clean the building. All you want is to dump her back washing floors instead of the Arab. The way my mother used to clean for you. That is why we hate you here.

> When I was a little kid my kindergarten teacher was white, and her assistant was black. In school my teacher was Iraqi, and the principal was Polish. On the construction site where I worked, my supervisor was some redhead from Solel Boneh. At the

clinic the nurse is Egyptian and the doctor Ashkenazi. In the army we Moroccans are the corporals, and the officers are from the kibbutz. All my life I've been at the bottom and you've been on top.

Amos Oz, after 21 pages of such views, concludes sadly: "What I have written of the things I heard from the people of Bet Shemesh is only a small part of what they said, because the discussion went on for five or six hours. What will become of us all I do not know. If there is someone with an answer, he would do well to stand up and speak. And he had better not tarry. The situation is not good."

Anti-Semitism

Anti-Semitism, used as a description for specifically anti-Jewish behaviour, is of course semantically incorrect. The Arabs are Semitic people too. Nevertheless, I adopt the term. More important than semantics is the fact that, after a generation of quiescence, anti-Semitism is on the rise again throughout Western Europe. And, as a survey by *Los Angeles Times* reporters showed in November 1982, Jewish leaders are increasingly worried by this.

The level of anti-Semitic acts varies from country to country, with France and Italy the worst infected. In 1982, Paris saw the machine-gun attack on the Goldenberg restaurant in August; while Rome saw the assault on a synagogue in October, both with heavy casualties. In London the Israeli ambassador was shot. In Brussels four people were hurt when a synagogue was bombed. In Austria the homes of prominent Jews were bombed. In West Germany Jewish graveyards were desecrated; the federal justice minister reported 323 illegal acts of anti-Semitism in West Germany in 1981, compared to 263 the year before.

According to the *Los Angeles Times,* virtually every Jewish leader they interviewed ascribed the increase in anti-Semitism in Western Europe to three basic causes: widespread unemployment (encouraging workers to seek out traditional scapegoats); growing political support by European governments for a Palestinian state; and, most important, Israel's invasion of Lebanon.

Despite this governmental support for the Palestinians (which the Jewish leaders naturally deplored), the European governments themselves were acquitted of anti-Semitism. "The British Government is not anti-Semitic," one Jewish leader in London declared. Another in Paris pointed out that President Mitterand's cabinet contains three Jews, while another is among his senior advisers.

What really worried the Jewish leaders was the relationship they sensed between this anti-Semitism and the actions of the Israeli government. Thus, in seeking to combat this anti-Semitism, they felt themselves to be in a dilemma. Many believed that Begin's policies were in large part responsible for the upsurge in anti-Jewish feeling; yet if they criticised those policies, they feared they might be adding fuel to the fire. What almost all agreed, however, was that anti-Semitism in Western Europe is linked as never before to events in the Middle East. And it was one of the Jewish leaders in France who surely pointed to the root cause of the problem when he drew attention to what he called the reversal of the traditional David and Goliath relationship between Israel and the Arab world. Nobody has much sympathy for Goliath.

2

The Superpowers and The Arab-Israeli Conflict

The Superpower Balance

The Path to Parity

Through the late 1940s and early 1950s, America's virtual monopoly of intercontinental nuclear systems—atomic bombs and the long-range bombers to deliver them—led the United States and its allies to believe that their requirements for conventional defences were relatively small. The US could respond to any Soviet attack, however limited, upon America or its allies by unleashing an atomic strike against the Soviet Union. This policy was called "massive retaliation."

As the 1950s became the 1960s, however, the Soviets began developing their own long-range nuclear capabilities. Now the United States, too, began to feel itself vulnerable. Accordingly, to protect its Western European allies while at the same time limiting the risks to the territory of America itself, the US pressed upon its reluctant allies a new policy: "flexible response." Under this concept, the US and its NATO partners supposedly committed themselves to strengthening their conventional forces so they might fare better against a Soviet conventional attack. At the same time, the US promised to increase its nuclear capabilities so that they could now be used either to support those NATO conventional forces, or to respond selectively to a limited Soviet nuclear strike—limited, in particular, to Western European targets. The US did not abandon the option of massive retaliation. Now, however, this was to be kept to deter the possibility of a major Soviet nuclear attack—in practice, an attack upon the United States.

Even this revised strategy of flexible response depended upon American nuclear superiority. (How else could the US ever dare to initiate nuclear war, if necessary, to support NATO's conventional forces?) Through the 1960s the US indeed retained superiority. Soviet strategic nuclear capabilities were small by comparison with those of the US: too small to give the Soviet leadership real freedom of action. If the Soviets, for example, were to target their missiles on America's hardened missile silos and front-line bomber bases—those where the nuclear bombers were on constant alert—the Soviet missiles were still too few in number to disarm America's capacity to retaliate. So the Soviet Union would face an American counter-strike that might even be against Soviet cities, because the Soviets—having expended their own missiles against American military targets, and with any missiles held back now being vulnerable to American strike—would have no further means of deterring a vengeful America. If, on the other hand, the Soviets targeted American cities, then the full weight of the undamaged US nuclear forces would inevitably descend upon Soviet cities in retaliation. No matter what the Soviet Union did in a first strike, in other words, the United States was certain to be able to inflict unacceptable punishment by way of retaliation. Hence the name given to this state of affairs: "assured destruction."

In the course of the 1970s, however, the Soviet arsenal grew steadily in quantity and quality. Finally, towards the end of the decade, the situation was reached where both superpowers became able theoretically to absorb a first strike from the other and still have the weapons to inflict unacceptable punishment in retaliation. The balance of terror hung level: the era of "mutual assured destruction" had arrived. Both superpowers have been adjusting to this state of affairs ever since.

Mutual Deterrence

Faced with a continuing need to provide at least a superficially credible nuclear defence for Western Europe at a time when the United States itself is now vulnerable to retaliation, the American response has been to seek ever more flexible and "limited" targeting options—essentially in the hope that any nuclear exchange could be held short of an attack upon the territories of the superpowers themselves. Of course, the US cannot admit this to its NATO allies, so the new doctrine is disguised as reply to alleged Soviet actions. The classic statement of this was by Defense Secretary Harold Brown on 20 August 1980:

The US has never had a doctrine based simply and solely on reflexive massive attack on Soviet cities. Instead we have always planned both more selectively (options limiting urban-industrial damage) and more comprehensively (a range of military targets). Previous administrations, going back well into the 1960s, recognised the inadequacy of a strategic doctrine that would give us too narrow a range of options. Our nuclear modernisation program emphasises the survivability of our forces, and it conveys to the Soviets that any or all of the components of Soviet power can be struck in retaliation, not only their urban-industrial complex.

The Soviet leadership appears to contemplate at least the possiblity of a relatively prolonged exchange if a war comes, and in some circles at least they seem to take seriously the theoretical possibility of victory in such a war. We cannot afford to ignore these views, even if we think differently—as I do. We need to have, and we do have, a posture, both forces and doctrine, that makes it clear to the Soviets and to the world that any notion of victory in nuclear war is unrealistic.

Nothing in our policy contemplates that nuclear war can be a deliberate instrument for achieving our national security goals, because it cannot be. But we cannot afford the risk that the Soviet leadership might entertain the illusion that nuclear war could be an option—or its threat a means of coercion—for them. In declaring our ability and our intention to prevent Soviet victory, we have no illusions about what a nuclear war would mean for mankind. It would be an unimaginable catastrophe. We also know that what might start as a supposedly controlled, limited strike could well escalate to a full-scale nuclear war.

Further, we know that even limited nuclear exchanges would involve immense casualties and destruction. But we have always needed choices aside from massive retaliation in response to grave but still limited provocation. The increase in Soviet strategic capability over the past decade, and our concern that the Soviets may not believe that nuclear war is unwinnable, dictate a US need for more, and more selective, retaliatory options.

Grasp that by "grave but still limited provocation" Brown meant a Soviet attack upon Western Europe, and his message becomes clear: the US has all but abandoned the doctrine of nuclear first use in defence of Western Europe; and should a nuclear war break out in Europe it would seek to confine its spread.

Brown's successor as defence secretary, Caspar Weinberger, has been franker still. Abandoning the convenient fiction of supposed Soviet plans to "win" a nuclear war, Weinberger gave the Senate on 14 December 1982 the real reason why the US was seeking to add yet more weapons to its nuclear arsenal:

As the Soviets began tipping the theatre nuclear balance in their own favour while maintaining their superiority in conventional forces, the risk became greater that a limited attack would appear attractive to the Soviet military. The strategic modernisation program which President Reagan set forth in October 1981 is designed to address in part this adverse and imbalanced situation. It restores the margin of safety we require in order to continue to deter successfully Soviet strategic aggression.

In essence the program is designed to accomplish two general goals: first, to improve the survivability of our present and planned forces; and secondly, to sustain the credibility of our deterrent policy by developing the capability to threaten and destroy if necessary the full spectrum of potential Soviet targets. This combination of improved survivability and military capability is intended to assure that the Soviet leadership will continue to recognise clearly and unambiguously that they can realise no conceivable benefit from initiating nuclear aggression.

Since the era of nuclear weapons began, the United States has sought to prevent a nuclear war through a policy of deterrence. That policy has worked successfully for almost four decades. We are dedicated to ensuring that it continues to do so.

Rearrange Weinberger's statement into its five salient points, and you see the American dilemma. *First,* Weinberger is saying that the Soviets have responded logically to the stalemate at the strategic nuclear level by building up their nuclear forces targeted on Western Europe: the so-called theatre nuclear forces. *Second,* he does not say that the Soviets intend to use these forces in a first strike against NATO. He says only that, given theatre nuclear superiority, the Soviets might think a "limited attack" an attractive option: he does not specify a limited nuclear attack. *Third,* in essence Weinberger is saying that the Soviets might feel able to launch a conventional assault upon Western Europe, in the confidence that their theatre nuclear superiority forecloses NATO's options for the first use of nuclear weapons to avert conventional defeat. *Fourth,* he is saying that the US has decided to leap-frog this problem by re-establishing superiority—he uses the euphemism "a margin of safety"—at the strategic nuclear level as a precondition for restoring extended deterrence. *Fifth,* he is saying that the US would propose to use its strategic weapons selectively in defence of Western Europe, in the hope of limiting the nuclear war.

More immediately, of course, NATO tried to leap-frog the perceived Soviet theatre nuclear superiority—in particular the threat posed by the Soviets' new SS-20 missile—by installing in Western Europe Pershing 2 ballistic missiles and ground-launched cruise missiles, both capable of striking the Soviet Union and thus, by common definition, strategic weapons.

The Soviet Union's response to these developments was given in a statement by the then-general secretary of the Soviet Communist party, Yuri Andropov, on 21 December 1981:

The imperialists have not given up their scheme of economic war against the socialist countries, of interfering in their internal affairs in the hope of eroding their social system, and are trying to win military superiority over the USSR and over all the countries of the socialist community. Of course these plans are doomed to failure.

The main road to confidence, to preventing any wars, including an accidental one, is that of stopping the arms race and returning to calm, respectful relations between states—to detente. We consider this important for all regions of the world, and particularly for Europe, where a flare-up of any kind may trigger off a world-wide explosion.

The Soviet Union is prepared to go very far. As is known, we have suggested an agreement renouncing all types of nuclear weapons—both medium-range and tactical—designed to strike targets in Europe. But this proposal has been met by deaf ears behind a wall of silence. I want to reaffirm that our proposal remains on the table. We have also suggested a variant: that the USSR and NATO countries should reduce their medium-range weapons by more than two thirds. So far the USA will not have it. For its part, it has put forward a proposal which, as if in mockery, is called a "zero option." It envisages the elimination of all Soviet medium-range missiles not only in the European but also in the Asian part of the Soviet Union, while NATO's nuclear missile arsenal in Europe remains intact and may even be increased. Does anyone seriously believe that the Soviet Union can agree to this?

We are prepared to agree that the Soviet Union should retain in Europe only as many missiles as are kept there by Britian and France—and not a single one more. This means that the Soviet Union would eliminate hundreds of missiles, including dozens of the latest missiles known in the West as the SS-20. In the case of the USSR and the USA, this would be a real "zero option" as regards medium-range missiles. And if, later, the number of British and French missiles were scaled down, then the number of Soviet ones would be further reduced by the same number.

Along with this, there must also be an accord on reducing to equal levels on both sides the number of aircraft carrying medium-range nuclear weapons based in this region by the USSR and the NATO countries. We call on our collocutors to accept such a clear and fair accord and to take advantage of this opportunity while it still exists. But let no one delude himself. We shall never let our security or the security of our allies be jeopardised. Thought should also be given to the grave consequences that the deployment of new medium-range weapons in Europe would entail for all further efforts to limit nuclear weapons in general. In short, it is now up to the USA to respond.

Andropov, in other words, was saying that the Soviet Union was sufficiently confident of its conventional forces in Europe to be willing to abandon its theatre nuclear weapons—if NATO would do the same. And in response to American plans to fight a limited strategic war in defence of Western Europe, Andropov warned that the Soviet Union might not be willing to play by the same rules.

That the American dilemma—how to give nuclear protection to its allies in an age of strategic nuclear parity—went far beyond Western Europe was evident from the US State Department's response the same day to Andropov's statement:

The Soviet proposal contained in Mr. Andropov's speech today is unacceptable because it would leave the Soviets with several hundred warheads on SS-20s, while denying us the means to deter that threat. We cannot accept that the US should allow the Soviets superiority over us because the British and French maintain their own national deterrent forces. Nor can we agree that medium-range nuclear force limits should apply only to Europe. This would leave the Soviets free to threaten our Asian friends as well as to maintain a highly mobile missile force that could be moved at any time into position to threaten NATO.

America's Nuclear Arsenal

In December 1983, the United States possessed 1885 strategic offensive weapons, carrying 7297 nuclear warheads with a total destructive capability of 2202.8 megatons. It was made up as follows:

1045 ICBMs	(the land-based missiles Titan, Minuteman-1 & Minuteman-2, with ranges of 11,000–15,000 kms)
568 SLBMs	(the submarine-launched Poseidon & Trident-1, with ranges of 4600–7400 kms)
272 heavy bombers	(the B-52s, with ranges of 9900–16,000 kms)

The US also possessed 393 intermediate-range offensive nuclear weapons, with 393 warheads of a total destructive capability of 95.3 megatons. It was made up as follows:

149 land-based missiles	(Pershing-1, Pershing-2, and the cruise missile BGM-109A, with ranges around 1800 kms)
44 sea-launched missiles	(BGM-109 cruise missiles, with a range around 2400 kms)
200 air-launched missiles	(AGM-86B cruise missiles, with a range around 2400 kms)

The US also possessed a range of tactical nuclear warheads and delivery vehicles, with a total destructive capability of 234.7 megatons. These were as follows:

36 Lance missiles (range 110 kms)
1140 short-range air-launched missiles, SRAM (AGM-69A, with a range of 55–160 kms)
452 artillery projectiles fired by the 203mm howitzers.

From which it is clear that in 1983 the total destructive capability of the American nuclear arsenal was 2532.8 megatons.

The Soviet Nuclear Arsenal

In December 1983, the USSR possessed 2521 strategic offensive weapons, carrying 8342 nuclear warheads with a total destructive capability of probably 5112.4 megatons. This force was made up as follows:

1398 ICBMs   (SS-11, SS-13, SS-17, SS-18, SS-19, with ranges from 10,000–11,000 kms)
980 SLBMs (various types, with ranges from 1400–8300 kms)
143 heavy bombers (Tu-95 & Mya-4, with ranges of 11,200–12,800 kms)

The Soviet Union also possessed 599 intermediate-range offensive nuclear weapons (the SS-4, SS-5, SS-20) with 1320 warheads and a total destructive capability of 401 megatons.

Finally, the Soviet Union possessed several thousand tactical nuclear warheads, on a range of delivery vehicles, with a total destructive capability of probably 856.6 megatons. So the total destructive capability of the Soviet Union is probably 6370 megatons.

Britain's Nuclear Arsenal

Though tiny by comparison with the superpowers' forces, the British nuclear force still possesses, by any conventional measure, immense destructive capability. The force comprises four Polaris submarines, each carrying 16 missiles with three warheads apiece. Total destructive capability: 38.4 megatons.

France's Nuclear Arsenal

18 land-based S-3 missiles, range 300 kms, each with a single warhead. Destructive capability: 21.8 megatons.
6 submarines, each carrying 16 M-20 missiles, of range 3000 kms. Destructive capability: 96 megatons.

Total French destructive capability: 117.6 megatons.

China's Nuclear Arsenal

100 land-based CSS-3 missiles, each of range 7000 kms, and carrying a single warhead.
Total destructive capability; probably 200 megatons.

The Consequences of Nuclear War

Together, the US, USSR, Britain, France, and China have approximately 30,000 nuclear warheads, with a total destructive capability of about 9,258.8 megatons—that is to say, about 500,000 times the destructive power of the bomb which destroyed Hiroshima. The detonation of even a few hundred of these warheads would destroy civilisation around the world, perhaps forever, certainly for decades.

Theoretically, there is more than enough explosive to kill every single person on this planet: that megatonnage is equivalent to two tons of explosive for every member of the earth's population. In practice, of course, the blasts of a nuclear war would impact most heavily upon the countries waging it. Assuming such a war were limited to the NATO and Warsaw Pact counties plus China, the likely blast per head of population works out as follows:

US and Canada: 10 tons of explosive per head
USSR: 9 tons/head
NATO (Europe):   4.5 tons/head
Warsaw Pact
(exc USSR):   4.5 tons/head
China: 2 tons/head

The destruction this would cause is unimaginable. To grasp the scale, recall that the utter destruction of the US Marines' building in Beirut in October 1983, with the death of 241 people, was caused by an estimated 900 kilograms of explosive.

Confronting this prospect, we may be sure, neither the leaders nor the peoples of the opposing superpower blocs for one second want a nuclear war—however much they may differ about the means to ensure that. Of all the former US defence secretaries, Robert McNamara has been the most outspoken on this topic, but there is no reason to think that his views are unrepresentative of his fellow officeholders. "We must act to reduce the risk of a nuclear war," he told *Newsweek* in December 1983. "We should begin by accepting two overriding principles. First, we must recognise that each side must maintain a stable deterrent: a nuclear arsenal powerful enough to discourage anyone else from using nuclear weapons. Neither the US nor the Soviet Union should move in a way to destabilise the other's deterrent, or to provide an incentive for a pre-emptive strike. That's absolutely imperative. Second, we must recognise that nuclear weapons have no military value whatsoever other than to deter one's opponent from their use."

The implications of that attitude for NATO, clinging as it does to a threat to use nuclear weapons first in the event of a Soviet invasion of Western Europe, are of course profound.

The Balance in Europe

The Warsaw Pact has a clear though not overwhelming superiority over NATO in conventional forces. The Pact has 25,490 tanks against NATO's 20,722; 11,830 artillery pieces against 8996; 3715 anti-tank weapons against 3027. Accentuating this numerical imbalance is the geographical disparity between the alliances. The Soviet Union could double the Warsaw Pact forces in a matter of days. The United States, separated from the battlefield by thousands of miles of ocean, would need several weeks to reinforce its troops in Europe by less than 50 per cent. Nor does it look as if NATO could emulate the Israelis and use air-power to buy time for this mobilisation. The Warsaw Pact has superiority in the air too: 7786 combat aircraft and 786 armed helicopters, against NATO's 3433 combat aircraft and 1195 armed helicopters.

The gloomy conclusion Western leaders draw is that the Soviet Union could successfully invade Western Europe with its conventional forces alone. NATO's Supreme Allied Commander, the US Army General Bernard Rogers, said on 28 September 1983 that NATO forces could not last much longer than seven to ten days against a full-scale assault from the east. Facing the prospect of a rout, he said, he would be forced to ask permission to use nuclear weapons in the early days of battle. If Western European governments wanted to relieve the anxieties of their publics about NATO's reliance upon nuclear weapons, they would have to spend more on conventional forces. Rogers called for a four per cent annual increase in military spending—a real increase, after inflation—to finance an impressive array of sophisticated weapons that Rogers wants to see in the NATO arsenal.

The question inevitably arises why NATO clings to a nuclear strategy so clearly suicidal. Why do the Americans, in particular, allow the West Europeans to persist in the belief that the United States would initiate global immolation on their behalf. It is, on the face of it, strange that Robert McNamara should have been one of the few Americans of prominence to advocate NATO's renunciation of the first use of nuclear weapons. One answer, voiced publicly by some strategists and believed privately by many European political leaders, is that the United States is, in the American phrase, holding Europe's feet to the fire. So long as the US holds publicly to the doctrine of first use, the public unrest this generates in Western Europe will force NATO governments to increase their spending on conventional arms. But whether the United States government really plans to use nuclear weapons to stave off defeat in Europe, knowing that to do so would almost certainly trigger a global holocaust, is a very different question.

The balance in the European theatre has a direct bearing upon the Arab military option in the Middle East. The link is the United States: at once the mainstay of NATO and the bulwark of Israel. And the point to ponder is that circumstances can be envisaged in which the United States could be forced to choose between those two commitments. To take the simplest example, the US has plans to airlift its 24th and 101st divisions from their American bases to forward positions in West Germany in time of crisis in Europe. But those divisions are also part of the Rapid Deployment Task Force, now renamed the US Central Command, which has the job of reinforcing American interests in the Middle East. Similar choices whould have to be made with regard to military equipment: if both superpowers were stocking up their forces in Europe in time of crisis or even limited conflict, neither would have much to spare for its friends in the Middle East. So we see that the status of the European theatre—the balance and the tensions—is of potentially paramount importance to the outcome of any future conflict in the Middle East.

The United States and Israel

American Interests

Whatever its other manifold failings, the administration of President Jimmy Carter was remarkable for its candour. On no topic was it franker than America's interests in the Middle East.

In a speech on 6 March 1980, Carter's defence secretary, Harold Brown, defined US interests in the region as being fourfold. One, to ensure Western access to adequate oil supplies. Two, to repel Soviet expansion in the region. Three, to promote stability in the region. Four, to advance the Middle East peace process, while ensuring— indeed, in order to ensure—the continued security of the State of Israel. Brown continued: "Oil is the lifeblood of modern industrial societies. Sixty per cent of the world's imported petroleum comes from this region. About 13 per cent of the oil consumed in the United States, and much higher percentages for our allies—45 per cent for Germany, and 75 per cent for France—comes from this region. As President Carter said in his State of the Union speech, an attempt by any outside power to gain control of the Persian Gulf region will be regarded as an assault on the vital interests of the United States. It will be repelled by the use of any means necessary, including military force."

The link which President Carter saw between support for Israel and the maintenance of America's wider interest in the region was direct, as he explained in his memoirs: "Before being president I believed very deeply that the Jews who had survived the Holocaust deserved their own nation. I considered this homeland for the Jews to be compatible with the teachings of the Bible, hence ordained by God. These moral and religious beliefs made my commitment to the security of Israel unshakeable. These were thoughts I shared with many other Americans; but now I had been elected president and needed a broader perspective. For the well-being of my country, I wanted the Middle East stable and at peace; I did not want to see Soviet influence expanded in the area. In its ability to help accomplish these purposes, Israel was a strategic asset to the United States."

The consequence was a Niagara of American aid. In his 1980 re-election campaigning, President Carter told the Jewish organisation B'nai B'rith: "I am proud that since I have been president we have provided half the American aid that Israel has received in the 32 years since its independence. This is not a handout, but an investment in America's own security."

To my mind those constitute the frankest statements ever made by a US administration about America's perceived interests in the Middle East. Their importance is that they dispel the popular misconception that the Jewish lobby in the US is the most important factor in the formulating of America's foreign policy in the region. Certainly the effect of this lobby cannot be discounted or minimised. But it must be understood: the task of the lobby is to shape America's foreign policy so that it is compatible with Israel's interests. Not even the lobby dares to elevate Israel as such to primacy of place among America's interests in the Middle East. Israel sidles in as the instrument of wider US interests. From which it follows, first, that this lobby could not have succeeded—and cannot succeed in the future—if the interests of Israel ever contradicted those wider interests the US perceives itself to have in the region. It follows, second, that the link between Israel and the United States, though strong, is not unbreakable.

Nor is it a question of party, in my opinion. The Republicans and Democrats differ on many issues, but there is consensus on the relationship with Israel. Support for Israel is accepted as part of America's strategic design for the Middle East. That explains why aid to Israel increases inexorably whatever the idiosyncracies of the man in the White House. That also explains the importance of the dissenting voices: that swelling number of Americans, mainly intellectuals, who question national policy towards Israel. For the thrust of their dissent is that American policy is shortsighted and does not serve America's own long-term interests. In other words, they question the link between Israel and American regional objectives.

The most outspoken critique of America's present position came in July 1982 from George Ball, from 1961–1966 US undersecretary of state and in 1968 the US representative to the United Nations, who told the Senate Foreign Relations Committee: "It has been 25 years since an American president has had the political fortitude to use this country's influence to make Israel back down from these aggressive adventures, [the last instance being] when Dwight Eisenhower forced the withdrawal from Sinai after the Suez War. In US foreign relations since 1967, Israel seems to be the exception to every rule, every principle America stands for. When Turkey invaded Cyprus in 1974, we suspended all military assistance to the aggressor for two years, because the Turks illegally used weapons we had given or sold to them for self-defence. When Israel invaded Lebanon eight years later, however, America—in particular the US Congress—seemed to have misplaced its last copy of the Arms Export Control Act. Our response was to promise delivery to Israel of 75 more advanced F-16 fighter aircraft."

In his study of American policy in the Middle East, *Taking Sides,* the historian, Stephen Green, dates this loss of perspective fairly precisely: "In the years 1948–1963, presidents Truman, Eisenhower, and Kennedy firmly guaranteed Israeli national security and territorial integrity, but just as firmly guaranteed those of Jordan, Lebanon, and the other nations of the region. The boundary line between US and Israeli national security interests was drawn frequently and usually decisively. Then, in the early years of the Johnson administration, 1964–1967, US policy on Middle Eastern matters abruptly changed. It would be more accurate to say that it disintegrated. America had a public policy on the non-proliferation of nuclear weapons; but suddenly had a covert policy of abetting Israel's nuclear weapons program. We had a public policy on arms balance in the region, but secretly agreed to become Israel's major arms supplier."

American Aid to Israel

Even for an economy the size of America's, the burden of Israel is onerous—and is growing heavier every year. It is doubtful, indeed, whether many Americans realise quite how much Israel is costing them every year; and equally doubtful that they would support this burden if they knew its true weight. From 1946 to 1983 the US provided more than $27 billion in official economic and military assistance to Israel. In the three fiscal years 1981–1983, US official aid averaged $3400 a year to an average Israeli family of five. Those figures do not include private gifts and donations, or proceeds of the sale in the US of Israeli development bonds. Of this official US aid, 70 per cent has been military. In all, America has given Israel $17 billion in military assistance since 1946. And virtually all of this—99 per cent—has been provided since 1965.

An effort to quantify the unofficial and indirect American aid to Israel, on top of this official assistance, was made in 1983 by the

Washington lawyer Frederick Dutton. Dutton estimated that total US assistance to Israel in 1983 came to $10.335 billion. He uncovered:

$2,685 million:	Official US aid
$200 million:	Support for the Israeli arms industry
$750 million:	Humanitarian aid from individuals and organisations
$450 million:	From the sale of Israeli bonds in the US
$3,000 million:	Short-term debt
150 million:	American private investment in Israel
$1,500 million:	Loss of excise duty on Israeli exports to the US enjoying special exemptions
$1,500 million:	Loss of US wages as a consequence of the impact of those Israeli exports
$100 million:	Miscellaneous aid

According to Dutton's calculations, American aid to Israel, direct and indirect, official and unofficial, in the year 1983, amounted to $3,130 for every single Israeli. Over the previous ten years, Dutton estimated, such US aid had totalled $75 billion. And he predicted that over the coming decade the total would top $100 billion.

The policy watershed which Stephen Green identified in the early Johnson years coincided with an equally decisive surge in American assistance to Israel. During the Eisenhower administrations, US aid to Israel averaged about $70 million a year. But under Johnson the totals at once began to rise steeply: from $70 million in 1963 to $130 million in 1964, and so upward. The kind of assistance changed too. Prior to Johnson, the US aid to Israel was mainly economic. Since then, 70 per cent of the assistance has been to enable Israel to buy American military equipment. This growth in US aid has to be seen in context. The reason for its surge in the Johnson years was not some upwelling of American generosity, but rather the ending of the brief illusion of Israeli independence. Up to the mid-1960s, Israel did not need lavish American aid, because it was getting money from elsewhere: 75 billion Deutschmarks from West Germany as compensation to the Jewish state for the Nazi atrocities against the Jews. For almost 20 years, from 1948 to 1967, Israel got these reparations; and most of the money went to buy armaments from France. Both parts of that policy were of American making. It was the US which pressured the defeated Germans into paying reparations to Israel. It was the US who pressed the idea that the Israelis should then buy French military equipment—thus helping to rebuild France's industries after World War Two. When these reparations were due to end, America stepped in as Israel's next source of subsidy; this came during the Johnson administration.

Whether President Johnson or the American taxpayer realised the scale of the commitment thus casually assumed is doubtful. For Israel has proved a voracious client. By the mid-1970s, during the Carter administration, US aid to Israel was running at $2.2 billion a year. (Even that excludes $3 billion paid to Israel as "compensation" for its withdrawal from Sinai in 1979 as part of the Camp David settlement.) Under the Reagan administration, Israel's appetite has grown further: by 1983, US aid was almost $2.7 billion; in 1984, $2.6 billion; in 1985, $3.4 billion; and $3.7 billion has been allocated for 1986. Yet even these awesome figures conceal the full extent of American official aid, because the type of assistance has altered too. American aid commonly comes in three ways: outright grants, which do not have to be repaid: so-called "waived loans," on which the interest is a nominal two or three per cent a year, and repayment is deferred for ten years and then spread over a further 20 to 30 years, and, finally, loans at close to commercial interest rates. The proportion of American aid to Israel given as outright grant has steadily increased. Out of the $2.6 billion in aid for 1984, $1.75 billion was outright grant; the remainder was "waived loans." For 1985 and 1986, the entire $3.4 billion and $3.7 billion will be gifts.

Yet still Israel is asking for more. On his visit to Washington in October 1984, the Israeli prime minister, Shimon Peres, requested that American aid for 1985 should be increased to a staggering $4 billion. Peres' reported argument was interesting: In keeping Israel strong, the United States was getting an excellent return on its money, compared with the much larger amounts spent to keep American troops in Europe and other parts of the world. He said the US spends $130 billion a year on NATO, and had to keep thousands of US soldiers (in fact, 355,000) in Western Europe. In Israel the US had an ally which did not ask for US troops to help it do the job. "We are doing it ourselves."'

The significance of Peres' argument was not his wearying reassertion of Israel's role as America's policeman in the Middle East. Clearly foreseeing the time when Israel's needs will force even the United States to look carefully at its priorities, Peres was playing the anti-European card: choose gallant little Israel over the soft Europeans. That is a dangerous card for Israel to play; because, as I indicated in my analysis of the military balance in Europe, the United States might indeed one day be forced to choose in time of crisis between Europe and Israel. If that time ever comes, then on no rational basis could the United States place Israel first.

American Technical Transfers

Israel's economic dependence upon the United States, as these figures show, is close to absolute. Its technical dependence is no less total. The apex of American collaboration was the technical know-how which the CIA gave the Israelis' nuclear weapons programme in the mid-1960s—the first account of which was given by the investigative reporter Seymour Hersh in *The New York Times Magazine* in 1978. But virtually all of Israel's burgeoning arms industry is, in fact, based on American technology and technical help.

The most blatant example of recent times is the American decision to grant access to the technology Israel needs to produce its new Lavi fighter, destined to be the teeth of the Israeli air force in the 1990s. After a meeting with Prime Minister Peres, the US Defense Secretary Weinberger announced on 17 October 1984: "The Lavi phase-three composite production technology has been released to Israel. This technology is the one that is essential to the production of the new aircraft." (Weinberger also announced that the US had agreed to a joint working group with Israel to study Israel's submarine requirements. What possible need does Israel have for submarines? Answer: to blockade Arab ports in the Mediterranean and to interdict the oil traffic in the Gulf. Why is it in America's interest to abet them in those plans?)

The Lavi transfer demonstrates, in fact, how America now has to bend its own rules to accommodate Israel's ever-increasing demands.

The rule is that US military credits are to be used by a foreign country to help finance its purchases of US military equipment; the money thus goes to support American jobs. But on 11 November 1983, the Congress approved legislation allowing Israel to use $550 million in US military credits to finance the construction of the Lavi—in Israel. When the Lavi competes with American aircraft in the world export market in ten years time, will US aircraft workers really think that money well spent?

Intelligence Cooperation

Cooperation between Israel and the US in military intelligence matters is particularly close. Following the 1973 war, the Pentagon set up with the Israeli armed forces a joint "data acquisition team" as a high-level part of the Defence Department's own weapons systems evaluation group. The group's job is to study the relative performances of US and Soviet weapons sytems when matched against each other. Israel's experiences were judged invaluable. Reportedly, the group's reports carry the classification stamp "No Foreign National Except Israel."

This unprecedented cooperation is duplicated across the whole spectrum of military intelligence and even in political intelligence about the Middle East. Despite this, Israel is unsatisfied and spies on the United States. In its 1979 report on Israel, the CIA noted: "Israel's program for accelerating its technological, scientific, and military development as rapidly as possible has been enhanced by exploiting scientific exchange programs. Mossad, the Israeli intelligence service, plays a key role in this endeavour. In addition to the large-scale acquisition of published scientific papers and technical journals from all over the world through overt channels, the Israelis devote a considerable part of their covert operations to obtaining scientific and technical intelligence. This has included attempts to penetrate certain classified defence projects in the United States and other Western nations."

Arms Deals

The Israeli government spent $6.461 billion on its armed forces in 1983. One in every four of those dollars came from the US Treasury. Israel's military dependence on America is total. Of Israel's 830 front-line combat aircraft, 570 were acquired with American grants or waived loans. Another 150 of the aircraft, the Israeli-assembled Kfir, relies upon a General Electric engine. Pratt & Whitney is developing the power plant for the new Lavi fighter. In all, Israel buys $500 million-worth of military parts each year from 15,000 American companies.

With the exception of some French aircraft and British tanks, virtually all the equipment operated by the Israeli armed forces has been obtained under the US foreign military sales programme. And Israel is a uniquely favoured customer: invariably the first country to get the latest and most sophisticated American equipment. Israel was the first to get the F-15, F-16, and E-2C aircraft—and the first to use them in combat. For America, of course, that is the pay-off. The Americans see little chance of testing in combat any of their most modern weaponry; so the Israelis are useful guinea-pigs. The information is fed back through that joint US-Israeli "data acquisition team."

But conflicts loom in the US-Israeli relationship. Israel is expanding its arms industry faster than its Third World clients can afford to increase their purchases. New markets have to be found; Israel has turned to the West, and to the United States in particular, competing with firms in those countries to sell the most advanced material. To give only one instance; Tedrian, a US-Israeli company based in Israel, beat a Dallas company, E-Systems, for a $40 million contract to supply sophisticated radar equipment for the US army's tanks and fighting vehicles.

Since 1979, the United States has bought $150 million-worth of Israeli-manufactured military equipment; now a one-billion-dollar deal is reportedly in the offing. A toehold of that size in the American market would provide the base for a dizzying expansion of the Israeli arms industry. But when will American taxpayers begin to ask whether they really want to subsidise Israeli jobs over their own?

American Combat Support

The US has consistently been reluctant to provide actual operational support to Israel in time of conflict—reluctant, at any rate, to provide overt support. The US is quite willing to arm Israel, but has so far stood aloof from open involvement in combat. There are three main reasons for this. First, the US must fear that combat support of Israel would provoke the Soviet Union to intervene militarily on the side of its friends in the region. Second, America's Arab collaborators can—and do—argue at the moment that their alignment with the US is what prevents America from intervening openly on Israel's side; however threadbare the argument, the US is presumably unwilling to destroy it. Third, the fact is that the Israelis have so far been able to do the job themselves, without need of direct operational support.

Alongside this overt policy, however, has crept an equally consistent pattern of covert support for Israel in its various wars. Slowly over the years, details have emerged of these operations.

The best-known case came during the 1967 war: the ill-fated cruise of the USS Liberty. The Liberty was an electronic-intelligence gathering vessel. In the early hours of 21 May 1967, the Pentagon ordered it to sail with all possible speed to a point off the coast of the Sinai some thirteen miles west of Gaza. From there, cruising just behind Egyptian lines in the Sinai, the Liberty could intercept virtually any radio communication in the area, including short- and long-distance military and diplomatic traffic, telemetry data, rocket guidance, and satellite control signals. These the Liberty could process and in many cases decode on the spot, relaying the most interesting back to the United States by bouncing a microwave signal off the surface of the moon. For its time, the Liberty was a very advanced spy ship.

It is reasonable, given Israel's relationship with the US, to think that anything the Liberty gleaned about Egyptian actions or intentions would have been fed straight to the Israelis. Yet on 8 June, Israel attacked the Liberty with aircraft and torpedo-boats. Why? Washington was more anxious to quell the outrage in America than to ask such awkward questions in public. As *Newsweek* wrote in its account of the incident: "Although Israel's apologies were officially accepted, some high Washington officials believe the Israelis knew the Liberty's capabilities and suspect that the attack might not have been accidental. [Israel had promptly claimed the attack had been a terrible mistake.] One top-level theory holds that someone in the Israeli armed forces ordered the Liberty sunk because he suspected it had taken down messages showing that Israel started the fighting. [Israel of course was claiming to have been attacked by Egypt—a lie.]" A later theory was that what Israel feared was not the Liberty's reception of its previous transmissions but the knowledge it would give Washington of Israel's future plan of campaign.

The US provided more direct help to Israel in the 1967 war. It is now clear that on 3 June 1967, four F-4C aircraft, then America's most advanced combat reconnaissance plane, were flown secretly to Israel—complete with their American pilots. The aircraft flew several photo-reconnaissance missions over the Egyptian, Syrian, and Jordanian fronts before they returned to their US Air Force bases in Europe on 12 June.

The same help was given in the October 1973 war. The US sent its high-flying strategic reconnaissance aircraft, the SR-71, over the Egyptian front. It is now known that the information gathered by the SR-71 was passed to Israel and materially helped the Israeli high command plan its counter-attack over the Suez Canal to penetrate Egyptian positions around Deversoir. The Israelis did not select that precise crossing point by chance. It was chosen as being the point of maximum vulnerability on the Egyptian front, because it was the boundary between sections of front covered by two different army corps. The Israelis may have learned this from their own field intelligence, but the SR-71 reconnaissance would have supplied the proof. Most crucially, the over-flights would have told the Israelis before they launched their assault that there was no Egyptian armour in or around the area to counter-attack.

Steadily, though, America is being drawn into ever more direct involvement in Israeli combat operations. During the October war, American pilots were flying Israeli aircraft on combat missions. Some were shot down and taken prisoner by the Egyptians. We found that they were American Jews, some actually living in the United States, but having dual nationality, American and Israeli. Now, American law forbids dual nationality and also prescribes that any American citizen who serves in the armed forces of another country automatically loses US citizenship. Only one country and one people are exempted from this wise prohibition: Israel and the American Jews. The effect of the loophole, of course, is to turn all Jews serving in the United States' services into potential Israeli reservists to be summoned to join the Israeli armed forces whenever Israel decides it needs them. They can then return, as if nothing had happened, to their units back in the States.

Looking to the future, though, it must be doubtful if the United States will be able to draw the line even there—and it looks as though senior officials of the Reagan administration realise this. Israel is saturated with military equipment: it can absorb no more. Already, in terms of conventional military equipment per head of population, it is the most heavily armed nation in the world. In other words, though Israel may hope to increase the firepower and combat-effectiveness of its forces with ever-newer American equipment, its potential for a real increase in military strength is now marginal. The Arabs, by contrast, have more resources, a vastly greater man-power pool to draw upon: inexorably, the Arabs are gaining strength. What the Soviets like to call "the correlation of forces" is tilting against Israel: its greatest military successes are in the past; ahead lie no more easy victories.

That, to my mind, was the rationale underlying the so-called strategic agreement concluded between the US and Israel on 30 November 1983. One of the main points of this agreement—indeed its only point of operational significance—was that the US can now stockpile in Israel heavy equipment needed for the American Rapid Deployment Task Force. In the guise of a logistics agreement, a crucial principle was quietly established: in future the United States is willing to deploy American troops on Israeli territory. Ask then: "Against whom, and for whose benefit, is this new American task force going to act?" The answer is clear.

American Political Support

The American support for Israel is so slavish that in the international arena they might be clones. President Reagan, addressing Jewish organisations in America on 18 March 1984, noted that the United States and Israel vote the same way in the United Nations nine times out of ten; whereas the Western European members of NATO vote with the US only six times in ten. The difference, which of course President Reagan forebore to point out, is that the countries of Western Europe are truly independent of the US; Israel is not. Or perhaps it is the other way round: perhaps it is the United States which is not independent of Israel. When President Reagan reiterated in the same speech that if Israel were ever expelled from the United Nations the United States would withdraw too, it was the logical culmination of twenty years in which US policy at the United Nations has been distorted—and to a large degree rendered ineffective—by its obsessional support for Israel. This support is independent of party. The Republicans were in the White House from the end of 1972 to the end of 1976 and again from the end of 1980. The Democrats alternated with them. The justification for Israel's every action never faltered.

- 10 November 1975: UN General Assembly adopts resolution declaring Zionism a form of racism. Votes for: 72. Votes against: 35, including the US and Israel.
- 15 December 1975: UN General Assembly adopts resolution condemning Israeli practices in the occupied territories [such as the destroying of Arab homes, the confiscation of Arab lands, and the continuing programme of annexation through the construction of new Israeli settlements]. Votes for: 102. Votes against: 3, including the US and Israel.
- 30 April 1980: US vetoes Security Council resolution calling for the establishment of a Palestinian state.
- 31 May 1980: President Carter announces that the US will veto any attempt by America's European allies to introduce at the Security Council a resolution on the right of Palestinians to self-determination.

- 30 June 1980: UN Security Council unanimously—with the US abstaining—denies Israel the right to change the status of Jerusalem and declare it Israel's capital. Even this bare resolution was a compromise: the US had threatened to veto an Arab-Islamic resolution calling for economic sanctions against Israel in response to its decision to declare sovereignty over the whole of Jerusalem.
- 29 July 1980: UN General Assembly adopts a resolution calling for Israel's withdrawal from all Arab territories captured in 1967. Votes for: 112. Votes against: 7, including the US and Israel.
- 20 January 1982: US vetoes Security Council resolution calling for measures against Israel in response to its annexation of the Golan Heights.
- 9 June 1982: US vetoes Security Council resolution condemning Israel's invasion of Lebanon, and calling for immediate Israeli withdrawal.
- 26 June 1982: US again vetoes Security Council resolution calling for Israel's withdrawal from Beirut—this despite the fact that the wording was deliberately milder than that of the previous resolution.
- 26 June 1982: In emergency session, the General Assembly adopts a resolution demanding immediate withdrawal of Israeli forces from Lebanon, and asking for consideration of punitive action if Israel does not comply. Votes for: 127. Votes against: the US and Israel.
- 17 October 1982: US Secretary of State George Shultz announces that Washington is suspending an $8.5 million payment owed to the International Atomic Energy Agency because of the vote of its general conference the previous month to reject Israel's credentials. Shultz warns that the US would withdraw from the United Nations and suspend payment of those dues too if Israel were to be suspended from that forum.
- 17 November 1982: General Assembly adopts a resolution condemning Israel for its attack on the Iraqi nuclear reactor. Votes for: 119. Votes against: the US and Israel.
- 10 December 1982: General Assembly adopts a resolution supporting the Palestinians' right to an independent state. Votes for: 113. Votes against: 4, including the US and Israel.
- 20 December 1982: General Assembly adopts a resolution calling upon Israel to withdraw from all Arab territories occupied since 1967. Votes for: 122. Votes against: the US and Israel.

- 14 October 1983: International Atomic Energy Agency, at its annual general conference, votes 52–24 to recognise Israel's credentials after the US warns that it will withdraw its support, equivalent to about a quarter of the agency's $96 million budget, if Israel is rejected.
- 15 December 1983: General Assembly adopts resolution calling upon the International Atomic Energy Agency not to cooperate with Israel. Votes for: 99. Votes against: the US and Israel.
- 15 December 1983: General Assembly adopts resolution calling upon Israel to cease all work on its project to drive a canal from the Mediterrranean to the Dead Sea. Votes for: 141. Votes against: the US and Israel.
- 15 December 1983: General Assembly adopts eight other resolutions condemning Israeli policies and practices in the occupied Arab territories: confiscation of Arab lands; construction of Israeli settlements; punitive actions against parents of Arab children protesting against Israeli occupation; detention of Arab leaders in villages where trouble occurs; collective punishment of those villages; detention without trial; humiliating treatment of prisoners; the right of civilian Jews to bear arms on the occupied West Bank, endangering the lives of the Arabs living there; interference in Arab schools and other educational establishments. The resolutions called upon other countries to end cooperation with Israel, especially support that might encourage the continuation of such practices or of the occupation of Arab territories. The United States and Israel voted against all eight resolutions.
- 29 December 1983: US tells the United Nations Educational, Scientific and Cultural Organisation [UNESCO] that it will withdraw at the end of the next year. The reason given: "There has been a serious problem of politicisation throughout these agencies with issues coming up such as South Africa, Israel, and disarmament issues well beyond their area of specialisation."
- 6 September 1984: US vetoes a Security Council resolution calling on Israel to lift all restrictions imposed on Lebanese civilians travelling through Israeli-occupied southern Lebanon.
- 13 November 1984: UN General Assembly adopts a resolution holding Israel responsible for the safety of the Palestinian refugees

living in Israeli-occupied southern Lebanon. Votes for: 105. Votes against: US and Israel.

- 7 December 1984: UN General Assembly adopts a resolution calling on Israel to cease work on its project to drive a canal from the Mediterranean to the Dead Sea. Votes for: 115. Votes against: US and Israel.
- 11 December 1984: UN General Assembly adopts resolution to establish an independent Palestinian state and calls for an international conference on the Middle East. Votes for: 121. Votes against: 3, including the US and Israel.
- 14 December 1984: UN General Assembly adopts eight resolutions condemning Israel for its policies, among them the violation of human rights, in the occupied Arab territories. Votes for each resolution vary. Votes against: US and Israel.

The relationship between the US and Israel grew closer still in March 1985, when the US defence secretary, Caspar Weinberger, stunned the world with the announcement that Israel had been invited to participate in the research programme towards the Strategic Defence Initiative, President Reagan's plan for the "Star Wars" defence against nuclear missiles. Arguably, an invitation to America's NATO allies to participate was inevitable; but an invitation to Israel seems inexplicable. Two possible explanations present themselves.

The first is that the US knows that Israel has already become a nuclear power and fears that the Arabs may soon acquire the same capability. It intends, therefore, to supply Israel with defences to nullify the potential threat from an Arab nuclear force. The second possible explanation is that the US intends to deploy its own nuclear weapons in Israel, as it has done over the past 25 years in Europe. That would, of course, make Israel an automatic target for a Soviet nuclear strike—which, given the size of the country, would inevitably spread beyond the confines of military bases to engulf its cities as well. The prospect can scarcely appeal to the Israelis. To reassure Israel, therefore, the Americans—on this hypothesis—have offered to share whatever capability the Strategic Defence Initiative can ultimately provide.

To supply Israel with such advanced capabilities, for whatever reason, would be seen by the Arabs as further provocation. It is reasonable to assume that some would feel obliged to reply by seeking Soviet assistance—perhaps even inviting the Soviet Union to balance Israel's nuclear force by deploying Soviet weapons in Arab territory.

Voting Against Israel

The United States makes no secret of the fact that it regards itself as Israel's bodyguard—though, naturally, Americans prefer to cloak the point in more resounding phrases. But President Carter was surprisingly frank in his memoirs: "The Arab world and its many allies in international organisations continually raised the question of settlements in the occupied territories, the status of Jerusalem and the West Bank, altercations in Lebanon, and Palestinian rights. One after another of these resolutions, all condemning Israel, were introduced in the United Nations and other meetings, where they almost always passed overwhelmingly. Only the threat of a United States' veto in the Security Council prevented the adoption of more serious proposals involving political and economic sanctions by the international community against Israel."

In its utter disregard for the actual rights of the issues being raised, its unquestioning assumption that it is proper and prudent for the United States to ally itself so totally with one small country in a troubled region of great strategic importance to the West, Carter's flat recital is a revelation not merely of bankruptcy but, more dangerously, of blindness. But then, under Carter the US support for Israel degenerated into outright farce.

On 3 March 1980, the United States astounded the rest of the world by voting against Israel. The resolution before the Security Council rebuked Israel for increasing the number of its settlements in the occupied Arab territories, and referred in particular to the status of Jerusalem and the special need for protection and preservation of the unique spiritual character of the city and its holy places. The US joined with other Security Council members to adopt the resolution. Arab Americans were overjoyed; Israel and the American Jews were furious. That same evening, Carter issued a statement saying that the American vote against Israel had been an error caused by a failure in communication.

Under President Reagan, there has been a superficial hardening of US resolve. On 19 June 1981, the UN Security Council unanimously adopted a resolution condemning the attack on Iraq's Osirak nuclear reactor in Baghdad. The oddity was that the resolution thus condemned the attack but not the attacker. The US had warned it would veto any resolution explicitly condemning Israel. Still, it could be argued that it was an historic moment: the first time the US had ever voted against Israel at the UN. I disagree. Leaving aside the point that the resolution was wholly inadequate as a response to the enormity of what Israel had done, the affair was to my mind a tactical manoeuvre agreed between Israel and the US to disguise American encouragement and assistance to Israel in the execution of the raid. The US vote in the General Assembly on 17 November 1982 *against* a resolution condemning Israel for the attack surely demonstrates America's true stance.

The Reagan administration adopted the same manoeuvre on 18 September 1982, when it joined the rest of the Security Council in a unanimous vote to condemn the Israeli assault on West Beirut and to call for Israel's withdrawal to its previous lines. But once again the spare and weakly phrased resolution was in no way commensurate with the horrors which followed upon Israel's occupation of West Beirut—culminating, of course, in the atrocities visited upon the Palestinian families in the Sabra and Chatila camps. The resolution was a mere sop to assuage a Western public outraged by what TV had shown them of the horror sprawled along the alleys of these shanty-towns. On the real issue, how to force Israel to withdraw not just from Beirut but from the whole of southern Lebanon, the US was as unyielding and uncritical a supporter of Israel as ever.

The United States and the Arabs

American Objectives in the Arab World

The primary objective of the United States in the Middle East is to enforce an American hegemony over the nations of the region. The US perceives this to be necessary to ensure that Arabs as well as Iranians continue to export their raw materials, mainly oil, to the US and the industrialised West at cheap prices, while themselves comprising open markets for American and European manufactured goods.

To achieve that goal, the US has, since the ending of World War Two, followed a consistent set of policies towards the region. First, to eliminate Soviet influence there. Second, to ally itself with Israel, the one country in the region with no option (indeed, as we have seen, no *raison d'être*) but to act as a client state of this new Western imperialism. Third, to encourage inter-Arab disputes, rivalries between non-Arab countries bordering the region and their Arab neighbours, and racial and religious disputes within each Arab country. Fourth, to resist, subvert and if necessary destroy any genuine and thus potentially threatening move to create a strong and unified Arab state within the region.

Elimination of Soviet Influence

Since the fall of the Ottoman Empire—in fact, for almost a hundred years before its final collapse—the Arab world was recognised by the international order of those days as being within the Western sphere of influence. After World War Two, the United States virtually inherited this imperial legacy from the old and now impoverished colonial powers of the region: Britain, France, and Italy. For a decade, the region slumbered under the American umbrella.

In 1955, Gamal Abdel Nasser, then president of Egypt, became convinced that the Western powers were willing to help Arab nations neither to improve their economic state nor to achieve their political aspirations. He realised that the West saw any improvement in the conditions of the Arab people as, by definition, coming at the expense of American and European interests. The determinant for the West was the price of oil. In the years of American domination, the region sold its most precious resource for less than one dollar a barrel. (When that dominance was finally challenged, the price of oil jumped to about $40 a barrel.) It was exploitation: the West was buying the Arabs' raw material at an artificially low price and selling the region its manufactured goods at artificially high prices.

It followed that it would be foolish to expect the West to help the Arabs build their own industries: that would mean a loss of Western markets. It would be equally foolish to expect the West to supply the Arabs with modern weapons: armed, the Arabs could challenge the West's economic exploitation. Besides, a militarily powerful Arab world would be a rock to break the cudgel of Israel, the West's policeman in the region. Reviewing this network of oppression, Nasser decided to seek a new ally: the Soviet Union. The alliance was sealed with the arms deal concluded between Egypt and Czechoslovakia in 1955.

That was the door through which the Soviet Union first peeped into the Middle East. The door opened: people passed, and contact flourished between the Soviet Union and the Arab world, both at the official level between governments and on the unofficial level between peoples. Scores and eventually hundreds of students went to Soviet universities and technical schools, while thousands of Soviet experts swarmed across the Arab world in a genuine and wholehearted effort to help its nations develop. Agriculture, industry, health, education, science, communications, energy—no field was untouched by this surge of technical assistance. Inevitably, as first the Egyptian people and then the peoples of other Arab nations saw—on the ground, tangible before their eyes—what the Soviet Union was doing for them and their countries, their attitude towards the Soviets steadily warmed. The Arabs are neither naïve nor fools: they realised that the Soviets had their own motive for helping. The point was that they *were* helping; for the Arabs by now had learned, from leaders like Nasser, that the West would never help.

Soviet-Egyptian cooperation set the example for the rest of the Arab world; and year by year the Soviets became more involved throughout the Middle East. And the Arabs benefitted. Hundreds of factories were built, faster than the Arabs had ever believed possible.

The Soviet Union was generous in transferring its technology, and it did so without conditions. It was equally generous in its willingness to supply the Arab nations with arms: for the first time, the Arabs began to acquire the sophisticated weapons they needed to confront Western domination. For the West, of course, was the loser in this partnership, to such a degree that, fairly swiftly, Western leaders realised this new Soviet-Arab cooperation had to be challenged and broken or it was only a matter of time before the complete collapse of Western, and especially American, influence in the region.

If there was general agreement that Soviet influence had to be eliminated, it seems to me Western leaders were divided on the question how best to achieve this. The French and British, true to their colonial traditions, saw military intervention as the solution. The Americans certainly did not rule out the use of force, but they wanted to employ it indirectly and only after other less risky methods had been tried. That, I think, was the fundamental disagreement between them in 1957. The Americans wanted to try propaganda first; as befits a nation lying between Hollywood on one coast and Madison Avenue on the other, Americans place a good deal of faith in propaganda. And the American message to the Arabs was simple. Most Arabs are Moslem; Communists are by definition atheists. Arabs have a traditional respect for debate and for the authority of leaders elected by their communities; the goal of Communism is the dictatorship of the proletariat. So the theme of American propaganda was obvious and powerful: Collaboration with the Soviet Union will inevitably lead to dictatorship and the abolition of religion. Should that message fail, however, the Americans set about preparing other, more forceful means of persuasion.

Alliance With Israel

For the United States a powerful Israel is simultaneously a goal in its own right and a means to other goals. America has always seen a powerful Israel as an instrument of its wider interests in the region—above all, as a means of challenging and checking the expansion of Soviet influence. Israel is America's cudgel, its baseball bat to beat and punish any Arab country which has the temerity to challenge American hegemony. When propaganda fails, the killing begins. And Israel is willing to do the job for the same reason any hired gun does: the pay is good. In territorial expansion and political and economic support, Israel has been generously rewarded.

Neither party even bothers to conceal this now. The reality has been acknowledged with increasing candour of recent years. Carter was the first American president to say publicly that Israel was a strategic asset to the United States; and Peres was the first Israeli prime minister to talk openly of his country's role as America's instrument. When he came to the United States in October 1984 he declared: "The Israelis are not eating their planes or their tanks or their ships for breakfast. You can say that this is an investment in the posture of the free world and the posture of Israel. The United States spends $130 billion a year on NATO and still has to keep thousands of American soldiers in Western Europe. In Israel the United States has an ally which does not ask for US troops to help us do the job. We are doing it ourselves." Nothing could be clearer.

Dividing the Arab World

Divide and rule is the classic principle of imperialism. Before they withdrew their troops from the Arab lands, the old colonial powers had already built conflict into the region by their establishment of rival Arab regimes. As if afflicted by some terrible hereditary disease, the Arabs today live with that colonial legacy. Look at the map: the Arab people possess all the elements needed to created a United Arab State; they share the same landmass, the same language, for the most part the same religion, and the same culture and history. Yet instead of drawing together they remain plagued by divisions which seem only to intensify over time. Three diseases ravage the Arab world, debilitating its potential strength.

The first is the disease of ideology. There are 22 member nations in the Arab League; no two share the same political system, and indeed for the most part their systems conflict. Some are monarchies, yet each kingdom differs from the others. There are republics and emirates, but each of those too is unique. Some nations reject any form of party; others have a one-party system; a few accept the

politics of pluralist parties—though even they differ in their view of
the proper role of opposition parties, and the restrictions placed upon
them vary widely. In some countries, the restrictions have effectively
silenced opposition; in others, the opposition survives only because it
has been domesticated, neutered. In no case is a government-
tolerated opposition anything more than window-dressing. Some
countries have parliaments; others do not even have this; and what
parliaments there are all select their members by different means; nor
do any two parliaments have the same authority. The bitter truth is
that over the length and breadth of the Arab world, no two regimes
are the same.

The second disease of the Arab world is the mal-distribution of its
riches. Some among the Arab nations sit at the very top of the
pyramid of global wealth, while elsewhere in the region millions
struggle hopelessly at the bottom of the heap. Some nations face the
future with permanent and renewable natural resources—notably
their fertile lands—while others, especially those now floating on a
golden torrent of oil wealth, can hope for what, in the lifespan of a
nation, is no more than a short-term boom. So the long-term benefits
of Arab unity clash with the short-term interests of the rich, because
for the foreseeable future, unity would require sacrifice and sharing
on their part. Thus the richer Arab nations, and especially the
wealthy in those nations, resist for the present any moves toward
unity.

The third disease which disfigures the Arab world is ambition.
Arab unity would mean, if not the disappearance of the present
generation of leaders, at least some curtailment of their present near-
absolute powers. But power in the Arab world tends to be permanent: it is ended only by death—usually assassination or coup. In the
Arab world there is no tradition of the voluntary transfer of power,
and it is hard to see the present leaders stepping aside voluntarily
either.

The Arab world is a mosaic: seen from afar it looks whole, but
examined closely it reveals itself as no more than a pattern of glint-
ing, multi-coloured fragments. The bleak but inexorable verdict has
to be that it is impossible to see how Arab unity can be achieved in
the foreseeable future. Certainly the Arab people will remain divided
until those three diseases are lifted from them; and any Arab, politi-

cian, or intellectual, who truly seeks unity must first find a way of treating these plagues. The most serious, to my mind, is the first: the incessant conflicts of ideology. Cure that, and the way is open to tackle the rest. Aside from geography, the countries of Western Europe have nothing in common except their political system; yet their foreign policy is to all intents and purposes united. For rather different reasons, the same is true of Eastern Europe.

So the first question which faces the Arabs is: what sort of political system can they, or even a majority of them, unite around? The answer has to be Democracy—and, as a first step, the democratic right to express opinions about a choice of political system.

The United States is perfectly aware of these diseases weakening the Arab world. It is not in the interests of America or the industrialised West to see the Arabs cured of them. Weak and fragmented countries can be exploited in a way that big and powerful nations cannot. Besides, a United Arab State would pose a real threat to Israel's function as America's beachhead in the Middle East. It follows that one of America's foremost strategic objectives in the region is to keep the Arabs divided—even if, to do so, the US has to form expedient alliances with regimes whose ideologies and political systems run flatly counter to everything the Americans profess to believe in.

In opposing Arab unity and encouraging division, the United States does not stand out against all and every regional grouping. To the contrary, the US encourages collaboration—so long as it is under American auspices and ultimately subject to American control. Just as the old colonial powers raised native armies to do their work for them, so the US today encourages regional pacts and local alliances as a way of achieving its own strategic goals. All we need observe is that the Arab countries in those pacts are being groomed and trained to fight other Arab or Islamic nations: carefully, they are not equipped to fight Israel. Thus the alliance will succeed only in shedding the Arabs' own blood and deepening further the divisions in the Arab world—all in the service of America's strategic goals.

Limiting Arab Power

The first man to try to create a powerful and United Arab nation was Mohammed Ali Pasha, ruler of Egypt in the first half of the 19th century. At its peak, his power extended over Egypt, Sudan, the Arabian Peninsula, and the Greater Syria of those days, which comprised what are now Syria, Palestine, Jordan, and Lebanon. The European powers united against him, defeated him, and forced him to sign the London Treaty of 1840, which stripped him of all those Arab lands except Egypt and Sudan. As we discussed earlier, the creation of a Jewish state in Palestine was then conceived by British strategists as a way of blocking any repetition of Mohammed Ali's success.

Just over a century later, Gamal Abdel Nasser tried to unite the Arabs, though by means very different from those of Mohammed Ali. Mohammed Ali brought unity at the point of a sword. Nasser used the radio—reaching literally over the heads of the Arab rulers of the day to speak directly to their peoples, inciting them to action against the imperial powers occupying their countries, and against the collaborationist rulers who acquiesced in this domination because they too were exploiting the people they ruled. Nasser's challenge to great-power interests in the region brought swift retaliation: the tripartite aggression against Egypt in 1956.

The Israelis, French, and British were united in their political aim, which was to topple Nasser and the radical Egyptian regime each saw as a threat. Their assault failed largely because both of the superpowers were, each for its own reasons, opposed to it. The Soviet Unions' position was straightforward: it supported Nasser because his policies for the region accorded for the moment with the Soviets' own. The United States opposed the assault on Egypt for a more complex set of reasons. First, the US feared that the attack might draw the Soviet Union to intervene directly on Egypt's behalf, escalating the conflict immeasurably. Second was the fear that the attack would provoke anti-American and anti-Western feelings throughout the region and, more widely, among Moslem people across the world. Third was the conviction that US support for the aggression would only drive Egypt more firmly into the arms of the Soviet Union. Fourth was the corollary: that an American stand against the attack could bring a pay-off in improved relations with

Egypt. Last, there was the United States' determination to remind Britain and France that they were powerful empires no more: in the Middle East, they no longer had authority to act without the prior permission of the United States.

So Egypt survived to continue its challenge to Western hegemony, while the US and its allies continued their endeavours to contain Egypt by a never-changing blend of threat and inducement. Then came the earthquake of the October 1973 war. For the West, the implications were awesome. For the first time, Egypt and Syria contrived to launch a truly coordinated attack upon Israel, and for the first time, they achieved real victories. Despite their mistakes, the Arabs demonstrated beyond question that they could, if they concerted their military efforts, defeat Israel. And if Egypt and Syria alone could do that, what could be achieved if all other Arab nations played their due part in the conflict against Israel?

The United States and Israel saw the danger looming. They also saw the answer. Egypt, the most powerful country in the Arab world, must be eliminated from the fray. The US exerted all its political and economic muscle to that end. Duly, on 17 September 1978, Egypt, Israel, and the US, initialled the Camp David accords and, on 26 March 1979, the peace treaty between Egypt and Israel was signed. The parallels are striking between the London Treaty of 1840 and this treaty 139 years later. Both treaties had the same aim: to isolate Egypt from the rest of the Arab world, and at the same time to weaken its armed forces so as to reduce its power to act independently. The London Treaty limited the Egyptian army to 18,000 men. The provisions of the Camp David agreement achieved the same end by a backdoor. In the five years after the signing of the Camp David agreement, the correlation of forces between Egypt and Israel slipped from near equality to a staggering 2:1 imbalance in tanks and a 4:1 imbalance in combat aircraft, both in Israel's favour. In the strength of its forces, Egypt fell from first place among Arab nations to fourth. All this was the logical consequence of the Camp David agreement. In signing it, Egypt had implicitly acknowledged that it would not help any other Arab country resist attack by Israel. Egypt had been eliminated from the conflict.

The Camp David agreement was a body-blow to the Arab world, and especially to its radical regimes. Nothing could fill the gap left by

Egypt's defection, but the regimes in Syria and Iraq at least tried to shelve their differences and, in October 1978, began talks aimed at uniting their two countries—but then, in July 1979, the negotiations were abruptly broken off and relations between the two fell to the point where they seemed more enemies than Arab brothers. In September 1980, Iraq went to war with Iran, and is enmeshed still. In June 1982, Syrian troops entered the fighting in Lebanon. Far from uniting against a common adversary, the Arab world was tearing itself apart in internecine conflict.

It is hard to credit all this to mere chance. The principle of *cui bono?* would justify a search for the hidden hands of Israel and its protector in this catalogue of fiasco. Whatever their role, though, they could not have succeeded without the eager cooperation of some Arab leaders themselves. Some were guilty only of poor judgment: forgetting the central task of uniting against Israel, they sought what they thought would be easy pickings in other directions. But other leaders wittingly collaborated with the United States and Israel in pursuit of America's strategic objectives in the region. History will be harsh to both.

On 30 November 1983, the United States and Israel took their relationship to its logical next step. They signed a "strategic cooperation" agreement. The accord provides for the stockpiling of American military equipment in Israel, the sharing of intelligence, and joint planning—all against what the US piously asserted were "outside threats" to the Middle East. Moshe Arens, the Israeli defence minister, was more frank: "We share with the US common interests and goals in the area." Note, *in* the area. And the US secretary of state, George Shultz, angrily blurted out the truth when he was cornered by journalists' questions during a visit to Tunisia and Morocco in December 1983 to sell the agreement. "The United States," he said, "has had, does have, and will continue to have a strong and supportive relationship with Israel."

When the stockpile which the US plans is in place in Israel, the readiness of its Rapid Deployment Joint Task Force will increase dramatically. In less than two weeks, the US will be able to deploy in the Middle East no fewer than five divisions of ground troops and 15 tactical fighter squadrons. The Arabs have to ask themselves the question: against whom will this force be used? Against the Soviet Union, says the US. The military facts of life argue against this: against the Soviet Union, such a force would be wholly inadequate. The truth is that the equipment is poised for use against the Arabs—serving either to replenish Israel's own stocks when necessary, or there to be manned by Americans and Israelis on some larger expedition. Who can doubt that the targets would in that case be those Arab nations which dare to challenge America's hegemony?

Increasingly, Israel takes on the appearance of America's 51st state —except that the US taxpayer might reflect that Israel is getting all of the benefits while paying none of the costs. In April 1985, for example, the US and Israel signed a duty-free trade agreement, the first the US had signed with any foreign country. It lays down that all duties, excise tariffs, and other barriers to trade between the two countries shall gradually be lifted until, by 1995, there will be no barriers at all. What this means is that American companies based in Israel will manufacture for the Middle Eastern market goods of Israeli origin disguised by US labels. Transparently, that is the purpose of the agreement: to enable Israel to penetrate the Arab market beneath an American cloak. Again, the US taxpayer might wonder, first, whether the export of jobs from the US to Israel that this agreement must represent is really in the interests of the American worker; and, second, what the effects upon US trade will be if even moderate Arab regimes begin to boycott all American goods for fear of being accused of trading with Israel? For there is no doubting the scale of what the two leaderships have in mind. On 18 August 1985, an American trade official predicted: "The trade balance between the two countries was $3.6 billion in 1984. It is expected to be four times that amount within a few years."

How America Achieves Its Goals

The United States is a versatile power. To achieve its goals in the Middle East it relies on several different means, some public and others secret. They can be grouped into five broad categories: propaganda, arms sales and military aid, economic aid, demonstrations of force, and intrigue.

Propaganda

American propaganda in the Middle East plays three themes. One, that cooperation between the Arab states and the Soviet Union must lead to the spread of Communism and ultimately the establishment of Communist regimes in the area, which in turn will bring the discrediting of religion, the abolition of private property (from the rich man's palace to the peasant's small plot), and the dictatorship of the proletariat. Two, that the Soviet Union is thirsting to occupy the Arab Gulf states for its own economic and strategic reasons. Three, that whatever it professes, the Soviet Union is not in fact whole-heartedly behind the Arab cause and will never supply Arab nations with the sophisticated weaponry that the United States makes available to Israel. (This last point is, for obvious reasons, not one the Americans themselves shout about; rather, it is passed on in whispers by those Arabs who consider themselves America's friends.)

The first theme is utter nonsense. The truth is that most Third World regimes are dictatorial. But it was not collaboration with the Soviet Union which made them so. If that were the case, how would the US explain the Somosa regime in Nicaragua, the Pinochet regime in Chile, the Park regime in South Korea or the Marcos regime in the Phillipines—all valued clients of the United States? In no way does dealing with the Soviet Union require or lead to the adoption of Communist ideology. Algeria, Iraq, Syria, Libya, all have close ties to the Soviet Union, yet none could remotely be called Communist. Islam is simply too deeply embedded in the hearts and minds of its adherents—as the Soviet Union has cause to know. Sixty seven years of Communist rule in the Soviet Union have not sufficed to abolish Islam within the Soviet empire. About 20 per cent of the entire Soviet population, some 50 million people, remain Moslems, and by the end of the century the proportion is expected to reach 25 per cent. If there is any transfer of ideology between the Soviet Union and the Arab world, the traffic is to and not from the Soviet Union; and it is the Soviets rather than the Arabs who have cause for concern.

Besides, the Soviet Union is a superpower. The Arab world cannot cease to deal with it just because its official ideology is atheistic. By the same token, should the Arab world abstain from contact with countries such as Japan, India, South Korea, or Taiwan, all of whom are from the viewpoint of Islam non-believers?

The second theme of American propaganda—that the Soviet Union intends to occupy the Gulf—fares no better under examination. Why should the Soviet Union want to occupy the Gulf? Through their friends in the region, the Americans reply: to deny Gulf oil to the West; to reach the warm waters of the Indian Ocean. The assertions are strategic nonsense. The oil from the Gulf constitutes 60 per cent of the world's imports; and virtually all of it goes to the West or to its allies round the world. Cuting that supply would bring the West to a halt—something that neither the United States nor its NATO allies could possibly tolerate. Thus, if the Soviet Union were ever to try to take over the Gulf it would without doubt provoke a third world war—a war in which nuclear weapons would be used. And the Soviet Union knows this. Which means that a Soviet expedition to the Gulf is literally an incredible scenario.

As for the lure of the Indian Ocean, Iran and not the Gulf provides the Soviet Union with a logical route to those warm waters. The Indian Ocean lies 1500 kilometres from the borders of the Soviet Union, but only 600 kilometres from Afghanistan, where the Soviets already have troops. To pass through the Gulf states on their way to the Indian Ocean, Soviet forces would have to travel through—bluntly, invade—Turkey, Iraq, and on southward: a route of 3600 kilometres. Once again, why should the Soviets want to do that? A Soviet invasion of Iran would no doubt provoke a full-scale crisis, but nothing approaching the convulsion that would follow a Soviet takeover of Turkey and six Arab states. Turkey is a member of NATO, and the Arab Gulf states are friendly to the US, whereas Iran proclaims America the "Great Satan." Unlike an invasion of the Gulf, moreover, a Soviet seizure of Iran would not be a mortal threat to the West: Iranian oil does not go to the US or Western Europe.

But the whole scenario is ludicrous. Why should the Soviet Union want the Gulf? It does not need the oil. The Soviet Union is the largest producer of oil and natural gas in the world. In 1983 it was producing 12.4 million barrels of oil a day; the United States produced 10.2 million barrels a day; while Saudi Arabia came third with a production of only 5.1 million barrels a day. In the same year the Soviet Union was producing natural gas equivalent to a further 9.1 million barrels of oil per day, which was as much as the US was producing. If the Soviet Union thus has no need of the Gulf's resources, what is the evidence that it seeks to deny them to the West? Right now the Soviet Union is a net exporter of oil and natural gas. It brings much-needed hard currency. So, far from seeking to starve the West, the Soviet Union is eager to sign long-term contracts to *supply* Western Europe. The Soviets have invested billions of roubles to construct the giant pipeline bringing natural gas from Siberia to European markets. The line first flowed in 1984, with a capacity of 10 billion cubic metres of natural gas; but when completed its capacity will be 32 billion cubic metres a year. Does that really sound like the investment project of a country bent upon starving the West—in the process provoking a nuclear war?

The closer the American scenario is examined, the more it resembles a ghost-story told at bedtime to frighten children.

The third theme of American propaganda—that the Soviet Union is unwilling to supply the Arabs with military equipment in sufficient quantities or of appropriate sophistication—is simply a reversal of the facts. By 1984, the Arab nations deployed 12,745 main battle tanks, 1633 front-line combat aircraft, and 193 naval combat vessels —all Soviet made. By contrast, from Western suppliers, the Arabs had acquired only 2092 tanks, 743 combat aircraft, and 77 combat vessels. If anything, then, the arsenals seem to demonstrate not reluctance by the Soviets but, on the contrary, generosity. Nor does the Soviet equipment lack sophistication. The Soviets have always been willing to supply their most modern equipment to Arab allies—and, as the 1973 war demonstrated, that is more than a match for what the United States gives in such abundance to the Israelis. When the Americans call Soviet equipment unsophisticated, what they really mean is that it lacks the gold-plating and over-elaboration which is the curse of American weapons systems. In truth, the rigorous simplicity (and consequent reliability) of Soviet equipment is another mark in its favour.

Arms Sales

Weapons of war are a strategic commodity; as such their sale is not subject to the iron laws of supply and demand. Thus, the price of a weapons system is never fixed. Nor is the price always, even usually, a monetary one. Some cash will commonly be demanded, but the real price is calculated in other ways. Just as the supply, the availability of a particular weapon, will be subject to factors such as the ideology, foreign policy, and strategic and tactical goals of both seller and buyer nations, so the seller will not reckon his profit as the neat accountant's difference between production cost and price tag. The profit sought is commonly wider, less tangible. That is why the same piece of equipment will be offered to one country gratis, to a second country at half price, to a third at full price, and to yet a fourth at double price. The big arms manufacturers, and the United States and Soviet Union in particular, use arms sales as a way of winning friends and influencing people: spreading their own influence, or just as often seeking to eliminate the influence of their rival. With that as a primer—and recalling that in the 1986 fiscal year the United States is *giving* Israel as a grant $1800 million-worth of military equipment, a figure expected to rise still further in future—let us examine the terms the Americans impose, the price they demand, for their arms sales to the Arabs.

The then-secretary of state, Alexander Haig, said in a statement to the Senate Foreign Relations Committee on 1 October 1981:

The Saudis have agreed to ensure an important US role in the development of the Saudi air defence system, and to move forward in other ways to deepen the long-standing security cooperation between our two countries, in which we have played a key role in training the Saudi air force. Within this framework, we have reached understandings on a number of specific provisions governing the AWACS [early-warning reconnaissance] aircraft that provide important benefits for US security interests. These arrangements have been reached in the context of firm Saudi agreement on information-sharing, security of equipment, no unauthorised transfer of data or equipment, and use of AWACS only in a defencive mission within Saudi borders. This means:

One: there will be no sharing of AWACS data with other parties without US consent;

Two: only carefully screened Saudi and US nationals will be permitted to be involved with these aircraft. Given the shortage of Saudi aircrews and technicians, this means there will be an American presence in the aircraft and on the ground well into the 1990s;

Three: there will be no operation of Saudi AWACS outside Saudi airspace;

Four: there will be extensive and elaborate security measures for safeguarding equipment and technology, including:

a) US inspection team will monitor the performance of all equipment associated with the AWACS sale;

b) special facilities will be constructed to provide round-the-clock security protection against unauthorised entry;

c) all the agreed arrangements for protecting the security of AWACS must be approved by the US at least one year before any AWACS are delivered to the Saudis.

The United States is fundamentally and unalterably committed to the security of Israel. A strong Israel is required by our interests and our hopes for peace and security in the Middle East. For our part, we are determined to take steps to minimise any adverse impact of the sale and to maintain the qualitative edge upon which Israel depends. President Reagan would not have authorised this sale if he believed it would jeopardise Israel's security. On the contrary, we believe that the risks for Israel are greater if US-Saudi cooperation is disrupted and Saudi Arabia is left insecure or forced to turn elsewhere for equipment. . . .

To underscore what his secretary of state had said, President Reagan then, on 28 October 1981, sent a letter to Senator Howard Baker, detailing additional US demands of the Saudis:

One, the US has the right of continual on-site inspection and surveillance by US personnel of air and ground security arrangements for all equipment during the useful life of the AWACS. Two, computer software designated by the US government will remain the property of the US government. Three, it will be 1990 at the earliest before the eight Saudi crews needed to operate all five AWACS aircraft will be trained. Replacement and refresher training of individual Saudi crew members will require USAF technical assistance field teams during the 1990s. Four, critical AWACS maintenance, logistics, and support functions, particularly radar and computer software support, will of necessity be performed by US personnel in Saudi Arabia and in the United States for the life of the AWACS.

President Reagan concluded:

I am confident that the Saudi AWACS will pose no realistic threat to Israel. I remain fully committed to protecting Israel's security and to preserving Israel's ability to defend against any combination of potentially hostile forces in the region. We will continue to make available to Israel the military equipment it requires to defend its land and people, with due consideration of the presence of AWACS in Saudi Arabia. We have also embarked on a program of closer security cooperation with Israel. This proposed sale to Saudi Arabia neither casts doubt on our commitment nor compromises Israeli security.

Self-explanatory, I think—and humiliating. The AWACS sale is more for the benefit of the US and of Israel than of the Saudis. Who can doubt that whatever information the US gathers from the AWACS will be passed straight to Israel? At the same time, it must be doubtful if the Saudis will be told everything picked up by "their" aircraft. The aircraft add nothing to united Arab strength, since the Saudis must seek US permission to pass on information—which, by definition, will be denied if the prospective recipient is hostile to Israel. The question has to be asked: what exactly are the Saudis buying for the $6 billion these five aircraft are costing them, plus another $1 billion a year for their running costs and maintenance?

From their humiliating treatment by Washington, nobody would guess that the Saudis are America's firmest friends in the Arab world; or that these conditions are being imposed not upon beggars but upon a regime actually buying the equipment. Paying a high cash price too—for as well as imposing humiliating terms, the US charges its Arab clients top dollars for equipment that rarely turns out as capable as its salesmen boast. Even among America's most devoted allies, this treatment has begun to rankle. King Hussein of Jordan remarked in an interview in November 1984: "The United States' conditions for selling arms to us [the Arabs] are humiliating and unacceptable. It is an affront to our national pride. We must refuse to buy American arms under such conditions. We must turn to Western Europe or to the Soviet Union for our requirements."

In the 1984 fiscal year, Egypt got from the US $1300 million worth of military aid—$450 million of that in grants, the rest as loans. The aid was to be delivered in American weaponry. But what were the conditions? If the Americans impose the terms we have described on clients actually buying their arms, imagine what secret restrictions they must enforce on those buying American arms with borrowed American money.

Even then, even with all those conditions in place, the United States doctors the equipment it sells the Arabs. US aircraft, especially, are stripped of their most sophisticated electronic capabilities before being delivered, to ensure that the weapons sytems will not match those given to Israel. Thus the F-16s delivered to Egypt, and the F-15s delivered to the Saudis, do not match the same types delivered to Israel. But then, who could expect otherwise? The United States has repeatedly made clear its commitment to the security of Israel; its determination to help Israel keep its qualitative edge over its neighbours; and its refusal to sell to any Arab country a weapon which might jeopardise Israel's security. In this, at least, the Americans have been frank. The message is loud and clear—for those in the Arab world who want to listen.

Economic Aid

In the 1985 fiscal year, the United States allotted $1966 million in aid to the Arab world, the recipients including Egypt, Jordan, Lebanon, Oman, and North Yemen. Egypt was the biggest single beneficiary, getting $988 million—almost exactly half the total—with $750 million of that as grants and the other $238 million in soft loans (three per cent interest over 40 years, with a ten year grace-period on repayments). Generosity? Not exactly. As Miss Antoinette Ford, assistant director of the US economic aid program, explained: "Much of this economic aid is offered to the countries who offer facilities to American forces in the area, and which will facilitate their deployment in times of crisis." Not aid: rent.

Demonstration of Force

The United States has an extensive repertory of intimidation and compulsion, and the full range is on display in the Middle East: the Sixth Fleet, the Rapid Deployment Force, bases, manoeuvres, spy-ships, and spy-aircraft—the Arabs are daily made aware of them all.

The Sixth Fleet in the Mediterranean is a continuous presence just over the horizon—and not always that far. It was the Sixth Fleet which landed American troops in Lebanon in July 1958 and again in September 1982. In August 1981, it was the Sixth Fleet which patrolled the Gulf of Sidra, deliberately provocative in the knowledge that

Libya considered the Gulf its territorial waters, and then shot down the two Libyan interceptor aircraft sent to investigate. It was 28 fighter-bombers from the Sixth Fleet which on 4 December 1983 attacked Lebanese and Syrian troops outside Beirut; and in the days following, the guns of the Sixth Fleet pounded Syrian and Lebanese positions with hundreds of tons of shells.

The landward component of American muscle is the Rapid Deployment Force. Since 1981, the force has carried out at least one manoeuvre in the region each year, in cooperation with the forces of Egypt, Sudan, Somalia and Oman. The message of these manoeuvres is not even disguised: they are designed to put pressure on the neighbouring states, chiefly Libya and South Yemen.

And the US military investment in the region is increasing. Despite denial by both countries, the US now has bases in Egypt and Morocco. The details may be gleaned in Washington: in 1985 the US will spend $50 million on its base in Morocco and $95 million on its base in Egypt. The Egyptian base is at Ras Banas, on the Red Sea near Egypt's border with Sudan; and its importance emerged from testimony given to a Congressional committee in February 1983 by Major-General Richard V. Second, then-deputy assistant secretary of defence for Near-Eastern and South Asian affairs:

> The US air force has established a secret contingency air base in an unpopulated part of Egypt and has 100 airmen stationed there. Military supplies totalling about $70 million are stored at the facilities in the middle of nowhere, and thus it is a very good base for secret operations. The base has been used for deployment of AWACs and for training missions in the Middle East. It could support up to perhaps two Tactical Air Command fighter squadrons. The base was kept secret at the request of the Egyptians. The base is a matter of great sensitivity to them because there is a continuing presence of US troops there.

Again the question has to the faced: against whom will be troops from those US bases in Morocco and Egypt act? And the answer, of course, is: Arab nations which dare to challenge America. So now we know the true price Egypt paid for those American weapons. And now we know why the Egyptians and Moroccans deny the existence of the bases. But if they are ashamed of them, why did they accept them in the first place?

Intrigues

The American Central Intelligence Agency is notorious for its conspiracies against regimes which stand in the way of US interests. Everyone knows of its role in the Middle East in that informative decade after World War Two; and everyone knows, too, the questions that must be asked about its role today in the upheavals of the Middle East. What part did the CIA play in enticing Sadat to sign the Camp David agreement? What hand did the agency have in the collapse of the Iraq-Syria unity talks? What substance is there to the stories of a hidden hand igniting the war between Iran and Iraq? And how exactly did the CIA succeed in its long-sought goal of fracturing the PLO? So far we have no solid answers to any of these questions—nor to the question which in each instance must follow: who else collaborated with the US and Israel to bring about those disasters to the Arab cause? But perhaps, at long last, some answers are on the way. The storming of the US Embassy in Tehran, on 4 November 1979, supplied the Iranians with thousands of pages of the most sensitive American documents, most of them CIA cables and memoranda detailing its activities not only in the Middle East but around the world. I do not think we shall have to wait much longer for the truth.

The Soviet Union and the Middle East

Historical Background

After World War Two, Soviet ideologists considered it inevitable that the nations of the Third World—fighting as they were to struggle free of colonial rule—would be the friends and potential allies of the socialist camp. But the Soviet leadership had no time to ponder the point, still less to act upon it. Moscow was preoccupied by the need, first, to rebuild the Soviet Union after the catastrophe of war and, second, to consolidate and stabilise the position in Europe. In the immediate aftermath of the war, therefore, the Soviet Union devoted little time or attention to the countries newly emerging onto the world's stage. The Soviets contented themselves with public criticism of Western influence in the Third World and with modest secret support of the local Communist parties.

Not until Khrushchev came to power in 1953, after the death of Stalin, did the Soviet Union begin to take a more active interest in the problems and opportunities presented by the Third World. Two developments led the new leadership to activism. The first was the success of the Soviet Union's own reconstruction programme; for the first time its leaders could, if not relax, at least take stock and look around. The second factor was the utter failure of those local Commmunist parties to achieve success anywhere. Clearly, if the Soviet Union were to interest itself in the Third World, it needed new allies. But who?

Enter Gamal Abdel Nasser. He was the first Third World leader publicly to challenge Western influence, and he was looking for allies in his struggle. He turned to the Soviet Union. For their part, and for the reasons I have outlined, the Soviets were enthusiastic at the idea of supporting Nasser's regime. The alliance was sealed by the arms deal between Egypt and Czechoslovakia in 1955. Yet Moscow was cautious, as its decision to hide behind Czechoslovakia demonstrated. The Soviets realised they were infiltrating an area traditionally within the Western sphere of influence. They knew that, if their first opening led to a wider understanding, Egypt would be the door through which the Soviet Union might sidle into other countries not merely in the Middle East but throughout the Third World. They also foresaw, therefore, that the US and the other Western powers would not stand idly by. In sum, Moscow viewed the 1955 arms deal as marking the start of a long and, it predicted, harsh struggle between the two superpowers for influence in the Third World.

The West obliged by committing hara-kiri. A year after that arms deal—and in large part as a reaction to it—Britain, France, and Israel launched a concerted attack upon Egypt. The Soviet Union stepped forward, gave international support to Nasser, and threatened action against the aggressors. It was the death knell for the old colonial powers' influence in the region. Between 1955 and 1984, the Middle East saw six major wars and hundreds of skirmishes. When the dust of those thirty years settled, the map of political influence and allegiance in the region had changed beyond recognition. Neither superpower could claim with any confidence to have won. But what was clear was that the West could no longer assert that the region was its captive.

Soviet Objectives

The Soviet Union is a great power; and the first law of great-power behaviour says that great nations will always tend to exert influence, and if possible, dominance over smaller ones. In that regard the superpowers of today are no different from the imperialist powers of the 18th and 19th centuries. What differentiates the modern quest for hegemony, however, are two conditions—the rules of the game. The first is that neither superpower may gain influence at the expense of the other's vital interests: that could lead to military confrontation and is thus too dangerous. The second is that, unlike the 19th century, the expansion of superpower influence is today largely a voluntary affair: where the countries of the Third World accept it, the influence spreads; where they have the determination to resist, it is checked. (History provides precedents for this. The old empires carved most of the world in areas of influence; yet some small nations still succeeded in staying aloof.)

Those rules explain why the Soviet Union was so cautious in launching its political and diplomatic offensive in the Middle East in 1955. What still persuaded it to take the risk was the calculation that whatever changes resulted from its appearance on the scene must be to its long-term benefit. For the superpower stakes in the region were asymmetrical. The Soviet Union did not have to seduce anyone from the West into the Socialist camp: a new status merely as neutral or non-aligned would still represent a loss to the Western camp and a net profit to the Soviet Union and its allies.

So the first and overriding objective of the Soviet Union is to eliminate Western, and especially American, influence from the region. In that, the interests of the Soviets and the Arabs themselves are as one.

It is then only prudent to believe that the Soviet Union has as its second objective the replacement of American influence by its own. The point is that there is no inevitable linkage between the two objectives; and the Soviets' success in achieving the second depends upon the Arab themselves. It is up to the Arabs to accept or to resist interference in their internal affairs—up to the Arabs to accept help while rejecting domination. Logic dictates that it would be folly to struggle against Western hegemony only to replace it with the Soviet brand.

The same is true of ideology. No doubt the Americans are correct in shouting that the Soviets want to see Soviet-style regimes installed in the Middle East. What else should we expect? The Soviets have an ideology, and they lose few chances to propagate it. In this they are no different from the Americans. But to weigh this ideology and to accept or reject it is, once again, up to the Arabs themselves. To my mind, the Soviet dream is an impossible one, at any rate in the Moslem world; no ideology can challenge Islam. If the West really is concerned about the spread of Soviet ideology, it is not the Middle East which should give it concern. Between 1955 and 1973 cooperation between the Soviet Union and Egypt could not have been more intense or, within Egypt, more pervasive. Yet in that time Communism gained no ground in Egypt at all. Where did Communism gain ground? Western Europe.

The third Soviet objective in the Middle East is a balance of power. Israel is aligned with the United States in what the leaders of the two nations proclaim is nothing less than "strategic cooperation." It is in the interest of the Soviet Union to support and sustain its Arab friends, to prevent the scales from tilting too sharply in favour of the US and its allies. But in the nuclear age the balance of power is just that: a balance. What weight of arms and influence the Soviet Union can throw on to the scales is limited by the rule that the vital interests of the other superpower must not be threatened. Thus, the Soviet Union has declared it will support its Arab friends in their endeavour to regain the territories taken from them by Israel in 1967.It is a declaration not calculated to please those Arabs who would like to see Soviet support for the recapture of territory lost before that date. But it is as far as the Soviet Union considers it wise to go. This Soviet prudence is an instructive contrast to America's irresponsibility in encouraging Israel to continue its occupation even of those lands it took in 1967.

Arms Sales

Ever since the Soviet Union made its entrance into the Middle East arena with the 1955 arms deal between Egypt and its proxy, Czechoslovakia, the provision of arms has been the Soviets' chief means of winning friends in the Arab world. Critical to the success of this arms sales policy are the vast stocks of weaponry which the Soviet Union possesses, and the extraordinary capacity of its arms industries.

The scale of Soviet prodigality to its Arab allies is hard to grasp. Despite the Arabs' losses in their six major wars and innumerable skirmishes with Israel between 1956 and 1983, the Arab arsenal of Soviet-made weapons at the end of 1983 included 12,745 tanks, 1633 combat aircraft, and 193 naval combat vessels. By comparison, the United States has 11,769 tanks and all other NATO countries together possess 15,722.

If all the Soviet military equipment now in the hands of the Arabs were at the service of a unified political leadership, the Arab nation would be a great power on the world's stage. That will not happen: for the foreseeable future, in my judgement, the Arabs will remain divided. For that reason it is irrelevant in operational terms to compare what the Arabs as a whole possess with the arsenal of Israel or anyone else. I make the comparison with NATO only to demonstrate that, thanks to the Soviet Union, whatever else the Arabs may lack, it is not weaponry. The bitter truth is that this Arab arsenal, so generously supplied, has never been directed against Israel in anything like full force. Some of it has been squandered in fratricidal strife of Arab against Arab—Soviet weapons wasted fighting themselves. Some has been misapplied to suppress the people. Some has been frittered away in pursuit of secondary and for the most part mistaken ends. And some has stood idle, spectator of the struggle. In none of their wars with Israel have the Arabs deployed more than 20–25 per cent of their arsenal. And that too is not, in my view, going to change in the foreseeable future. So long as its causes go un-cured—so long as the Arabs cannot resolve their differences and join forces together—this haemorrhage of Arab strength will continue unabated. And the Arabs, not their supplier, will be to blame.

The Soviet Union supplies its weapons subject only to two conditions: that they not be used against Soviet interests, and that their secrets be preserved. For reasons already given, the Soviet Union considers that the struggle against Israel is in its interest. And the insistence upon security reflects the fact that the Soviet Union supplies to the Arabs virtually the same weapons that it relies upon for its own security and that of its allies in Europe. In that regard, we may expect the Soviets to be in the future a good deal more demanding in their security requirements after the betrayal by Sadat. When he broke with the Soviets in 1974, Sadat put all the sophisticated Soviet weaponry Egypts' armed forces possessed at the disposal of America.

The damage this did to the Arab cause was incalculable; its effects will be felt for years. When reports began to surface in the late 1970s that Sadat had even delivered four MiG-23 fighter aircraft to the United States, they were indignantly denied in Egypt. On 26 April 1984, the death of the US air force General Robert Bond while piloting a MiG-23 confirmed the secret that even Sadat had been ashamed to confess. But of course the result of his betrayal has been, and for years to come will be, not American but Arab deaths. The success of the Israeli air force in destroying 18 Syrian battalions of the Soviet-made SAM-6 anti-aircraft missiles in Lebanon in June 1982, a victory which opened the door to Israel's slaughter in Lebanon, was possible only because American experts had passed to Israel the results of their long study of those missiles, courtesy of Sadat, and their perfection of electronic counter-measures to defeat them.

The Soviets have been as generous to the Arabs in price as they have been in quantity. Soviet weapons are cheap anyway: about half the price of their nearest Western equivalents. In addition, the Soviets offer munificent repayment terms, especially to countries in real need. Commonly, the Soviets will write off half the purchase price and give a loan for the remainder at perhaps two per cent interest a year, with a grace period of three to seven years and repayment over a further 15 years.

Economic Aid

The Soviet Union appreciates why the West wants hegemony over
the Third World: to exploit it. To counter this—to help those countries emerge from economic dependence upon the West—the Soviet
Union stands ready to supply them with the technologies they need to
satisfy most if not all of their industrial and consumer demands. The
Soviets, in short, offer economic liberation. (To repeat my earlier
point: of course the Soviets do this for their own ends; what matters
to the Third World is that they do it.) Egypt's experience under
Nasser was an outstanding example of what Soviet help can make
possible. Soviet know-how coupled with Soviet soft-loans enabled
Egypt to construct and equip a thousand factories, which in turn
began to produce most of Egypt's consumer goods. The esssential
point is that the aid was not misused—or spirited to Swiss bank accounts, where so much Western aid ends up. Instead, it was devoted
to producing what the people actually needed. From 1955 to the end
of 1973, Egypt made phenomenal investments: deploying mighty
armed forces; fighting four wars; constructing the High Dam;
building a thousand factories; electrifying much of the countryside;
bringing schools and clinics to the mass of its people for the first time.
Yet in that period, Egypt's foreign debt rose only to $2 billion. Most
of those projects Egypt financed itself from the import-savings
generated by those thousand factories. That is the right way to use
economic aid.

Soviet Naval Power

Through the 1960s, the Mediterranean was a Western lake over which
the US Sixth Fleet and the navies of America's allies sailed unchecked
and unchallenged. Without that supremacy, America would never
have dared to intervene in Lebanon in 1958, sending the Marines so
bravely charging up the Beirut beaches through the serried ranks of
sunbathers and their Coke cans. The appearance of the Soviet Navy
in the Mediterranean in the late 1960s signalled the end of such
casual Western adventurism. By their presence, the Soviets were indi-

cating not a desire to clash with the Americans, but their readiness to protect the Arab nations around the Mediterranean from foreign intervention and intimidation. It was sufficient to encourage more of them to take a stand against the United States and its ally Israel.

The Soviet Mediterranean fleet remains, by comparison with the US Sixth Fleet, small and defensively deployed—most of the time at anchor off Crete. Yet its presence is of continuing value. It is still, as it was intended to be, a decisive restraint upon American intervention in the region. We may reasonably assume that it relays to the Soviet Union's friends in the area the latest information about movements of American ships or aircraft which might constitute a threat to those friends. And in time of crisis it protects Soviet supply-lines. The cargo-ships bringing military replenishments to Egypt and Syria during the October 1973 war would never have reached their destination, we may be sure, had the Soviet navy not been on alert in the eastern waters of the Mediterranean.

The Soviet Union and Israel

Soviet policy towards Israel was slow to evolve, for the same reason that Moscow came only late to an interest in the region as a whole. It was within the Western sphere of influence, and the Soviets had neither the means—apart from words—nor the incentive to intrude. They were unmoved even by the first Arab-Israli conflict of 1948, viewing it as a squabble between Western client states, fought on both sides with Western weapons, and assuming therefore that the West would resolve it as the West saw fit. Against that background, the Soviet Union's recognition of the State of Israel in 1948 was a formality, no more.

1955 was the watershed year. But it is easy now to underestimate the caution with which, even then, Moscow shifted policy. Without the presence of Nasser as the towering regional figure in alliance with whom they could enter the arena, it must be doubted whether the Soviets would have come in at all. Even so, they weighed not merely the sincerity and passion of Nasser's desire to rid the region of Western influence, but also his chances of success. Only because those odds looked favourable in the long term did the Soviets enter their initial understanding with him and seal it with that arms deal. Once the Soviets had taken the plunge, however, it was a decisive commitment. They were on the Arabs' side and against Israel. Ever since, the Soviet Union has been untiring in its international support for the Arab cause, always being the first to condemn Israeli aggression, always the unflagging ally of the Arabs in the United Nations.

Yet it was the West, not the Soviet Union, which forced the pace of this new alliance. When British and French paratroopers landed in Port Said at dawn on 5 November 1956, in blatant collaboration with the Israeli forces which had launched an attack upon Egypt a few days before, the Soviet Union stepped forward to help its new allies.

The warnings that Soviet Premier Nikolai Bulganin delivered to the governments of Britain, France, and Israel were impossible to ignore—and were not ignored. To Britain and France, Bulganin threatened nuclear destruction. To Israel he expressed only contempt: "The government of Israel, acting as an instrument of external imperialistic forces, perseveres in its senseless adventure, thus defying all of the people of the East who are conducting a struggle against colonialism and for freedom and independence of all peace-loving peoples in the world. The government of Israel is criminally and irresponsibly playing with the fate of peace and with the fate of its own people, which cannot but leave an impression on the future of Israel as a state. Vitally interested in the maintenance of peace and the preservation of tranquillity in the Middle East, the Soviet Government is at this moment taking steps to put an end to the war and to restrain the aggressors."

Years later, Moshe Dayan revealed the effect of this Soviet ultimatum on the Israeli prime minister of the time, David Ben-Gurion: "What particularly infuriated him was the difference between the letters sent to Britain and France and the letter sent to Israel. The one to us was couched in terms of contempt and scorn, and it threatened the very existence of Israel as a state. The message to Britain and France also contained the clear and explicit threat to use military force and to bombard them with ballistic missiles, but there was no calumny, no threat to their political independence, and there was none of the coarse mockery that marked the text of the ultimatum to Israel."

In 1967, the Soviet Union again stepped decisively forward to help its Arab allies. When Israel occupied the Golan Heights and advanced to within 70 kilometres of Damascus, Moscow warned the American president that if the US did not halt the Israeli advance the Soviet Union would intervene militarily to help the Syrians. Once again Moshe Dayan later revealed the reaction: "Secretary of State Dean Rusk got in touch with our foreign minister Abba Eban and our ambassador in Washington and asked them in near-panic where we thought we were heading. He warned that our situation in the Security Council was getting worse, and he demanded that we obey the council's cease-fire forthwith."

The same day, 9 June 1967, a hurriedly convened Warsaw Pact summit meeting in Moscow—with Yugoslavia an extra participant—resolved to sever diplomatic relations with Israel (Rumania dissenting from this); to provide military supplies to the Arabs; and to inform Israel of drastic measures to come if it did not immediately accept the Security Council resolution calling for a cease-fire. The Israeli ambassador to Moscow was then summoned to the foreign ministry and handed a sharply worded note containing threats as well as notification of the ending of diplomatic relations. To this day, no Eastern Bloc country—with the exception of Rumania—has relations with Israel.

In October 1973, the Soviet Union prepared to intervene in its most decisive fashion yet after Israel breached the cease-fire to complete its encirclement of the Egyptian Third Army. It was transparent that Israel was doing this to destroy Egypt's ability to bargain at the negotiating table; and equally clear that the United States, with all its reconnaissance resources, must have known of the Israeli advance as soon as it began and, probably, had picked up the preparations for it beforehand. Publicly, the Soviet Union criticised Israel in harsh terms at the United Nations for its action, and condemned the United States for its apparent complicity and for the massive military aid which was now merely reinforcing Israeli intransigence. (President Nixon had pledged $2.2 billion worth of aid for Israel.) Privately, the Soviet Union prepared to go much further. On the evening of 24 October 1973, Brezhnev sent a personal letter to Nixon. The full text has never been published, but those who saw it described its tone as "brutal." The key sentences are known, however; "I will say it straight, that if you find it impossible to act together with us in this matter, we should be faced with the necessity urgently to consider the question of taking appropriate steps unilaterally. Israel cannot be allowed to get away with the violations."

To add substance to this threat, the Soviets put on alert six airborne divisions—about 45,000 men; set up an airborne command post in the south of the country; and the military transport aircraft which had been lifting supplies to Egypt and Syria were diverted to assembly bases in Hungary and the Soviet Union, in readiness to pick up those divisions. All these preparations were monitored by the United States, as no doubt the Soviet leadership intended. Taken together with the fact that the Soviet naval presence in the eastern Mediterranean had by this time been augmented to 85 ships, the activities persuaded Washington that the Soviets were indeed on the brink of sending in combat troops.

The American response took two forms, the effective and the ineffective. The ineffective was a decision that same night to place all US military forces on a Defence Condition Three alert, which means on standby and awaiting orders. Presumably, Washington hoped thereby to deter the Soviets from unilateral intervention; but the alert caused more consternation among the American public and the NATO allies than it seems to have done in Moscow. The effective American response was to put pressure on Israel to abide by the ceasefire and to pledge publicly to supply the encircled Third Army.

The Soviet Union and the Arabs

Until 1955, the Arabs' thinking about the Soviet Union was conditioned largely by what they gleaned from Western media. The picture was uniformly hostile: a godless country, its rural population herded onto collective farms, and its townspeople crammed into concrete ants' nests; a permissive society, without marriage or family life, with children taken from parents to be reared in state institutions; an economy in which the all-embracing state paid everyone the same meagre wage, with no rewards to distinguish engineer from labourer, doctor from paramedic, general from private; a society in which the Communist party elite treated people as machines rather then human beings; a ruthless government so intolerant of dissent that a bullet or the living death of a Siberian labor camp awaited the few brave enough to speak out.

When the Arabs started going to the Soviet Union to see for themselves—first the Egyptians in the late 1950s, then the Syrians and Iraqis; and first to Moscow and then throughout that vast land—they came home with a very different picture. Certainly, the Soviet state does not believe in religion and does not build churches or mosques; but the Arabs found millions of Moslems following at least some religious observance, and many well-versed in the *Qur'an*. Certainly, Soviet marriages are civil ceremonies; but the Arabs found Moslem couples who, before or after the state registration, had also elected to be wed by an Imam. And family life appeared to be much as it is the world over. As for the economy, those first Arab visitors—coming from countries where for millions life is a daily struggle—were attracted by the fact that there is no unemployment, and reassured to find that, contrary to Western practice, skills are rewarded in proportion to their social worth.

In sum, it was by personal contact that the Arabs found the Soviet people and their lives to be nowhere as alien as Western propaganda had suggested, and for the most part little different from the people of the West whom the Arabs had long known. In one crucial respect, however, the Soviet Union was indeed different from the West: the Soviets were genuinely willing to help the Arabs develop. The torrent of technical assistance was proof of that: immediate help in the Arab countries themselves; help for the future in the training of thousands of Arab technical students in the Soviet Union—a programme which in time would transform the Arab world.

Of course, this change in Arab perceptions of the Soviet Union did not happen overnight; and governments were, in most cases, slower than their people to respond. Despite the scale of the assistance programme they could see around them, many Arab governments remained sceptical of Soviet sincerity and wary of its presence in the region. Only graudally did the official ice start to thaw. The Soviet Union's entry into the Middle East was thus slower, and more difficult, than its present acceptance there might suggest.

Now, of course, the Soviet Union is an established power in the region; indeed, if arms sales are the criterion, the Soviet Union is *the* established power. No fewer than 15 Arab countries have equipped their forces with Soviet arms. Only six Arab countries have not: Saudi Arabia, the Gulf states of Bahrain, Qatar, and the United Arab Emirates, Djibouti and—alone in North Africa—Tunisia. The superiority of Soviet weaponry is so acknowledged, in fact, that even though Egypt and Somalia are now closely aligned with the United States, the bulk of both countries' armaments are still of Soviet manufacture—and, significantly, the West has not offered to step in and replace them.

Inevitably the Soviet-Arab relationship has had its ups-and-downs. But by any measure the last thirty years have brought a net gain for the Soviet Union. In 1955, it had no presence in the Middle East at all. Now it has excellent relations with at least five Arab countries: Syria, Iraq, Libya, Algeria, and South Yemen. For some of these, friendship with the Soviet Union is fundamental to their security: it is the bulwark against their enemies. From 1982–1984, for example, the Syrian leadership warned repeatedly that, if attacked by Israel, Syria would not stand alone.

For its part, the Soviet Union loses no chance to reinforce that message. As one American expert on the Middle East, Robert Newman, reported in January 1984 after a visit to Moscow: "The Soviet Union is determined to stay in the Middle East, and will never accept the elimination of its influence. The Soviets regard Syria as the window through which they look out upon the region. The Soviet Union will thus supply Syria with whatever she needs to preserve her own position and with it the Soviet position in the region. We were given that message many times."

The United States was given the same message more officially too. On 9 July and 3 August 1982, according to *Pravda,* Brezhnev sent two letters to Reagan warning that if American troops were sent into Lebanon, the Soviet Union would respond with appropriate measures. Reagan must have ignored or underestimated the warning, because the next month US Marines landed in Lebanon as part of the multi-national force. The Soviets did not parade their response—but it came nonetheless. In January 1983, it was reported in Tel-Aviv and Washington that the Soviets had started to build two SAM-5 missile bases in Syria. The SAM-5 is the Soviets' longest-range air-defence missile: its range of 300 kilometres means that, from Syrian bases, it can cover much of Israeli airspace. The Soviets are cautious people;

the decision to install in Syria weapons of that capability must have been taken at the very highest level. It was the first real Soviet challenge to Israeli air superiority; and it was a message to Israel and its patron that the Soviet Union was serious when it pledged to stand by its friends.

In February 1984, the US Marines were withdrawn from Lebanon, their 18-month stay having accomplished nothing. Even so, their presence was a portent—an augury of further superpower interventions to come. It also signalled a reversal of American policy.

The Soviet leadership's decision to intervene unilaterally with combat troops in the final days of the October 1973 war—for we have to assume that was their decision—had been averted, in part perhaps by American counter-preparations overnight, but largely by Israel's belated acquiesence next day in the ceasefire. But after the episode, the then US secretary of state, Henry Kissinger, was at pains to spell out American policy on the question of direct super power intervention: "It is inconceivable that the forces of the great powers should be introduced [into the region] in the numbers that would be necessary to overpower both of the participants. The US is even more opposed to the unilateral introduction by any great power, especially by a nuclear power, of military forces into the Middle East in whatever guise those forces should be introduced."

That was in 1973. Nine years later, US troops intervened in the region twice in the guise of multi-national forces: in Egypt in March 1982, in Lebanon in September 1983. Under the same cover, they intervened in Grenada in October 1983. In Egypt, the American intervention passed off without trouble because the Egyptian regime accepted the troops within the terms of the Camp David Treaty. The US invasion of Grenada "succeeded"—if such a display of military incompetence can be called a success—because Grenada is a tiny country marooned within an area traditionally considered as being under American influence. The American intervention in Lebanon, by contrast, was a dangerous fiasco.

There were several local reasons for America's failure in Lebanon, among them the resistance of the Lebanese people themselves, and the resolute stand of Syria. But Soviet support for both was, to my mind, the crucial strategic factor in their success.

The Soviet challenge to America's presence in Lebanon took two forms. The first was increased supplies of weaponry to Syria, sufficient in quantity and quality to sustain Syria's position in Lebanon against any American or Israeli threat. This re-equipment of Syria, in fact, was little short of awesome in its speed and scale. In June 1982, Syrian forces in Lebanon had suffered heavily in their confrontation with Israel. Syrian losses were put at 400 tanks, 100 aircraft and helicopters, and 18 battalions of SAMs. The Soviet Union promptly replaced them all—with more modern equipment. On top of that, the Soviet Union then gave the Syrians an extra 200 T-72 tanks; a battalion of the SS-21 battlefield missile; strengthened Syria's air defences with a further 68 battalions of SAMs—including eight battalions of the long-range SAM-5; and gave its air force another 54 combat helicopters, 25 MIG-23s, and 25 MIG-25s.

The Soviet investment paid off. On 4 December 1983, the Syrians shot down three American aircraft over Lebanon. It was a humiliating blow to America's prestige. For the first time, an Arab country had shot down American aircraft and taken American pilots prisoner. Of course, Americans had been shot down during the October 1973 war; but these were American Jews with dual Israeli nationality, and they were flying aircraft, albeit American-made, which bore Israeli insignia. This was different. For once an Arab country had found the means and will to defend itself. If enough Arabs would follow the Syrian lead, then the days of gun-boat diplomacy—and the years of Arab timidity from the fear of gun-boat diplomacy—would be over. The Syrian example showed what could be done by an Arab state able to play the game of nations.

The second Soviet counter to the American intervention in Lebanon was to give support to those groups of progressive Lebanese nationalists fighting all foreign occupation of their country, be it Israeli, American, or nominally international. The Soviets supported these directly and through an Arab intermediary. This policy too was successful. The Lebanese government had been set up at the point of Israeli bayonets; it had no validity, nor any prospects except as a puppet of Israel. Duly, on 17 May 1982, these straw-men signed a peace-treaty between Lebanon and Israel—under the auspices, inevitably, of the United States. The treaty was an utter failure: neither the

Lebanese nor the Israelis were ever able to put it into effect. The resistance of the Lebanese progressive nationalist groups, fighting Israel and its puppets within Lebanon alike, prevented it. In the end, even the Lebanese government was forced, on 5 March 1984, to abrogate the treaty.

In swift succession, then, the Lebanese progressive groups forced American and other foreign troops to withdraw from the country in February and March 1984, and forced the Lebanese government to reverse its policy towards Israel. These were considerable victories, both for the groups themselves and for the Soviet Union backing them. By contrast, what did the United States get from its Lebanese adventure? Nothing except the coffins of its Marines. It was a salutary lesson that the days are over when the United States and Israel can impose their will upon the people of the Middle East. It was a warning, too, that the price of trying to do so is rising inexorably. In my view, however, the lesson has not yet sunk home to the United States. The Rapid Deployment Force seems to me the precursor of further efforts to turn back the clock in the region.

The Soviet Union, by contrast, has quietly and systematically set about cementing its ties with the Arab world. In April 1972, it signed a 15-year treaty of friendship and cooperation with Iraq—an agreement renewed at the end of 1978. Similar treaties were signed in October 1979 with South Yemen, and in October 1980 with Syria. Libya's ties to the socialist camp have been more circuitious, even circumspect. In November 1982, Libya signed with North Korea a "friendship and cooperation" treaty in which the parties agreed to exchange military data, specialists, and equipment. In January 1983, Libya signed treaties with Bulgaria and Rumania. But though it was widely reported in mid-March 1983 that Libya had taken the logical next step of signing a treaty of cooperation with the Soviet Union, that has never been officially announced. However, in a speech on 28 March 1983—only a fortnight after those reports—Gaddafi threatened that American installations in southern Europe were within striking range of bases along the length of Libya's 2000 kilometre coast. The military assessment would have to be that such threats are meaningful only if Soviet missiles were to be deployed in Libya—and that is a development which would swiftly be spotted by American reconnaissance satellites.

Soviet success in the region has by no means been confined to progressive regimes. The Soviet Union has ties now with some Arab countries commonly considered to be strongly Western-oriented, such as Morocco and Kuwait. In March 1979, the Soviet Union concluded with Morocco a trade treaty under the terms of which, over a period of 20 years, the Soviet Union will develop giant phosphate mines in Morocco and import vast quantities of the mineral.

The flourishing relationship between the Soviet Union and Kuwait is still more interesting. It first flowered in April 1981, when Kuwait's foreign minister, Sheikh Sabah al-Ahmad al-Jabir Assabah, paid an official visit to Moscow. The subsequent communiqué made interesting reading:

One: Both sides expressed their opposition to the Camp David accords, and agreed that these obstructed efforts to achieve a just peace in the Middle East. They pointed to the importance of Arab unity on the basis of the resolutions of Arab summit conferences in order to reach a just settlement of the situation in the Middle East and in order to confront the policy of separate agreements hostile to the Arabs.

Two: the USSR and Kuwait expressed their resolve to continue efforts to achieve a just and lasting peace in the Middle East, based on the complete withdrawal of Israel from all Arab territories occupied since 1967, including Arab Jerusalem, and the Palestinian people's exercise of their inalienable national rights including the right of self-determination and independent statehood.

Three: They declare their opposition to the setting-up of foreign military bases in the region and the deployment of nuclear weapons there, and to all forms of foreign interference in the internal affairs of its states.

In other words, the United States—with its policy of fostering at all costs the interests of Israel—is alienating even those Arab nations which might seem the natural allies of the West. For Kuwait, this American priority has had direct consequences: in 1984 the United States refused to sell Stinger anti-aircraft missiles—defencive weapons, it should be noted—to Kuwait or to other Gulf states. On 15 August 1984, Kuwait signed a $327 million arms deal with the Soviet Union for the supply of, among other weapons, surface-to-surface and surface-to-air missiles.

As that deal demonstrates, the mere presence of the Soviet Union on the international stage is an unqualified blessing for the Arabs. The Soviet presence means that the United States and the West are no longer the monopoly supplier of arms—which means they no longer have veto power over Arab strategy. The Soviet Union stands ready to equip any country which genuinely has the will to arm itself. Inevitably, some Arab leaders have tried to play the two superpowers against one another: trying to get arms from the United States by hinting that they will otherwise deal with the Soviet Union. That is misguided. It never works. Neither the United States nor the Soviet Union can be bluffed—and for one overriding reason.

There are only two major sources of modern armaments: the Western Bloc and the Eastern Bloc. Neither source is independent. The Western suppliers—however "independent" some European nations pretend to be—operate within the constraints of American strategy in the region; Eastern Bloc suppliers operate within the framework of Soviet strategy. The question of which bloc to turn to for arms is thus for the Arab an issue of high policy, and that policy has to be dictated by the overall strategy of the country. Each Arab nation has to decide what are its strategic targets and to accept that, once decided, those targets cannnot in practice be concealed, since they will shape the totality of the country's foreign policy. The strategy will then dictate the choice of arms supplier, for the unavoidable reason that neither bloc is willing to supply its sophisticated armaments to a country whose strategy is fundamentally aligned with that of the other bloc. So each Arab nation, unless it is willing to seek refuge in humiliating torpor, has no choice but to face the truth about its own strategy—and equip itself accordingly. The one option the Arabs do not have is bluff.

The Rest of the World

Voting at the United Nations

The Global Groupings

Votes at the United Nations are important not primarily for their practical consequences, which are frequently slender, but for the information they convey about the voters. The pattern of a nation's votes at the UN reveals, more clearly than any other declaration, where that nation's allegiances lie. For the United Nations is a political forum, not a judicial one: voting there is only rarely dominated by concern for what is just or unjust; far more often it is influenced by the competing national, regional, and strategic interests which divide the modern world.

Analysis of votes at the United Nations shows that, from the Arab point of view, the world may be classified into five main groups. First: the United States, Canada, Western Europe, Japan, Australia, New Zealand, and South Africa. Second: the Soviet Union and the East European socialist states. Third: the neutrals, including Sweden, Finland, and Austria. Fourth: China. Fifth: the nations of the Third World. Let us now compare how each grouping votes when the Arab-Israeli conflict is brought before them at the UN.

The first group invariably votes for Israel. In the Security Council, this unanimity is often deliberately concealed. The group has three votes there: those of the US, the United Kingdom, and France. But since a single negative vote is enough to veto a council resolution, the United States tends to act alone as Israel's defender in the council, leaving Britain and France the option of abstaining (no doubt by agreement with Washington) in the hope of currying some Western favour in the Arab world. When the same questions are brought before the General Assembly, however—where the great powers have no veto—Britain, France, and the rest of Group One almost invariably vote for Israel. In rare cases, and for tactical profit, some may abstain. They have never yet taken the Arabs' side against Israel.

Only one exception to this Western unanimity has lately emerged: and that is Greece, since October 1981, when the Socialist PASOK party came to power. Greece under Andreas Papandreou is not merely more supportive of the Arab cause than any of its European allies; it is more supportive even than some Arab regimes. On 5 February 1982, Greece voted in favor of a resolution condemning Israel for its annexation of the Golan Heights into the Jewish State. The representative of Egypt abstained.

Group Two, the socialist bloc, invariably votes on the Arabs' side in the General Assembly and in all other UN organisations. But in the Security Council, the group has only a single vote: that of the Soviet Union. Invariably this is cast on the side of the Arabs; but that neither matches nor annulls the help Israel gets from its allies. Certainly the Soviet Union could veto any resolution condemning Arab aggression; but the Arabs are not the aggressors and thus no such resolution has ever been tabled. In fact, the Soviet Union has only twice had to threaten to use its veto on the Arabs' behalf. The first was to block any resolution authorising the United Nations to send troops to Egypt in 1979; the second to block a similar contingent in Lebanon in 1982. In 1979, the United States, by trying to get Security Council agreement to send a force to the Sinai to monitor Egyptian and Israeli compliance with the Camp David agreement, was in fact endeavouring to secure implicit UN endorsement of that treaty—which of course had been rejected by the great majority of Arab nations. Similarly, by trying in August 1982 to get UN troops into Lebanon, the United States was in fact seeking to give the Israeli-imposed government there a superficial legitimacy by wrapping it in the United Nations' flag. (The main task of that puppet government, which had no popular mandate, was to conclude with Israel a peace treaty on the same lines as the Camp David agreement. That was why the US supported it.) In both instances, the United States had patched together a notionally multinational force which in practice consisted almost wholly of troops from America and its Western allies. In both instances, therefore, the threatened Soviet veto served Arab interests:

in 1979, by preventing international endorsement of the Camp David agreement; in 1982, by preventing the US from cloaking its intervention in Lebanon.

Group Three, the neutrals, also vote regularly on the Arabs' side. This support is important because, though the neutrals are small in number, they enjoy considerable international prestige—not least because they are acknowledged to vote according to what they perceive to be the justice of the case. Their influence, in other words, is by example.

Group Four, China, stands aloof from other groupings both in the General Assembly and in the Security Council, of which it is a permanent member. Though on other issues it is concerned to distance itself from the Soviet Union, in Middle Eastern matters China invariably supports the Arabs.

Group Five, the countries of the Third World, is the biggest bloc at the United Nations—and the one most susceptible to the pressures of the great powers. It can be divided into three sub-groups: Latin America, Africa, and Asia.

The Latin American countries, with a few notable exceptions, are under American influence at least, American dominance at most. Some of the countries are virtually American satellites. Countries such as Costa Rica or El Salvador, for instance—and the examples could be multiplied—are little more than American protectorates. Only a handful of countries have summoned the will to break free of this hegemony. Cuba was the first to revolt against American domination in 1959, followed by Nicaragua in 1979, and Grenada in 1983. Against each the United States has intervened, overtly and covertly. The Kennedy administration supported dissident Cubans in their unsuccessful attempt to invade Cuba. In October 1983, US troops invaded Grenada. In March 1984, President Reagan ordered the CIA to mine Nicaragua's harbors. Despite its efforts, though, the US has succeeded in overthrowing only one of the regimes, that in Grenada. But nothing suggests Washington has relaxed its efforts to subvert the other two with all the covert means at its disposal: supplying arms and money to dissidents and rebels: turning neighbouring states against them; trying to destroy their economies—the traditional tools of US diplomacy in its own backyard.

The upshot at the United Nations is that the smaller Latin American countries, with the brave exceptions of Cuba and Nicaragua, invariably vote as America instructs—which means votes in support of Israel. On rare occasions, when world opinion is overwhelmingly on the Arabs' side, one or two of this sad fraternity may try to hide their status as American satellites by abstaining on the issue. But the usual posture is more craven. Costa Rica and El Salvador, for example, are the only countries in the world to have shifted their embassies in Israel from Tel-Aviv to Jerusalem, thus implicitly recognising the city as part of Israel—which is contrary to all UN resolutions. Not even the United States has taken this step; and indeed the Reagan administration claimed publicly that it had encouraged neither country's action. There may be people who believe that. A better guide to the truth is perhaps the fact that on 10 May 1984, less than a month after El Salvador's decision to shift its embassy—Costa Rica had moved its mission in May 1982—Congress approved Reagan's request to give El Salvador $100 million in military aid.

The bigger countries of Latin America—Brazil, Argentina, Mexico —are of course less vulnerable to American pressure and consequently are far more independent in their relations with Washington. Brazil, for example, was the only Latin American country to vote in favour of the UN resolution declaring Zionism a form of racism. Yet Brazil illustrates the limits to the independence even these bigger countries of the region can enjoy. A vast land of more than 8 million square kilometres housing 128 million people, Brazil is the fifth largest nation in size and the sixth largest nation in population in the world. Its scale, in other words, equips Brazil to be a regional rival to the United States. And Brazil does oppose the encroaching American influence both within its own country and in the region; but it does this within a Western context and without seeking the help or support of the Soviet Union. For technology as well as capital, Brazil has deliberately looked beyond the US to Western Europe. Brazil, in fact, can fairly claim to be one of the rare countries which is truly non-aligned. But that enviable status is now threatened by its economic troubles. By the end of 1983, Brazil's foreign debt stood at roughly $100 billion, and foreign bankers effectively controlled the Brazilian economy. Inevitably, the question must be whether that foreign capital will drag Brazil's political leadership into the American camp.

The African countries of the Third World, by contrast, are geographically far closer to the Arab nations than to the United States. They have for the most part long-standing ties to the Arab World: and many also have links with the Soviet Union and the rest of the socialist bloc. For all those reasons, most African countries vote at the United Nations on the Arab side. But even in Africa it may be observed that the closer a country's relations are with the United States, the more that country will support Israel. Zaire and Liberia are the prime examples of this: they are the only nations in black Africa which have diplomatic relations with Israel.

The Asian countries of the Third World are different again from those of Latin America and Africa. They lie close to the borders of the Soviet Union and China, and far from the United States. Islam is the established religion in many of them. And their size—many are medium-sized regional powers, and India is by any criterion a major power—leaves them relatively invulnerable to great-power pressures. As a consequence, most of these countries vote with the Arabs. Even in this region, though, it is noticeable that the stronger a nation's ties to the United States—South Korea, Taiwan, and the Philippines are prime examples—the more support it gives to Israel.

Non-Aligned Nations

When the seventh summit meeting of the non-aligned nations opened in Delhi in March 1983, no fewer than 97 states were gathered there. Are so many nations truly non-aligned? To be blunt, I do not think that more than three of those nations truly deserve the name. All the rest are aligned to some degree. Who could seriously argue that Costa Rica or El Salvador, Zaire or the Philippines, Cuba or Vietnam are truly non-aligned? Yet all came to Delhi.

The reality is that these summits of the nominally non-aligned are now no more than social occasions: talking shop where countries with sharply differing ideologies and foreign policies meet to debate issues they know in advance they will not resolve. All but at most a handful of the participants—and in my judgement fewer still—are in fact aligned to one of the two big power blocs, and despite the conference rhetoric everyone present knows this. Nor is the rhetoric even original: the views the participants present are invariably the dogma of the bloc to which they belong.

The inevitable, pre-ordained result of these summits is a sheaf of compromise resolutions which invite much mutual congratulation but which might as well die in the wastepaper bin for all the attention they get outside the hall where they are passed. Regularly the summits pass resolutions criticising US policy in the Middle East and condemning US encouragement of Israel in its expansionist policies; but never do the summits then propose positive action against the United States or even against Israel. Even this exercise will itself be the product of a compromise, because the pro-American participants will have insisted on a parallel resolution condemning the Soviet Union's actions in Afghanistan. In this fashion, the conferences and summits of the non-aligned produce a fine annual crop of resolutions, from which every participant can pluck at least one to its taste. Summit over, the countries pursue precisely the same policies as before, regardless of the resolutions passed. Those who support the United States and Israel continue unruffled; those who support the Soviet Union's policy in Afghanistan are equally unmoved.

In facing this I do not criticise the so-called non-aligned countries for being, in fact, aligned. Genuine non-alignment demands that a country enjoy three things. First, the good fortune to live in relative harmony with its neighbours. Second, the population, natural resources, and technological capabilities to undertake its own development. Third, the means to defend itself without need of help from an outside power. The requirements are manifest. The countries of a divided region have no choice but to seek the support of allies. Countries without the technology to develop their resources need a partnership with whoever will offer that technology on the most generous terms. And countries which cannot produce the weapons for their own defence have equally little choice but to seek the help of whoever will agree to supply those weapons. How many countries of the Third World enjoy those freedoms that permit true non-alignment?

Nor, in describing the utter predictability of the non-aligned summits, am I calling for their abandonment. The mere fact of so many countries talking together is itself an achievement not to be cast aside.

And the gatherings do exert some influence on the participants: they set, as it were, norms of alignment. If a country has become so closely identified with its patron as to be a virtual satellite, the prevailing ethos of the summit will be to coax it back towards a modest independence. And while the resolutions themselves may be predictable both in content and ineffectiveness, the dialogue of differing viewpoints must leave some traces on the participants—and with time and care after the conference even the faintest of impressions can be deepened. The best policy for the Arabs is to redouble their efforts to win friends among these non-aligned. They are the true sleeping giant of world politics.

The Posture of the Islamic States

The Islamic Charter

The first Islamic summit was convened hastily in Rabat on 22–25 September 1969, after the Aqsa mosque in Jerusalem, the third holiest shrine in Islam, was damaged by fanatic Jewish terrorists. Twenty-six Arab and Moslem states took part. The follow-up meeting came in Jeddah in the Spring of 1972, when representatives of 30 Islamic states agreed upon the principle of an Islamic Charter, the terms of which were finally accepted by the second Islamic summit at Lahore in 1974. The signatories to the charter agreed to:

—Abide by the United Nations Charter and the Declaration of Human Rights;
—Coordinate efforts to secure, preserve, and liberate the holy shrines of Islam, and to give support to the Palestinian people in their struggle to recover their lost lands and their inalienable human rights;
—Support Islamic nations in their struggle for dignity, national rights and independence;
—Declare the Islamic Conference to be a permanent organisation open to any Moslem state upon two conditions: that it declare its approval of the Islamic Charter, and that it be accepted by a two-thirds vote of the existing members.

It is hard to believe any of this was seriously meant. For among the founders of the Islamic Conference and initial signatories to the charter were Iran and Turkey, both of which had the closest links with Israel. The relationship between Iran and Israel, especially, went way beyond even good-neighbourly cooperation: the two countries were sharing intelligence and coordinating much of their military training; and Iran was Israel's main source of oil. How could a country with such links abide for one moment by the provisions of the Islamic Charter? And how could the other signatories accept this? The fact that the founders of the Islamic Conference did not limit its membership to Moslem states which had no relations with Israel surely demonstrates that the charter was viewed as nothing more than another piece of paper to wave at the Arab people—the latest in that long line of empty promises.

Even the terms of the charter were studiously vague. Precisely what help was to be given to the Palestinian people in their struggle against Israel? Would a few dollars tossed to the PLO suffice? Or was it the obligation of each Moslem country to join with its men and its weapons the *jihad* which Islam lays down as the duty of every Moslem? The fuzziness of the charter is further proof that its founders meant none of it. So it should come as no suprise that in the 15 years since that first Islamic summit in Rabat, while the members of the conference have risen from 26 to 45, the group has achieved none of the charter's targets nor taken any positive steps to do so.

The pledge on human rights remains a mockery. Human rights are routinely violated throughout the Moslem world. The citizens of Western nations enjoy elaborate legal protections of their rights, including the ability to take complaints to international tribunals. The citizens of no Moslem country have comparable protection.

Nor has the conference had the least impact upon Israel. Since that Rabat summit, Israel has annexed Jerusalem, destroyed the Iraqi reactor, annexed the Golan Heights, invaded Lebanon, shared complicity in the massacres of Sabra and Chatila, daily violated the human rights of the Arabs living in the occupied territories, and failed to bring to justice any of its own fanatics who continue to destroy mosques and churches in those same territories. What has the Islamic Conference done? Nothing.

The Taif Conference of 1981

The third Islamic summit was convened at Taif in Saudi Arabia on 25–28 January 1981. Two issues dominated the agenda: the war between Iraq and Iran; and Israel's annexation of Jerusalem. On neither issue did the conference take any effective decisions. Of course, the conference report bore stirring words:

—It is the obligation of Moslem states to liberate occupied Palestinian and Arab territories. Moslem states should mobilise all their capabilities—military, political, and economic, including their natural resources—to aid the Palestinian people in achieveing their inalienable national rights, and to confront foreign countries which support Israel militarily, economically, and politically.
—The Moslem countries call on Iraq and Iran to agree to a cease-fire and request that they both accept Islamic mediation.

Four years later, the Taif conference is easy to evaluate. It has had no effect at all. The United States continues to support Israel militarily, economically and politically. None of the Moslem states at Taif has taken the required action against the US. No Moslem state has mobilised any, let alone all, its national resources or military and political forces for the struggle against Israel. Nor have they even managed to stop the Iran-Iraq war.

The Casablanca Conference of 1984

The fourth Islamic conference was convened in Casablanca in Morocco on 16–20 January 1984. Forty two Moslem countries attended. Three did not: Iran, Afghanistan, and Egypt. (Egypt had been suspended from membership of the conference by a decision of an emergency meeting of the Moslem Foreign Ministers Council in Rabat on 9 May 1979, following Egypt's signing of the Camp David Treaty. Afghanistan was likewise suspended from membership in 1980 on the grounds that its government had been established by Soviet force of arms. Iran, however, boycotted this fourth summit of its own free will, alleging that the gathering was dominated by the United States and that most conference members were biased towards Iraq in its war with Iran.) The Casablanca conference decided:

—To re-admit Egypt into the Islamic Conference.

—To adhere to the Arab peace plan known as the Fez Plan. In addition, the summit asserted that no Arab country was permitted to search unilaterally for a solution to the Palestinian problem, or to the conflict between the Arabs and Zionism.

—To continue opposition to the Camp David accords and to demand their abrogation and the annulling of all their consequences.

—To request the Security Council to adopt a new resolution which states, this time in unambiguous terms, that Israel must withdraw from all occupied Palestinian and Arab territories, including Jerusalem; which asserts the Palestinians' inalienable rights, including their right to return to Palestine and their right to self-determination under the terms of several UN resolutions, especially Resolution 3236.

—To condemn the US for its opposition to the inalienable rights of the Palestinians; its non-recognition of the PLO as the sole and legitimate representative of the Palestinian people; and its lack of commitment to the objective that Israel must withdraw from all occupied Palestinian and Arab territories, including Jerusalem.

—To condemn the US for its policies, which are aimed at American domination of the people of the region and their incorporation into the American sphere of influence.

—To condemn the US for its continuous support of Israel in all fields: military, economic, and political, culminating in the 30 November 1983 signing of a strategic cooperation agreement between the two countries.

—To support the independence of Lebanon, and to call for the unconditional withdrawal of all Israeli forces from Lebanese territory.

—To condemn the presence of the American fleet in the eastern Mediterranean, which the summit considered a threat to the security of the Arab states of the region and an encouragement to the Zionist state. [The summit saw these American forces as the vanguard of the larger Rapid Deployment Force, the intervention of which, the summit concluded, would signify a return of the colonial powers to the area in defiance of the United Nations and its role as the sole international organisation responsible for peace. The summit also condemned the American air attacks on Syrian positions on 4 December 1983, and the published statements attributed to American officials asserting that the US administration was determined to continue its aerial reconnaissance of Syrian positions.]

—To express the summit's deep concern at the continued Soviet intervention in Afghanistan, and to repeat its request that all foreign troops be withdrawn from Afghanistan immediately and unconditionally.

—To accept Kuwait's offer to host the fifth summit meeting in 1987.

The Re-Admission of Egypt

In a press conference in Cairo on 30 January 1984, ten days after the Casablanca summit, the Egyptian president Hosni Mubarak declared that Egypt would abide by the terms of the Islamic Charter. That, it emerged, was the only condition imposed on the re-admission of Egypt—and even that was no more than a face-saving device. For Mubarak pointedly did not say that Egypt would abide by the resolutions adopted by the conference during Egypt's suspension, even though established law is that Egypt is so bound. So the question arises: does the return of Egypt to the Islamic Conference have positive or negative implications for the Moslem people and for Egypt itself?

To assess this, we need first to know Egypt's intentions. If Egypt were really minded to abide by those Moslem summit resolutions—to abrogate the Camp David Treaty and to play its full part in the Arab struggle to recover the lost territories—then its return to the conference would clearly be a positive step. Egypt's size and power would add strength to the struggle; while the support of its fellow Moslem nations would aid Egypt in its difficult withdrawal from the Camp David entanglement. If Egypt has no real intention of respecting the summit resolutions, on the other hand, its re-admission to the conference is a negative factor, a setback.

The evidence is all too plain from official Egyptian declarations. The Islamic Conference calls for the mobilisation of resources for the struggle against Israel; yet the Egyptian regime has declared in plain terms that it intends to pursue the normalisation of relations with Israel and condemns the use of force in solving the dispute. The Islamic Conference supports the Fez Plan for peace, and by implication denounces the Reagan Plan; yet the Egyptian regime continues to support the Reagan Plan. The Islamic Conference denounces the Camp David Treaty and calls for its abrogation; yet the Egyptian regime declares its continued commitment to Camp David.

On that basis, the only possible conclusion is that the re-admission of Egypt to the organisation of the Islamic Conference is a setback. This has wider implications, too. The Casablanca summit adopted the strongest and clearest resolutions of any Islamic conference.

Those resolutions, viewed in isolation, would represent a major step forward. But the re-admission of Egypt, in what must have been full knowledge of its attitude towards those and previous resolutions, casts doubt on the integrity of the entire summit. None of those who voted for Egypt's re-admission can possibly have been unaware of the Egyptian position. The suspicion has to be voiced that many voted for Egypt's re-entry precisely so that its failure to abide by those resolutions would give them too an alibi for inaction. Such cynicism, in my view, is disastrously short-sighted. In the long run so blatant a gap between rhetoric and reality can only undermine what popular legitimacy the Moslem regimes possess. And that in turn can only encourage the rise of extremists committed to violence within the Moslem countries themselves.

The Islamic Council

The Islamic Council is an independent non-governmental organisaton based in London. It is committed to striving for unity among Moslem peoples and for the establishment of an Islamic order under which the Moslem *ummah* [nation] may thrive. It has published three documents so far. The first, the Universal Islamic Declaration, was published in London on 12 April 1980. The second, the Universal Islamic Declaration of Human Rights, was published in Paris on 19 September 1981. The third, a model Islamic Constitution, was published in Islamabad on 10 December 1983.

The first document outlines the fundamentals of Islam, defines the salient features of an Islamic order, and concludes with a direct appeal to Moslems to unite as one *ummah* under the banner of Islam. It declares: "The affairs of the *ummah*, divided into nation states, are presently in disarray because:
a) In spite of public declarations of commitment to Islam, Islamic principles have not been implemented in the life of its people and institutions.
b) Real power is, by and large, in the hands of people whose hearts are not imbued with the teachings of Islam and the spirit of Moslem solidarity, and who tend to put their own interests above those of the Moslem *ummah*.

c) The vast resources of the *ummah* are being grossly wasted. In many cases they are being used for purposes held to be illegal and immoral by the *Qur'an*. Instead of being used for the righting of economic imbalance and social injustice in the *ummah,* wealth is being used in a way that benefits forces inimical to Islam and to the *ummah."*

The document ends with the appeal: "O people of the Moslem *ummah,* in every Moslem country where the prevailing order does not conform to the teachings of Islam it is your sacred duty to struggle for change. O people of the Moslem *ummah,* stand firm and do your utmost to fulfill your obligations to build a truly Islamic society. So help us Allah: You are the best protector and best helper."

The second Islamic Council document succinctly sets out a code of human rights and obligations, reminding Moslem governments of the divine origin of these rights and drawing the peoples' attention to the fact that it is their duty to struggle and prevail upon their governments to respect these rights, violation of which is a repudiation of Islam. The 23 clauses of this code are based on the *Qur'an* and *Sunnah,* and were compiled by eminent Moslem scholars and jurists, working with representatives of different Islamic movements and schools of thought. If governments were ever to pay heed to the code, justice would prevail in the Moslem world, millions of prisoners and detainees would be released, millions of emigrants would be free to return to their homelands, and the persecution of opposition movements and the flogging of journalists would come to an end.

But the third document from the council, a model Islamic Constitution, is its most ambitious production so far. It is, unfortunately, an unsatisfactory effort.

Moslems agree on the fundamental importance of the *Qur'an* and the *Sunnah;* but on the meaning and implications of many other rules there is debate. There is agreement, for example, on the principle of *shura*—meaning "the people sharing in decision making," it is the Arab word closest to democracy—but there is disagreement as to how it should be put into practice. There is agreement on the right to the freedom of private enterprise, but disagreement on what limits should be set to prevent the exploitation of the people. There is agreement that *jihad* is the perpetual and inalienable duty of every Moslem, but disagreement on what the people should do against rulers who themselves abandon the *jihad,* or who formalise relations with an enemy at war with other Moslem states, or who conclude a peace treaty with those who have made war on Moslem people and driven them from their homes.

On all these vital questions, the document is vague or silent. In case after case, it shies away from fundamental questions about the rights and duties of the people themselves by saying that a law should establish this or institute that. But that is precisely that trap the Moslem world has fallen into too many times. The real question is: who is to write the law? Unchecked, the *Imam* (ruler of a theocratic Islamic state) has total power to draft a law which, in practice, would permit dictatorial rule. What currently exercises many Moslem scholars is the debate about the role and power of the *majlis al shura* [parliament]. Are the decisions of the *shura* mandatory? Can an *Imam* veto them? The council's model constitution is silent on the issue. Similarly, it nowhere suggests the formation of political parties. Nor does it propose that an individual has the freedom to take his case to some international court—why not an international Moslem court?—if his human rights are violated by the government of his *Imam.*

In their willingness to rely on the benevolence and goodwill of the *Imam,* it seems to me the eminent authors of this document paid too little attention to the differences between the *Imam*s of the earliest days of Islam and the *Imam*s of today. When Omar ibn al-Khattab was chosen as *Imam,* his first speech to his followers was to tell them: "Obey me if I do good: challenge me if I do wrong." When one of his audience then brandished a sword and shouted that if Omar did wrong this would be used against him, Omar was not angry. On the contrary, he replied: "Thanks be to God who made an *ummah* from which comes one to challenge Omar, with his sword." If all *Imam*s were of the calibre of Omar, there would be no need to fear violation of human rights. But that is the point: the *Imam*s of today are not the giants of the past. Human rights are being violated. That is why we need strict guarantees, why we need checks on the power of the *Imam.* As things stand, we can at least complain that the human-rights violations we see around us are also violations of Islam. But to give the *Imam*s the further power so to write laws that they could then claim to be abusing human rights in the name of Islam would be a remedy more deadly than the disease.

The Ulema (Religious Experts)

Islam is more than a religion. Religions deal with the relationship between God and man. Islam goes further: it sets out the code for every
aspect of life—the belief among Moslems being that since Allah's
presence is eternal and universal, His writ must run through every
sphere of human life and conduct without distinction between
spiritual and temporal. Thus, a Moslem scholar has the right and duty
to speak his mind not merely on spiritual matters concerning the relationship of God and man but also on temporal questions concerning
man and his community. In practice, of course, the first is permitted
by the rulers while the second most decidedly is not. Any Moslem
scholar who dares to speak frankly about Islamic precepts of justice,
democracy, social relations, human rights, the duty of *jihad,* and the
obligations of an *Imam* to his people, will almost certainly find
himself accused of fomenting revolution.

What happens in practice is that those *ulema* who do speak on
such matters produce texts to justify the policies of the ruler. For this
they are rewarded: the *ulema* are the salaried employees of the state,
Naturally, there are *ulema* impervious to coercion or corruption; but
the system gives these no protection. If we are to restore the Moslem
ummah to health, it will be necessary to restore independence to the
ulema. Rather than being employees of the state, they should come
under an independent council with non-governmental financial
resources and sufficient other safeguards to keep it immune from
influence by the executive power of a particular country. Only then
could the *ulema* become true guardians of the people against the
excesses of their governments.

Moslem Public Opinion

There are about a thousand million Moslems in the world, of whom
perhaps 15 per cent are Arabs. In the absence of any democracy, it is
impossible to know in detail what those people think. Certainly no
public-opinion survey would elicit the truth: too many people have

learned the hard way not to speak frankly. Yet there is compelling evidence that a storm is brewing. Increasingly of recent years, the Moslem world has been torn by the violence of clandestine groups, as like-minded and determined people organise secretly for what is ever more clearly seen to be an inevitable clash between the oppressed and their oppressors. The Islamic revolution in Iran, the epidemic spread of fanatic Moslem organisations, the short but bloody occupation of the Grand Mosque in Mecca in December 1979, the assassination of Sadat, the Jihad organisation, the suicide attacks in Lebanon: in execution these may all have been isolated events, yet all are portents of the same cataclysm to come. They are the surface manifestations of deep discontents welling up with explosive force among the younger generation of Moslems.

A characteristic of this younger generation is its loss of faith in the present leadership. They look around, these younger people, and they see the yawning gulf between words and deeds. They hear honeyed words and they feel betrayed. As one of the greatest American presidents pointed out, you can fool all of the people some of the time, and some of the people all of the time, but you cannot fool all of the people all of the time. Across the Moslem world, people are waking from sleep and realising they have been fooled. How can leaders expect to retain allegiance when anyone may read of decisions taken, pledges given, resolutions solemnly passed, and then no action taken? How can leaders be trusted to defend Islam against its enemies without, when the principles and rules of Islam are so blatantly flouted within?

Viewing the Arab world today, an analyst must surely conclude that the tide of militant Islam is rising. A storm is brewing. There will be violence. The tragedy is that the violence will be Moslem pitted against Moslem. Can it be averted? Probably it is too late. Certainly the only hope of averting it lies in swift and far-reaching reforms in democracy, human rights, social justice, and foreign policy.

4

The Arab World

Economic Resources

Geography

The Arab world comprises 22 states accepted as members of the Arab League. [I do not count the proclaimed Republique Arabe Sahrawi Democratique.] Covering an area of 13.97 million square kilometres, the Arab territories are second in size only to the USSR. And with a coastline of more than 22,000 kilometres, having access to two oceans, the Arabs have the longest and most strategic shoreline in the world. The Arabs stand at the strategic fulcrum of the modern world.

Red Sea

The Red Sea covers 438,000 square kilometres. Its maximum length between Suez and the Straits of Bab-el-Mandab is 2100 kilometres. Its greatest width is 306 kilometres. It is one of the most intensively used waterways in the world, being the maritime artery between Europe and Asia. Apart from Eritrea, whose 1010 kilometre coastline is under Ethiopian control, and about ten kilometres still occupied by Israel in the area of Eilat, the rest of the Red Sea's 4860 kilometre shoreline is under the direct control of the Arabs.

The Red Sea is rich in natural resources. It has petroleum deposits, evaporite deposits—sediments such as salt, gypsum, and dolomite, laid down through evaporation—and the newly discovered heavy-metal deposits in the bottom oozes of the Atlantis II and Discovery Deeps, lying, between 21 15° and 21 30° North. The oil and gas deposits are being exploited to varying degrees by the littoral states. Through the 1970s, however, the evaporite deposits were exploited only slightly and then purely for local use.

The heavy-metal deposits have not been touched. Those in the sediments of the Atlantis II Deep are alone estimated to be worth $25 billion. Analysis of the mud down there reveals an average content of 29 per cent iron, 3.4 per cent zinc, 1.3 per cent copper, 0.1 per cent lead, 54ppm silver and 0.5ppm gold. (The sediments of the Discovery Deep have lower, though still significant, metal concentrations.) The deposits are in the form of fairly fluid oozes, about 85 per cent brine in fact. It is estimated that in the top 30 feet of the Atlantis II sea bed there are about 50 million tons of this mineral-rich sediment—that weight being exlusive of the brine. The deposits actually seem to go down about 60 feet, but below that upper 30 feet the mineral content is unknown. Recovery of these sediments, which lie beneath 5700–6400 feet of water, clearly poses technical problems. But the ooze is so fluid that it may be possible just to pump it to the surface like oil; and once on shore there are several proposals for drying it and preparing it for smelting.

The waters of the Red Sea are themselves an untapped resource. No rivers flow into the Red Sea, and rainfall is scant, but the evaporation loss—more than 80 inches a year—is made up by an inflow from the Gulf of Aden through the eastern channel of the Straits of Bab-el-Mandab. It is estimated that the waters of the Red Sea are renewed every 20 years. On average, then, the inflow of water at Bab-el-Mandab must run at about 100 million cubic metres an hour, which is more than ten times the average flow of water in the River Nile at the Aswan High Dam. The energy potential of that flow is clearly enormous.

Since the 1970s, the Red Sea has been the subject of intensive study, partly because of its unusual geology but more because of its vast and untapped economic potential. Further investigation of those mineral concentrations and swift action to recover them for the benefit of the Arab nations around its shores should be a priority task.

Arabian Gulf

The Arabian Gulf—known to some as the Persian Gulf—is the shallow sea, the marginal waters of the Indian Ocean, that lies between the Arabian peninsula and south-east Iran. It is 615 miles long, and with a width varying from a maximum of 215 miles to a minimum of

35 miles at the Strait of Hormuz. It covers an area of 92,500 square miles (240,000 square kilometres). The Gulf is very shallow, rarely deeper than 300 feet, though at its entrance and at isolated spots in its south-eastern part the bottom drops away to depths of more than 360 feet. In profile the Gulf is noticeably symmetrical, with the deepest water found along the Iranian coast and a broad shallow shelf, rarely more than 120 feet deep, running along the Arabian coast.

The nations around the Gulf produce approximately 31 per cent of the world's total oil production and sit on 63 per cent of the world's proven oil reserves. Offshore exploration beneath the shallow waters of the Gulf itself have revealed further large reserves of oil and gas. Other exploitable minerals appear to be scarce, though the surveys have so far been only cursory. The Arabs' economic zone in the Gulf, defined by the 200 mile offshore territorial limit, totals 46,250 square miles (120,000 square kilometres), and the shallowness of the water on the Arab side makes exploitation of the minerals on or beneath its bed a relatively simple proposition.

Mediterranean Sea

From east to west the Mediterranean stretches approximately 2,500 miles (4,000 kilometres); north to south it is about 500 miles wide. If the Black Sea is included, it is about 970,000 square miles in area, and the Arab economic zone covers approximately 40 per cent of this —some 388,000 square miles (a million square kilometres). The zone, in other words, is 2.5 times larger than the entire area of the Red Sea and more than eight times the Arab economic zone in the Gulf.

But the coastal shelf along the Arab shoreline in the Mediterranean is narrow and the sea bed then falls away into very deep waters. Only off the Gulf of Gabes along the eastern coast of Tunisia does the shelf widen to as much as 170 miles; and the only other significant shelf is a 70 mile width off the Nile delta. It looks as if the exploitation of the Mediterranean will have to await the advanced technology of the future.

Gross National Product

The gross national product of all Arab countries in 1983 was $421,743 million. Spread that among the Arab population of 176,295,000 people and it is evident that by comparsion with the industrialised nations, the per capita income in Arab countries—the Arab peoples' standard of living—is very low.

Country	Population in millions	GNP $ billions	Per Capita Income $
Britain	55,965	473,424	8459
France	54,270	537,353	9901
West Germany	61,600	659,153	10,700
Japan	119,400	1057,616	8858
Arab nations	176,295	421,732	2392

But, as table 10 shows, this low average figure for the Arab world conceals frightening disparities within the region. In the United Arab Emirates the annual per capita income is $28,858. In North Yemen it is $394. We must further distinguish between the present GNP of the Arab world and its economic potential for the future. At present, the natural resources of the Arab world are poorly utilised, and their fruits unjustly distributed. Fully utilised, and properly distributed, the economic capabilities of the Arab world are enormous.

Agriculture

The present dire state of food production in the Arab world is an inevitable outcome of the disparity between growth in demand and growth in production. Growth in demand is a natural, by which I mean effectively unstoppable, phenomenon—the product of population and income growth. The only realistic answer to the problem has to be faster growth in production. This has not come about because the Arabs, fragmented into 21 independent states, have not coordinated their natural and their financial resources.

About 80–90 per cent of the basic agricultural resources of the Arab world—that is, arable land and water to irrigate it—are to be found in Morocco, Sudan, Egypt, Syria, Somalia, North Yemen, Iraq, and Algeria. But those countries, in the main, are poor: they lack the resources to develop their agriculture as fast as they would like and the Arab world needs. Divide the Arab world crudely into seven main oil-producing countries and 14 non-oil economies. In the latter, agriculture accounts for an average 20.5 per cent of GNP; among the oil-producers it does not exceed two per cent. Yet the resources are being misplaced. The cash allocated for agricultural development per head of farming population varies from $1700 per head in one of those oil-rich countries to a mere $70 in one of the main agricultural producers.

If the oil-producers would invest even a fraction of their wealth in developing agriculture in the main production areas of the Arab world, the results would be beneficial to themselves and to those countries. The Arab world could fairly swiftly become self-sufficient in food. Without this coordination of resources, though, the Arab reliance on imports will actually increase.

Industry

Oil and gas dominate the extractive industries of the Arab world. Mining in general is of secondary importance, the exceptions being phosphate production in Morocco, iron-ore mining in Mauretania, and mercury extraction in Algeria. The Arab world has 51 per cent of the world's known reserves of phosphate, with 88 per cent of that in Morocco. Uranium has been found in Algeria, Egypt, Morocco, Somalia, and Saudi Arabia. Total uranium reserves in the Arab world are estimated to be 60,400 tons; though that does not count the uranium present as a trace element in phosphate which, with the rise in the world price of uranium, it is now economical for Morocco to extract.

In the manufacturing sector, the average per capita output of the Arab world was only $153.3 in 1980 and $150 in 1981. This is very low. By comparison, the per capita output of the manufacturing sectors in the Netherlands and Japan in 1977 amounted to $5129 and $4413 respectively (both at 1975 prices). Even a relatively advanced developing country such as South Korea managed a per capita output from its manufacturing sector of $557 in 1977. And though this sector of the Arab economy will undoubtedly grow, it is clear that on present plans it is not going to grow fast enough. The best projections suggest that Arab manufacturing industry will grow at about 11 per cent a year. But if we assume a 1981 per capita manufacturing output of $150, and factor in a population growth of three per cent a year, then the per capita value of Arab manufacturing output in the year 2000 will be only $590 (at 1981 prices). That will still leave the Arab world trailing far behind.

Energy

On the face of things, Arab energy resources are bounteous. The known oil reserves in the Arab world were put in 1982 at 349.7 billion barrels, which constituted 52.17 per cent of the world's total known reserves. At the same time, Arab natural gas reserves were put at 12,202 billion cubic metres, or 14.24 per cent of the world's known reserves.

But even if we assume that future world oil consumption stagnates at its 1982 level, those oil reserves will run out in just 34 years. Of course, new discoveries will be made. But the projection illustrates how transient the Arabs' present oil wealth could be. And if a July 1983 study published in Paris by the International Bank is accurate, those oil reserves could run out faster still. For the study projects that, while oil consumption will certainly diminish as a component of total world energy use—from 45.5 per cent of total energy consumption in 1980 to 35.4 per cent in 1995—the world's overall demand for energy is still likely to rise so much that in absolute terms oil consumption will also increase.

Year	Oil		Natural Gas		Solid Fuel		Hydrolique		Total World Production of energy million bpd
	Production million bpd	% energy	Production equivalent million bpd	% energy	Production equivalent million bpd	% energy	Production equivalent million bpd	% energy	
1980	61.4	45.5	36.5	27.0	24.8	18.4	12.2	9.0	134.9
1995	67.5	35.4	36.0	29.4	38.6	20.2	28.5	14.9	190.6

Add to this the fact that over the next ten years, oil production in the Arab world is expected to rise to compensate for the diminishing reserves of the non-Arab oil-producers—thereby, of course, depleting still faster the Arabs' own resources. What all this means is that the Arab oil-producing countries must look forward now to life without those resources, since their run-down will begin to be felt by the early years of the next century. Unless the Arabs use their present oil revenues correctly—which they are certainly not doing right now—they face catastrophe.

Nor could hydro-electric power begin to supply even the Arabs' own energy needs, still less replace oil as a source of wealth. The best available estimates suggest that the Arabs are currently utilising about 40 per cent of available hydro-electric resources. The commercial potential is put at 41.4 gigawatts per hour, or the equivalent of 12 million tons of petroleum. Solar power is of course another non-depletable energy resource, but so far it has found only the most limited use in the Arab world.

The Arab Armed Forces

Defence Budget

To repeat a basic point made earlier, a nation's defence budget—more especially the ratio of that budget to GNP—is the first index of a country's concern for its own security. But there is a complicating factor. Poor countries cannot sensibly allocate any sizeable fraction of their GNP to defence without undercutting other services necessary for social stability, and distorting their whole development.

Yet, as table 9 shows, in the Arab world today it is the poorer nations which are in fact making the greatest sacrifices to build their defences. Syria, for example, spends 15.8 per cent of its GNP on defence; Jordan spends 12 per cent; yet both are poor countries. Meanwhile, wealthy states such as Libya and Qatar are spending respectively 2.2 per cent and 2.4 per cent of GNP.

There is, however, another factor to be considered: value for money. What relationship is there between the amount spent on defence and the quantity and quality of weaponry obtained? The contrast here is equally striking. Libya comes top of the list; Saudi Arabia trails at the bottom. In 1983, Libya's defence budget peaked at $709 million. Saudi Arabia's defence budget the same year was $21,952 million, after several years at roughly that level. Yet Libya contrives to deploy 2900 main battle tanks and 496 front-line combat aircraft, while Saudi Arabia owns just 450 tanks and a pitiful 65 front-line aircraft. The question has to be asked: where has all that Saudi money gone?

The defence budgets of the Arab world are painful proof that among nations supposedly allied in a joint struggle against a common enemy, the sacrifices are being inequitably borne at the same time as mountains of money are deliberately squandered and embezzled. Unless the whole budget process is reformed, all those slogans about a collective Arab responsibility for defence will remain so much hypocritical posturing. It is vital that the burden on the poorer Arab countries be relieved, while the richer nations can well afford to spend vastly more than they do now. One possible way of allocating the burden would look this like:

Group	Arab Countries with Per Capita Incomes ($ per year)		Suggested Defence Budget (% GNP)
	From	To	
One	400	1000	3
Two	1001	2000	5
Three	2001	5000	10
Four	5001	10,000	15
Five	10,001	15,000	20
Six	15,000	20,000	25

Group one comprises seven Arab nations: Egypt, Morocco, Sudan, North Yemen, Mauretania, and Somalia. Yet, as tables 9, 10, and 45 show, these poorest nations are currently spending much more than many of the countries in income groups five and six.

As a first step, though, the Arabs could drastically improve their defences if they merely stopped squandering what they are spending already. The case of Saudi Arabia has already been pointed out, but the profligacy runs wider. In 1983, the total defence budget of all Arab countries totalled $46,052 million. The Gulf states alone accounted for $26,847 million of that, which is 58 per cent. Yet those states manage to deploy only 5.6 per cent of the total Arab tank force and only 6.6 per cent of the total Arab strength in front-line combat aircraft. Clearly, the defence spending of the Gulf states is overdue for hard questions and radical reform.

Armed Forces

The total strength of the Arab armed forces in 1984 was 2,276,270 troops (not counting reserves). The forces thus represent 1.20 per cent of the Arab population. Between the forces of particular countries, however, this ratio varies widely. The armed forces of Sudan are only 0.28 per cent of its population, while in Iraq they are 3.61 per cent and in Syria 2.41 per cent. Beyond a certain minimal level, though, the capabilities of armed forces are best assessed not by numbers but by the quantity and quality of the arms they possess, along with less tangible indices such as the standard of their training, their morale, and the ability of their political leadership properly to direct them. But the bedrock, the foundation on which all else is built, must be the standard of their weapons.

Modern weaponry is sophisticated and costly; to attract, train, and retain soldiers able to master this technology is also expensive. The more modern a force, therefore, the more it will tend to cost per head. In 1983, this is what various countries were paying per year for each soldier in their armed forces:

United States:	$112,619
USSR:	$29,703
United Kingdom:	$78,594
France:	$44,435
West Germany:	$38,182
China:	$2195

If we look at table 8, we find that the comparable costs paid by the Arab nations vary from $430,431 per soldier per year in Saudi Arabia to $1074 in Djibouti.

From tables 5, 6, and 7 we see once again that the relationship between money allocated to the armed forces of the Gulf states and the weaponry actually at their disposal is disquieting. In 1983, the Gulf states spent $26,847 million on defence; yet all they had to show for it were 114 front-line combat aircraft and 850 tanks. Libya, by contrast, spent $709 million and deployed 496 front-line combat aircraft and 2900 tanks. The profligacy of the Gulf states' military spending is the more shameful because if their combined budget were rationally and prudently spent it would equip them with armed forces equal to those of West Germany—which deploys 4254 main battle tanks, 7636 armoured fighting vehicles, 551 front-line combat aircraft, 24 submarines, 20 medium-sized surface vessels, and 38 missile-launching fast attack craft. And even after that, the Gulf states would have a surplus of $8,000 million which they could offer as military aid to the poorer Arab nations.

Ground Forces

The ground troops are in general the best equipped and best trained of the Arab armed forces. But this by no means implies that they are free from defects. On the contrary, they tend to share four main weaknesses.

The first weakness is an absence of professional and experienced military commanders. With the exception of Egypt, Syria, and Iraq, no Arab country has field divisional headquarters or any headquarters for higher formations still. Some armed forces do not have even field brigade headquarters.

The second weakness is organisational imbalance within the ground forces as a whole and between combat, support, and administrative units within the field formations. In some Arab countries, the combat units and formations are short of anti-tank guided weapons, artillery pieces, sappers, and engineers—and lacking administrative units.

The third weakness is a lack of mobility among the field units of many Arab countries. Modern warfare needs combat vehicles with cross-country capabilities: that means tracked vehicles.

The fourth weakness is air defence, and here I mean air defence deployed as an integral part of combat field units and field formations. Of course, the primary responsibility for the defence of air space over a country or a theatre of battle rests with the air force. But the speed of modern aircraft permits low-level attacks on ground forces so sudden and so quick that friendly aircraft can have no chance to intercept the raider. To survive, ground forces must possess anti-aircraft weapons able to repel, and if possible deter, enemy air attack—and that requires man-portable anti-aircraft missiles and mobile, vehicle-mounted surface-to-air missiles. Few of the Arab ground forces are yet equipped with mobile SAMs; without them, they will be so much meat on the counter for enemy pilots.

Air Defence

Air defence is the greatest single weakness debilitating, though to different degrees, all the Arab armed forces. The Israeli air force destroyed the Iraqi nuclear reactor with "smart" bombs in June 1981. Aircraft of the American Sixth Fleet shot down two Libyan aircraft over the Gulf of Sidra in August 1981. The Israeli air force destroyed no fewer than 18 Syrian SAM battalions in June 1982. The success of these multiple acts of aggression, all accomplished without loss, demonstrates the weaknesses of the air defence in all three victim countries. Yet Iraq, Syria, and Libya have the best air defences in the Arab world—which illustrates the severity of the weaknesses elsewhere.

Fortunately, and largely as a response to those acts, the Arabs—especially Iraq, Syria, and Libya—began to put matters right after 1982. Since then the air defences of those three at least have improved significantly. On 4 December 1983, an historic day, the Syrians shot down three US aircraft as they were raiding their positions in Lebanon. On 25 January 1984, the Libyans shot down two French aircraft, a Jaguar and an F-1, on a reconnaissance mission over their troops in Chad. And through 1983–1984, the Iraqi air force gained superiority over the Iranian.

A modern air defence system requires five main elements. First is warning: ground and airborne radars. Second is local defence: anti-aircraft guns and SAMs able to cover the entire dome of sky from ground level to the maximum height and range from which enemy aircraft could launch their air-to-surface missiles against those SAM batteries. Third is combat aircraft to deal with enemy intruders out-side the localities defended by SAMs. These must have capabilities at least equal to those of the enemy. If our enemies intrude in F-4s, F-15s and F-16s, then to pit against them obsolete aircraft like A-4s, F-5s and even Alfa jets is a waste of money and, more important, of pilots whose bravery and skill the Arabs cannot afford to squander. Fourth is an effective electronic warfare capability. Without that, all other elements are useless. By electronic warfare capabilities I mean the capacity to counter enemy attempts to jam our electronic equip-ment, as well as the capacity to jam the enemy's own. Fifth is a requirement for an Air Defence Command. Modern aircraft have reduced warning time to minutes; modern missiles cut it to seconds. To achieve anything, the elements of an air defence system have to cooperate. Lack of cooperation inevitably brings disaster: our own aircraft guided into combat against friendly forces, or shot down by our own SAMs. Only a trained and experienced Air Defence Com-mand, using modern and reliable communications, can avert such disasters.

That in turn requires computers, the brains of all modern air defence systems, and electronic networks to relay the computers' in-structions in the seconds which may be all an air defence system is given. The United States protects its forces with the E-2C Hawkeye aircraft and the E-3 Sentry AWACS; the Soviet Union does so with the Tu-126 Moss. Little is known about the Soviet aircraft's capabilities, but the American AWACS carries the communications device known as the Joint Tactical Information Distribution System (JTIDS). This, operating over a single communications channel secure against enemy eavesdropping, can link anything from two to 98,000 participants in a defence network. It is far less vulnerable to enemy jamming than more conventional communications sytems. In-evitably, the AWACS to be delivered at such cost to the Saudis in 1985 will not be equipped with JTIDS nor with the latest electronic protection systems.

No half-measures, no semi-solutions, suffice for air defence. The operations and equipment of offensive forces may to a degree be tailored to a country's own capabilities; but defencive forces—and especially air defences—have by definition to be tailored to the enemy's capabilities. The objective must be a defence system of such known and demonstrated capabilities that it deters enemy attack. Optimally, indeed, the defence should be able not merely to deter enemy attack but also to forestall and disrupt it by destroying military targets deep inside the enemy's own territory. The Arabs could achieve this. It can be done with aircraft or missiles. The Israeli air force is greatly superior to Arab air forces and will remain so for years to come. The surface-to-air and surface-to-surface missiles are thus the best option for the Arabs. Surface-to-surface missiles with a range of some 500 kilometres based in the Arab countries bordering Israel—Syria, Jordan, Lebanon, Egypt, and Saudi Arabia—would be a significant deterrent to Israeli aggression. Those Arab countries which rely on the US and the West for their arms have no hope of getting such missiles. But those with the Soviet Union as an ally and supplier could get the SS-12: its 700 kilometre range would be more than enough for the task to be done.

Coastal Defence

Like air defence, coastal defence comprises five main elements: warning; coast-based weapons; combat vessels; electronic warfare capabilities; and command.

The warning system for coastal defence may be integrated into the air defence network. Coastal guns and missiles must be able to repel ships at distances beyond the ranges of the ships' own weapons. To defend an entire shoreline with static installations is virtually impossible: the best solution is mobile defence units, with guns and missiles, while static defences are concentrated along the stretches most vulnerable to enemy amphibious assault. A coastal defence brigade—25 tracked missile-launch vehicles, carrying 50 missiles of 50–100 mile range, with another 25 support and command vehicles—can defend 200 miles of coast in time of war and guard 600 miles in peacetime.

To close the gaps between those coastal defence units, and to launch counter-attacks against enemy craft beyond the range of coastal weapons, the Arabs need naval forces. So long as Arab navies are for defence and limited counter-attack against forces within 200 mile territorial waters, the vessels need not be big. Naval ships of any size are expensive, painfully vulnerable to enemy air strike, costly in lives when they sink—and, for short-duration missions no more than 500 miles from base, no more effective than small, fast missile craft.

An electronic warfare capability and an overall command are as important in coastal as in air defence. Warning systems, missiles and other guided weapons, communications—whether our own or the enemy's—all depend upon electronic transmissions. In modern warfare, to disrupt the enemy's electronics is to disarm him; to lose one's own is a catastrophe. The primary responsibilities of any defence command must be, first, to ensure the secure functioning of the elements of that defence and then, second, to ensure communication between the elements. The status of the command itself, however, is a matter for debate. Should coastal defense command be independent? Integrated under the navy command? Under the ground forces? The proper answer depends on many factors—among them, what attacks the enemy might attempt; the size and sophistication of the coastal command relative to naval and ground forces; and the capability of either of those to direct specialised units—so the solution will vary from country to country.

Political Decisions

The Arab Summit, Baghdad 1978

Extracts from the Communique of 5 November 1978:

On the initiative of the Government of the Iraqi Republic and the invitation of President Field Marshal Ahmad Hassan Al-Bakr, the ninth Arab Summit Conference convened in Baghdad from 2 to 5 November 1978. The summit held discussions with deep awareness of pan-Arab responsibility and common care for the unity of the Arab stand vis-a-vis the dangers and challenges threatening the Arab nation, particularly following the developments resulting from the signing by the Egyptian government of the Camp David accords and their effect on the Arab struggle against the Zionist aggression and the interests of the Arab nation. Out of the principles in which the Arab nation believes, and based on the unity of Arab destiny and adherence to the traditions of the joint Arab cause, the conference has affirmed the following basic principles:

One: The cause of Palestine is the decisive Arab cause; it is at the heart of the struggle against the Zionist enemy. All sons and countries of the Arab nation adhere to this cause and are committed to struggle for it and to make all material and moral sacrifices for it. The struggle for the restoration of Arab rights in Palestine and the occupied Arab territories is a pan-Arab responsibility; all Arab countries must participate in it, each according to its position and its military, economic, political, and other resources. The struggle against the Zionist enemy transcends the struggle against it by the countries whose territories were occupied in 1967 and embraces the entire Arab nation in the light of the military, political, economic, and cultural danger the enemy constitutes to the entire Arab nation and its vital national interests, its culture, and its fate. This requires all members of the Arab nation to shoulder responsibility in the struggle with all the resources they possess.

Two: All Arab countries shall give all forms of support and aid and facilities to the Palestinian resistance struggle in all its forms through the PLO as the sole legitimate representative of the Palestinian people within and outside the occupied Arab territories, for the sake of their liberation and the recovery of their legitimate national rights, including the right to return, to self-determination, and to the establishment of their independent state on their national soil. The Arab states will adhere to the preservation of the Palestinian national unity and to non-interference in the internal affairs of the Palestinian nation.

Three: Commitment is reaffirmed to the resolutions of the Arab summit conferences, particularly the sixth and seventh summit conferences of Algiers and Rabat.

Four: In the light of the above principles it is impermissible for any party to act unilaterally in seeking to resolve the Palestinian question in particular and the Arab-Zionist conflict in general.

Five: No solution can be accepted until it is enshrined in a resolution of an Arab summit conference convened for the purpose.

The conference discussed the two agreements signed by the Egyptian government at Camp David and considered that they harmed the Palestinian people's rights and the rights of the Arab nation in Palestine and the occupied Arab territory. The conference considered these agreements had been reached outside the framework of collective Arab responsibility and contravened the resolutions of Arab summit conferences, particularly the resolutions of the Algiers and Rabat summit conferences, the charter of the Arab League, and United Nations resolutions on the Palestinian question.

The conference considered that these agreements did not lead to the just peace that the Arab nation desires. Therefore the conference has decided not to approve these two agreements and not to recognise their consequences. The conference also rejected all political, economic, legal, and other effects issuing from them.

The conference decided to call on the Egyptian government to abrogate these agreements and not to sign any treaty of reconciliation with the enemy. The conference hoped that Egypt would return to the fold of joint Arab action and cease to act unilaterally in matters concerning the Arab-Israeli conflict.

After studying the Arab and international situations, the conference asserted the Arab nation's commitment to a just peace based on the total Israeli withdrawal from the Arab territories occupied in 1967, including Arab Jerusalem; the guaranteeing of the inalienable national rights of the Palestinian Arab people including the right to establish an independent state on their national soil.

The conference also adopted a number of resolutions to safeguard the aims and interests of the Arab nation in light of developments. Among them were the following:

—Arab League meetings and conferences would continue to take place in Arab states by turn. If a peace treaty were finally to be signed by the Egyptian government, Arab foreign ministers would meet in Baghdad to take the necessary steps to transfer the Arab League's headquarters from Cairo to another Arab capital, and to suspend Egypt's membership in the League.

—Immediately upon Egypt's signing of a peace treaty with the Zionist enemy, Arab foreign ministers would meet to affirm a decision that the Arab embargo enforced against foreign companies dealing with Israel would be extended against any Egyptian companies dealing directly or indirectly with Israel. However, relations will continue between Arab states and the Egyptian nation, its companies and personnel who do not directly or indirectly deal with the Zionist enemy. (The Omani delegation reserved its position on both resolutions.)

Arab League Council, March 1979

On 27 March 1979, the day after Egypt had signed a peace treaty with Israel, Arab foreign and finance ministers met in Baghdad. At the end of their discussions on 31 March, they announced the following decisions:

One: Arab ambassadors in Cairo should be recalled immediately, and diplomatic relations with Egypt should be ended within one month.

Two: The suspension of Egypt's membership in the Arab League takes effect from the day it signed the peace treaty with the Zionist enemy. Tunis is to become the temporary headquarters of the Arab League.

Three: Efforts will be made by Arab states to suspend Egypt's membership in the non-aligned movement, the Organisation of the Moslem Summit Conference, and the Organisation of African Unity for its violation of resolutions adopted by those organisations concerning the Arab-Israeli conflict.

Four: All loans by Arab governments or their organisations to the Egyptian government or its institutions will be cut; all bank deposits, guarantees, and facilities withdrawn; all economic aid in cash, material, or technical assistance terminated.

Five: As the peace treaty with Israel includes an article under which Egypt is obliged to sell oil to Israel, no Arab state must supply Egypt with oil or oil-products.

Six: The rules and principles of the Arab embargo upon economic or financial dealings with companies and organisations which deal with the Zionist enemy will be enforced upon Egyptian companies, organisations, and persons who directly or indirectly deal with the Zionist enemy.

Seven: The United Nations will be asked to transfer its regional offices dealing with Middle Eastern affairs from Egypt to another Arab capital. Arab countries should make a collective effort to achieve that goal.

The Arab Summit, Tunis 1979

The tenth Arab summit conference, convened in Tunis from 20 to 22 November 1979, reaffirmed its commitment to Arab summits, particularly the ninth summit, and adopted several resolutions, among which were the following:

One: The conference expresses its concern at the efforts being made by some countries to re-establish diplomatic relations between those countries and Israel and to recognise Jerusalem as the capital of Israel. The Arab countries announce that they would respond with appropriate measures if such actions were taken.

Two: The conference condemns the Egyptian regime's decision to supply Israel with water from the River Nile and asks the secretary-general of the Arab League to contact the Sudanese government and the governments of other countries with rights in the waters of the River Nile in order to take the necessary steps.

Three: Arab kings and presidents renew their condemnation of the Camp David Peace Treaty with Israel and their rejection of all measures arising from it. They reaffirm that any solution to the Arab-Israeli conflict must be based on the total Israeli withdrawal from all Palestinian and Arab territories occupied in 1967; and the guaranteeing of the inalienable national rights of the Palestinian people including the right of return, the right to self-determination, and their right to establish an independent state on their national soil.

The Arab Summit, Amman 1980

The eleventh Arab summit conference convened in Jordan on 25 November 1980. It was boycotted by the Arab Solidarity Group which then included Syria, Libya, Algeria, South Yemen, Lebanon, and the PLO. The most important achievement of that summit was its approval of the Arab Economic Charter, which was prepared and presented to them by the secretary-general of the Arab League.

The charter calls for Arab economic integration, and blames the political leaders of the Arab world for their failure in past years to move towards economic integration, essentially because long-term objectives are always sacrificed to decisions made for immediate gain. The charter, drawn up by economists and financial and industrial experts, is a masterpiece. If those who signed it actually put it into effect, the Arab world would swiftly rid itself of its economic problems. Unfortunately but predictably, the economic charter proved merely another in the long list of documents to be signed by Arab summits and then cast into oblivion.

The Arab Summits, Fez 1981–1982

The twelfth Arab summit conference convened at Fez in Morocco on 25 November 1981. Within hours it broke up in dispute over a Saudi peace plan known as the Fahd Plan. The conference re-convened in the same place on 1 September 1982, and adopted an Arab peace plan which has become known in consequence as the Fez Plan. This will be discussed in Chapter Five.

PLO Resolutions

When the Palestine Liberation Organisation was formed in the mid-1960s, its declared aim was to bring about the creation of a secular state in Palestine where Arabs and Jews could live together with equal rights. This obective was gradually abandoned and, implicitly, the PLO shifted its aim to the following:

One: Total Israeli withdrawal from all Arab territories occupied since 1967.

Two: Acknowledgement of the inalienable legal rights of the Palestinian Arabs, among them their right to return to their country, their right to self-determination, and their right to establish an independent state.

To achieve these goals, the PLO lifted its gun; and it is undeniable that in so doing it achieved popularity within the Arab world, the respect of much of the international community, and the attention of everybody. By 1970, the PLO was sufficiently established that when Nasser accepted a 90-day cease-fire with Israel starting 7 August, the PLO felt able to criticise him in savage terms, going so far as to accuse him of treason against the Arab cause. When Sadat signed the Camp David accords on 17 September 1978, the PLO went further. Accusing him of being a traitor and an agent of America, the PLO called on the Egyptian and Arab people to liquidate him. When Khalid Islamboully and his group did assassinate Sadat on 6 October 1981, the PLO celebrated the event for several days in Beirut and their other locations—even putting tables spread with feasts into the streets for all to share.

The PLO remained adamant in its opposition to the Camp David Treaty and to President Hosni Mubarak, whom they considered Sadat's spirtual as well as temporal successor. But the Israeli invasion of Lebanon and the eventual evacuation of PLO forces from Beirut after almost three months of siege had a profound effect on the thinking of many PLO leaders. Some began to speak for the first time of political options. Though fearing the humiliation of renouncing the military course, they preferred to say that both political and military options would be pursued in parallel. Behind the scenes, this new thinking was encouraged by Egypt and other Arab regimes. Others within the PLO leadership opposed these views, however, and accused those advocating them of violating the PLO charter.

Amid this tempest of conflicting ideas, the Palestine National Assembly—the Palestinian Parliament—convened in Algeria on 23 February 1983. Dispute between radical and conservative groups over the future policy of the PLO was serious, but the factions managed at last to agree to resolutions which, in time-honoured fashion, contained something for everyone and were in some cases vague enough to allow rival interpretations. Among the resolutions were the following:

One: The PLO affirms the special relationship that binds the Jordanian and Palestinian peoples. The assembly visualises future relations between the two peoples as being in the context of two independent states within one confederation.

Two: The PLO condemns the Camp David agreement. The assembly demands that Arab relations with the Egyptian regime be conditional upon the abrogation of the Camp David Treaty.

Three: The PLO asserts the importance of the Brezhnev Plan, proposed on 15 September 1982, which acknowledges the inalienable and lawful rights of the Palestinian people.

Four: The PLO rejects the Reagan Plan, and considers it unsuitable as the basis for any just and permanent solution either to the Palestinian problem or to the Arab-Israeli struggle.

Five: The PLO considers the Fez Plan to be the minimum base from which the Arabs might move on the political front, but any political move must be coupled with military action aimed at tilting the military balance in favour of the Palestinian and Arab struggle.

Six: The PLO affirms that Syria and the PLO are together in the front line against their common threat, and that good relations between them are therefore a matter of strategic importance.

Seven: the Arab Solidarity Group was ineffective during the Israeli invasion of Lebanon. The assembly calls upon the executive committee of the PLO to undertake discussions with the countries of this group with a view to re-establishing it in such a way as to make it more effective in future.

Fatah and the PLO

Fatah is the largest group in the federation that is the PLO. Yasser Arafat announced the formation of Fatah on 1 January 1965. It has a majority on the executive committee of the PLO and a majority in the national assembly. It is supported by the leaderships of conservative Arab countries who consider it more moderate than other groups in the PLO. The fourth conference of Fatah convened in Damascus from 21 to 29 May 1980 and approved the following political programme:

One: Fatah is a revolutionary patriotic movement that aims to liberate the whole of Palestine and to establish a democratic Palestinian state on the undivided soil of Palestine. Armed popular revolution and armed struggle are the only ways to liberate Palestine.

Two: The Jordanian arena is of special importance to the Palestine revolution. It must be given special attention so that it may be restored as the spring-board of struggle against the Zionist enemy.

Three: We must strengthen the joint struggle with the Palestinian people, as represented by their patriotic and progressive forces, in order to foil the Camp David plot and its consequences and to restore Egypt to the Arab fold to take its natural position in the Arab struggle.

Four: The United States stands at the head of the enemies of our people and nation. It is pursuing a policy hostile to our people, our revolution, our Arab nation, and to all Arab and world liberation forces. The United States supports the Zionist entity and its agents in the area and establishes military alliances aimed at subjugating the area under its military hegemony so that it may continue to plunder our nation's resources. For this reason, the world front hostile to US policy must be strengthened and must fight to foil this policy and to strike at US interests in the area.

The Split Within Fatah

The gulf between rival views as to the military and political options was evident when the Palestinian National Assembly met in Algiers in February 1983, but it was papered over with compromise resolutions. By now, however, the factions distrusted each other. Arafat's decision to order the replacement of some senior officers by others more loyal to him personally was a spark to tinder. A group of officers led by Abu Moussa accused Arafat publicly of acting in complicity with reactionary forces in the area and heading towards an agreement with Israel similar to the Camp David accords and similarly under the auspices of the United States. His latest re-assignment of officers, it was said, would tend to eliminate from sensitive command positions those who believed in the military option, replacing them with supporters of the political course. The re-assigned officers refused to relinquish their posts. On 10 May 1983, the military mutiny against Yasser Arafat began.

The mutiny spread, and on 4 June, fighting broke out between the pro- and anti-Arafat forces: 40 men were killed or wounded. Arafat claimed that Syria was encouraging the dissidents and supplying them with arms and ammunition; Syria denied this. By November, the pro-Arafat faction had been expelled from the Bekaa Valley in Lebanon and had re-grouped its forces in the northern Lebanese city of Tripoli. The anti-Arafat forces moved west and put the city under siege.

Arafat's position soon became critical. He was surrounded by superior forces so close that the port was commanded by their artillery. Thus he could neither win nor break out. After mediation by

Syria and Saudi Arabia, however, the rebels finally agreed to let Arafat withdraw his forces from Tripoli. The question then arose, how to guard against Israeli vengeance upon the ships carrying Arafat and his men? The United Nations was brought in. On 3 December 1983, the UN Security Council approved a proposal to allow five ships provided by Saudi Arabia—they were chartered from Greece—to transport Arafat's forces to Tunisia and North Yemen. Through the mediation of the United States, Israel was induced to promise no interference with the ships, which were escorted by French warships.

Arafat Meets Mubarak

Arafat left Tripoli on 21 December 1983. In Cairo next day he had a surprise meeting with President Mubarak. It was Arafat's first visit to Cairo since the Camp David agreements had been signed back in 1978, and the reasons for the meeting have been debated ever since among Palestinians and the Arabs at large. Those who condemn the meeting have done so on the grounds that it was a clear signal that Arafat is on his way to a political solution along the lines of the Camp David agreement and sponsored by the United States. Those who applaud the meeting have claimed that, on the contrary, Arafat's visit was for the purpose of encouraging Mubarak to abrogate the Camp David Treaty and return to the Arab fold. Each side has produced evidence.

Those who applaud the visit recall that Mubarak has not yet been to Israel—and specifically has avoided a visit to Jerusalem—and that he recalled the Egyptian ambassador from Tel-Aviv after the Israeli invasion of Lebanon in June 1982. They also argue that Arafat's visit was at worst a courtesy call, to thank Mubarak for having supplied him with arms during the siege of Tripoli. And they go on to assert that all steps are proper to encourage Egypt to return to the Arab fold, since they date the Arabs' present misfortunes from the day of Egypt's departure.

Those who criticise the meeting view the same facts differently. They decline to give Mubarak much credit for not visiting Jerusalem, pointing out that such tacit recognition of Jerusalem as the capital of

Israel would be so flagrant a breach of United Nations' resolutions that no serving president of the United States has ever been to Israel either. Thus, Mubarak's absence from Israel may demonstrate prudence; it reveals nothing about policy. Similarly, his recall of the Egyptian ambassador from Tel Aviv means little. Relations between the two countries continue unchecked—business being handled in the usual way by the Israeli ambassador in Cairo and the Egyptian chargé d'affaires in Tel Aviv, supplemented by a stream of high-level contacts shuttling between the capitals. Nor does Mubarak's supply of arms to Arafat do him credit: they were being used, after all, to kill other Palestinians and even Syrians. If Mubarak really wishes to return to the Arab fold, let him give the Palestinians weapons to be used against Israel, and let him open Egypt as a base for their operations. The sceptics agree that it is important to draw Egypt back into the Arab camp—but an Egypt liberated from the shackles of Camp David, an Egypt that can once more take its place in the line. And what chance is there of that so long as Hosni Mubarak remains in power? For Mubarak has repeatedly said that he intends to abide by the Camp David Treaty, that he has no intention of abrogating it, and that the rest of the Arab world has no viable option but to follow Egypt's lead and conclude similar settlements with Israel.

The details are argued with this theological intensity because the dispute itself is symbolic. The real issue here is the question of the military option versus the political option as a means of resolving the Arab-Israeli conflict. Those who applaud Arafat's visit to Mubarak are covertly supporting a political solution. Those who condemn the visit still believe that the only way to a solution is through the military option. Both sides in the debate wrap their convictions in fine phrases; but both sides know that is the real issue.

The PLO Split

Abu Moussa and the mutineers of Fatah were backed by every other Palestinian organisation, though the degree of support ranged from actually joining in the battle against the Arafat faction to mere condemnation of Arafat's visit to Cairo. For Arafat, the break was decisive. After their withdrawal from Tripoli in December 1983, his forces steadily dwindled, until he could not have exercised the military option even had he wished. Now the Palestinian forces, in all about 23,800 men, are divided into three groups:

One: Regular troops, about 15,000 in all, serving in the armies of other Arab countries. The biggest contingent, about 12,000 men, comprises the two brigades of what is called the Palestine Liberation Army and is effectively part of the Syrian army. The other main contingent, about 3000 men, serves as a regiment of the Jordanian army.

Two: Guerrilla fighters loyal to Arafat. These number about 2800 men, and they are dispersed in penny packets through six Arab countries: 500 in Algeria; 500 in Tunisia; 600 in Sudan; 400 in North Yemen; 400 in South Yemen; and 400 in Iraq. Few if any of these governments let the guerrillas have guns; mostly they languish semi-captives in remote and fenced camps. Their camp in Sudan, for instance, is in the desert about 700 kilometres north-west of Khartoum.

Three: Guerrilla fighters opposed to Arafat. These men, about 6000, are still in Lebanon, divided between the Bekaa valley, a refugee camp outside Tripoli, and, a few in and around Beirut. They have some freedom to operate against the enemy, but their actions must be approved in advance by the Syrian military command.

Organisationally, some of these fighters are men of the Abu Moussa rebel faction within Fatah; others are members of Saiqa, the Palestinian wing of the Syrian Baath party; others owe allegiance to the Popular Front for the Liberation of Palestine/General Command; still others are dissidents from the Palestine Liberation Front. All these factions have been drawn together into a broad National Alliance, which is backed by Syria.

Somewhere in the middle, critical of Arafat but anxious to avoid an irreparable split in the PLO, stand the groups of the Democratic Alliance: primarily the Popular Front for the Liberation of Palestine, led by George Habash; the Democratic Front for the Liberation of Palestine, which is a Marxist group led by Nayef Hawatmeh; and the small and newly formed Palestine Communist Party. (The members of the Palestine Liberation Front and the Iraqi-backed Arab Liberation front have for the most part remained loyal to Arafat.)

Despite mediation by several Arab leaderships through 1984, the members of the PLO failed to resolve their differences. Finally Arafat decided to convene a meeting of the Palestine National Council. Initially he planned to hold it in Algiers; but the Algerian government wanted no part of his plan, so he had to choose Amman instead. The council meeting would commence, he announced, on 22 November 1984. The eight constituent organisations in the federation which is the PLO all had the right to attend. But the rebels of Fatah, under Abu Moussa, announced that they would boycott the meeting, and at that five of the eight elements of the PLO followed suit. Some individuals prominent in Palestinian affairs announced the same, notably Khalid el-Fahoum, the speaker of the council. It became clear the meeting would not be attended by the two thirds of its membership—252 out of a total of 378 members—needed for a quorum.

Despite this, the council convened in Amman. Only three organisations came: Fatah, shorn of its rebels; the Palestine Liberation Front, and the Arab Liberation Front. The meeting was boycotted by the Popular Front; the Democratic Front; Saiqa; the Popular Front/General Command; the Palestine National Front; and the infant Palestine Communist Party. So the first question was whether the meeting was legal under the terms of the PLO's constitution. If 127 members of the council were absent, then the meeting would fall one short of the two thirds needed. Those boycotting the meeting published a list of the names of 168 council members who were not at Amman. The meeting was thus 42 delegates short of a quorum. It had to be illegal.

They had reckoned without Arafat's bureaucratic cunning. Just before the meeting, he had arranged that 47 of those council members proposing to boycott Amman should be "expelled"—and replaced by delegates loyal to him. By this device, he produced a meeting with five delegates more than the two thirds he needed. Of course, those boycotting Amman protested that Arafat's manoeuvre was itself illegal. But, not being there, they could not press their case—and in Amman the council, declaring itself to have a legal quorum, proceeded to take momentous decisions.

Arafat's personal power was strengthened. The council changed the rules and elected him leader of the PLO in a direct vote. The previous practice had been for the council to elect the executive committee and for this inner group then to elect the leader. That system of course ensured that the leader was only the first among equals. Under the new system, by contrast, Arafat could claim a mandate to override the committee.

The council then voted, in effect, to give Arafat a free hand. It approved his visit to Cairo, and it ordered the executive committee to start work on defining the future relationship of the PLO to Egypt. In strategic terms, what the council was doing was to approve the establishment of a new political axis in the Arab world: Egypt, Jordan, Iraq, and the PLO—a grouping now set upon negotiation with Israel. With these decisions, the Amman council irrevocably split the PLO. The date was 28 November 1984.

Hussein and Mubarak

Jordan had not even bothered to wait for the outcome of that rigged meeting. On 25 September 1984, it was announced in Amman that Jordan had decided to resume full diplomatic and political relations with Egypt. The reasons King Hussein gave echoed those advanced by Arafat when he had visited Cairo: the move, he said, was in recognition of Egypt's support for the Arab cause, especially in Iraq, in Lebanon, and on the Palestinian issue. The announcement was scarcely unexpected: the rapprochement had been gathering pace for a year, with ministerial visits back and forth, and even the signing of a trade agreement. Nevertheless, the Jordanian announcement was welcomed rapturously in Cairo, and two weeks later Mubarak paid an official visit to Amman.

King Hussein's return visit to Cairo on 2 December 1984 was an occasion of some interest, however, because Hussein went out of his way to make clear his continued opposition to the Camp David agreement. His speech to the Egyptian Parliament was carefully worded, but the message was clear. And when he went to lay a wreath at the Tomb of the Unknown Soldier, Hussein deliberately avoided the tomb of Sadat, even though his memorial was only a few paces away. Once again, the message was clear.

Where Now?

There are many signs: the split within Fatah; Arafat's visit to Mubarak; the refusal of Algeria to host a meeting of the Palestine National Council—a decision unthinkable even three years ago—and

Jordan's selection instead; the final split in the PLO; the new axis of Egypt, Iraq, Jordan, and the rump of the PLO; the voices heard calling for Egypt's acceptance back into the Arab fold even without abrogation of the Camp David Treaty, which was the cause of its suspension from the Arab League in the first place; and now the debate over the legality of the Palestine National Council session in Amman. Can all this turmoil be traced to a single source, a single convulsion?

In my view, it can. Politicians hide their intentions behind a smokescreen of words. It is the task of analysts to penetrate that cloud. Behind the smokescreen, I see a single issue: the political option versus the military option. That is the issue convulsing the Arab world today. The Egyptian regime is the only one to have declared openly its conversion to the political option. No other regime feels it can yet risk such candour. Instead they speak in code-words and symbols: they call for the return of Egypt to the Arab fold. But to what end? To confront Israel once more? On that, they are silent. They divert the question by instancing all the other issues on which Egypt's presence, Egypt's weight, would benefit the Arab world. Helping Iraq in its war with Iran; supplying troops to the Gulf states to deter Iranian incursions or to suppress internal disturbances; deterring Gaddafi from further military adventures, especially against his neighbours; sending troops to Sudan before the fall of Numeiry in April 1985, or Somalia—the list is endless, and the examples cited have for the most part some cogency. A lot of Arab leaders undoubtedly want Egypt back in the Arab fold, for reasons which are serious. But the reason missing from their list is the fundamental one: that Egypt should return to the Arab world in order to fight Israel. By their silence, those leaders indicate that that is not what they have in mind.

How do these regimes propose to get Egypt back into the Arab fold? Specifically, how can its return to the Arab League be rigged? Since its inception, the League has taken decisions by consensus. But Syria and Libya have declared publicly that they would veto any resolution in the League calling for Egypt's return without abrogation of the Camp David Treaty. The response can already be heard, murmured in the corridors. Consensus, it is being said, is undemocratic: it gives one country veto power over the will of the many. It is surely time to institute the practice of voting in the Arab League: decisions should be by simple majority. The argument sounds plausible, constructive; the intentions behind it are wholly destructive.

Egypt's return to the Arab League before it abrogates the Camp David Treaty would not merely violate the resolutions of successive Arab summits. It would split the Arab League down the middle. It would signal the start of a new era, a civil war of Arab versus Arab.

Human Rights in the Arab World

The Brain Drain

In a report to the Arab summit conference in Amman in 1980, Dr. Al-Hassan Zalzaleh, assistant secretary-general of the Arab League, estimated that 150,000 professional workers have left the Arab world to settle in the developed countries. He categorised the losses: 24,000 doctors; 17,000 engineers; 7500 physicists; 200 nuclear scientists; the rest spread across virtually the whole range of modern science and technology. Dr. Zalzaleh estimated that the outflow of talent is increasing at the rate of 10–15 per cent per year. The emigration, he thought, has cost the Arab economy perhaps $100 billion.

This haemorrhage of talent is not unique to the Arab world. It is a phenomenon seen throughout the Third World. And there is general agreement about the damage it is doing to all developing countries. But how can it be checked? There have been suggestions that these highly skilled people are a natural resource and that, like other resources, their export should be controlled. But compulsion—even if it would work, which is doubtful—should be only the last resort. Before compulsion, the developing countries should try persuasion. And that requires the creation of suitable conditions within the Third World itself.

Arab inquiries into the Brain Drain have been notably reluctant to address the question of why these professionals are so eager to leave their native lands. That reluctance is itself symptomatic. Anybody who has bothered to seek out these émigrés and question them in their new homes is drawn time and again to the realisation that a major factor in their decision was the systematic violation of human rights in the Arab world. Everyone in the Arab world knows how scandalously human rights are being abused. Everyone knows of people thrown into prison, tortured, and even killed because of their political or religious beliefs. Why should those with the ability to seek a new life in a freer society stay to risk the torture of himself or his family? Why should anyone stay in a country where, if his views are not those of the ruling regime, the only prudent course is silence?

Freedom of Opinion

In Chapter One I quoted the views expressed by Professor Dwight J. Simpson in a lecture on the Middle East question. At a subsequent seminar, attended by many Arab intellectuals and diplomats, Professor Simpson repeated his views, in the process vigorously criticising American policy in the region.

A few days later, I met an Arab intellectual who had also heard the speech. I asked his impressions. "I am struck by Simpson's views," he said. "But I am even more impressed with the American political system which permits Simpson to say what he did. Were an Arab ever to express opinions as opposed to those of his government as Simpson's are, he would be put into jail at once and accused of treason." In my view, that assessment is correct. Effectively, there is no freedom of expression in the Arab world. The contrast with the United States is total. Professor Simpson not only holds views which are utterly opposed to US policy in the Middle East, he puts those views to his students in the state university where he works. Yet he is not dismissed from his job for inserting wrong or dangerous ideas into the heads of young Americans. He is not accused of treason or of being the agent of a foreign power. That would be the fate of an Arab teacher in Simpson's position. To be sure, Simpson will never become president of the United States, or even its secretary of state. But, as he said when I put that point to him: "Who said I want to be one of those?" The point, surely, is that one of his students might become president.

Words versus Deeds

The alienation of the Arab people from their governments is frightening in degree and in potential consequences. The cynicism with which the Arab media are viewed is a clear sign of this. People in the Arab world expect their media neither to tell them the truth nor to stand up for their rights. They have no illusions: the media exist to serve the interests of the man who is in power—no more, no less. That does not mean the Arabs are badly informed. Word-of-mouth is the true medium of the Arab people and rumours are its daily headlines. The Arabs are adept at analysing rumours—this one clearly put about by the government, that one probably circulated by the opposition—and then sifting truth from lies. From the established media, however, they expect only lies.

This loss of faith in the media reflects loss of confidence in the regimes which control them. How can the man in the street have faith in a newspaper which told him yesterday that the Camp David Treaty was an act of treason but which today tells him that Egypt must return to the Arab fold with that treaty intact? If yesterday he was asked to believe that those calling for rapprochement with the United States were traitors and CIA agents, why today should he believe that those who criticise American policies are Soviet agents? The same absurdities run through his daily life. How can he believe that the Arabs are boycotting Israel when he sees Israeli manufactured goods on open sale in every market? How can he take seriously the proclaimed Arab policy of liberating Jerusalem when he sees that the head of the Islamic Committee charged with that strategy hosts an international conference—this was in May 1984—in which 35 Israelis took part, eight of them members of the Knesset which sits in Jerusalem? How, finally, can he have the slightest belief in slogans about the struggle against Israel being a pan-Arab responsibility when he watched the Israelis invade Lebanon while the bulk of the Arab world stood idly by?

The Arab Human Rights Organisation

In January 1984, a group of Arab lawyers and intellectuals formed the Arab Human Rights Organisation. Its members were drawn from Egypt, Kuwait, Iraq, Sudan, and Jordan. Cairo was selected as its headquarters. By any standards, the need for such a committee is great, the task confronting it onerous. But the rulers of the Arab world need not quake. The committee swiftly announced that it would confine itself to making requests of Arab governments, and then purely on humanitarian grounds. And of course there would be no public criticism.

I was reminded of an incident in Cairo in the 1950s. It was at a seminar on the Arab poem, to which poets had come from all over the Arab world. At length a poet from North Yemen took the floor. "In Yemen," he said, "poetry has only two themes. The first is to praise the Imam. The second is to ask his forgiveness." Thinking he was being ironic, the audience broke into laughter. The poet was shocked. Not merely was he serious; it had not occurred to him that this state of affairs might be regarded as strange. Thirty years after that silly incident, it seems that the lawyers and intellectuals of the so-called Arab Human Rights Organisation are still content to ask the Imam's forgiveness.

Man and Machine

Without the engines of war, a country is powerless. Tanks, aircraft, guns, boats, are the ready-reckoning of power. But without the man to operate it, the deadliest weapon in the world is so much junk. And modern weaponry demands more than men alone: it demands able, trained, willing, motivated men. If he is to go to war with any prospect of success, a soldier has to believe that his cause is just, that he is fighting for his people, and not just for the benefit of the ruler or a tiny ruling clique. But if he is to believe that, he must also feel that social justice prevails in his society, that he shares in his country's wealth according to his efforts and abilities, and that he has the freedom to speak and vote on the political and economic decisions which will shape his future and that of his children. In short, an effective soldier is one who believes his human rights are respected.

The Arab world has a long way to go. Human rights are routinely violated, and the Arab people have no redress, either in their own courts or by way of appeal to an international tribunal. A people oppressed have only two options. Both are bitter. One is to rise in violence against their oppressors. The other is to live as slaves in their own land—and to renounce all thought of victory in war, because wars are not won by men who think themselves slaves.

5

Is There a Solution?

The Political Options

For Internal Consumption Only

When Arab leaders meet to discuss the Arab-Israeli struggle, they have no difficulty agreeing on the objectives. It is when they come to discussing the means that they differ. One will declare that he is ready to mobilise his country's entire military and economic resources for the war against Israel—so long, naturally, as all the other Arab countries do the same. Another will urge grand strategy: "Before fighting Israel, we must first decide on the Arabs' strategic goals. We must look to the balance of forces in the global arena. Because Israel is merely one factor in the international situation, and while of course we must deal with her, we must do so within the framework of our overall strategic concept." A third will say quietly: "I will agree to anything the rest of you agree upon."

Each will then go home from the summit with his reputation intact as a doughty warrior vibrant for battle but once again unaccountably let down by the others. The truth, of course, is that the position of each was a carefully constructed alibi for inaction. Each made a stirring pledge of mobilisation in the certain knowledge that his accompanying conditions would never be met. Almost every member of the Arab League has taken refuge in one of the three approaches I cite. In essence, they boil down to a single device: a demand for impossible unity. Merely to define the ploy is to see its disingenuousness. How can 22 countries differing in everything except language and religion —size, wealth, political systems, relations with the superpowers, skills of their populations—be expected to agree on all the details of everything? The result is rhetoric as a deliberate substitute for action. Every Arab leader finds it necessary to posture before his own people as the most unyielding in the struggle against Israel, the most ardent is the crusade to recover the Aqsa Mosque, and safeguard the holy shrines. So Arab summit after Arab summit passes thunderous resolutions. If Israel could be conquered by rhetoric alone, the Palestinians would have been home years ago. Unfortunately, the rhetoric has rarely been matched by deeds.

Voting in the summits of the Arab League is by consensus. High-flying resolutions calling for crushing sacrifices in lives and treasure ought therefore to be rare, and subject to the most painstaking scrutiny. What happens in practice, however, is that when one leader—not usually of a nation distinguished by its feats in the front line—tables such a resolution, the others tend to go along for fear of being accused of lacking the requisite devotion to the struggle, but without any real intention of carrying out whatever the resolution demands. The result over 20 years has been a fine crop of resounding resolutions, but a barren harvest of deeds—and a source of endless quarrels as each leader blames the others for his own inaction.

To achieve anything, the Arabs must reverse this pattern. Instead of seeking unanimity on everything, they should decide what they can agree upon, and build on that. Instead of setting unattainable goals, they should agree on modest ones that do have a chance for fulfillment. And any country which persists in calling for greater sacrifice should be told that it is free to take whatever action it wishes, but must not insist that others follow suit. In short, minimum goals which have a prospect of success offer more hope than maximum goals which die stillborn on the paper. There is, in my view, general agreement in the Arab world that the struggle with Israel transcends the particular grievances of those countries whose territories were occupied in 1967. There is, in my view, agreement that the struggle does involve the whole Arab nation. If that is so, Arab countries could usefully turn from criticism of the inaction of others to a recital of what they have done themselves.

The Fahd Plan

In August 1981, the then-Crown Prince Fahd of Saudi Arabia announced a set of proposals to solve the Arab-Israeli dispute. Later known as the Fahd Plan, his scheme comprised eight points:

One: The withdrawal of Israeli forces from all territories occupied in 1967.

Two: The dismantling of all Israeli settlements in those territories.

Three: Freedom of worship and the practice of religious rites for all religions in the holy places.

Four: Reaffirmation of the right of the Palestinians to return to their homes, and compensation for those who choose not to return.

Five: The West Bank and Gaza to be placed under United Nations supervision for a transitional period not to exceed a few months.

Six: The establishment of a Palestinian state with East Jerusalem as its capital.

Seven: The right of all countries in the region to live in peace.

Eight: The United Nations, or some of its member-nations, to guarantee the implementation of these principles.

The Fahd Plan got a mixed reception in the Arab world, and especially among the Palestinians. Critics voiced three main objections to the plan.

First, it did not mention the PLO as the sole legitimate representative of the Palestinian people. The vague reference to the Palestinians in article four could open the way for Israel and the United States to select compliant Palestinians living inside Israel or even the US and declare those to be the representatives of the Palestinians with whom they would deal. Nor did article four affirm the right of the Palestinian people to self-determination. Without that guarantee, Israel could manipulate a "government" of hand-picked Palestinians and annex the West Bank and Gaza under the pretence of fulfilling the wishes of the Palestinian population as transmitted by that collaborationist "government." (The example of South Africa manipulating the puppet governments of its Bantustans has not been lost on the Palestinians.)

Second, article seven implied the recognition of Israel. That could open the way for Israel to demand the establishment of normal relations with all Arab countries as it did with Egypt. Critics of this clause differentiated between security guarantees and the enforced normalisation of relations. They accepted that the United Nations Security Council should establish guarantees under which all states in the area agree to live in peace, but they rejected anything beyond this.

Third, the critics rejected article eight. They said it opened the door to the exclusion of the United Nations and the insertion of the United States as the arbiter—a role the US could not play because of its bias towards Israel. For their own protection, they said, the Arabs had to insist upon the United Nations itself playing the central role.

But Saudi Arabia persevered with its plan, despite these criticisms; and in October 1981, announced that it would seek approval of the Fahd Plan at the Arab summit, which was due to convene at Fez in Morocco on 25 November. On hearing this, Syria, Libya, Algeria, Lebanon, and the PLO boycotted the summit. Twelve hours after the conference opened, Saudi Arabia withdrew its plan and the meeting broke up.

The Fez Plan

To avoid a repetition of this fiasco, the Arabs realised the need to agree upon the outlines of a peace plan which everyone could accept. Progress was swift, and before the next summit gathered in Fez on 1 September 1982, all Arab states except Libya had agreed on the draft of a projected Arab peace plan. At Fez, this plan was formally accepted—Libya boycotting the meeting and accusing all who took part of treason. In effect, the Fez plan was a re-working and tightening of the abortive Fahd Plan. It too had eight points:

One: The withdrawal of Israeli forces from all territories occupied in 1967, including Arab Jerusalem.

Two: The dismantling of all settlements established after 1967 by Israel in the occupied Arab territories.

Three: Freedom of worship and the practice of religious rites for all religions in the holy places.

Four: Reaffirmation of the rights of the Palestinian people to return to their homes, to self-determination, and to the exercise of their inalienable national rights under the leadership of the Palestine Liberation Organisation as their sole legitimate representative, and to compensation for those who do not wish to return.

Five: The West Bank and Gaza to be placed under United Nations supervision for a transitional period not to exceed a few months.

Six: The establishment of an independent Palestinian state with Jerusalem as its capital.

Seven: The United Nations Security Council to establish guarantees of peace between all states in the area, including the independent Palestinian state.

Eight: The United Nations Security Council to guarantee the implementation of these priniciples.

The adoption of the Fez Plan represented a total victory of the so-called Steadfastness States, which had rejected the Fahd Plan and boycotted the 1981 Fez summit. Proof of this is the fact that the amendments the Fez Plan makes to the Fahd proposals—essentially, articles four, seven, and eight of the Fez Plan—were precisely the demands of those Steadfastness States. Libya alone of Arab League members dismissed even the Fez Plan, on the grounds that it surrendered to Israel the Arab lands it had occupied between 1948 and June 1967. For the opposite reason, Egypt—still suspended from the Arab League—also rejected the Fez Plan, not because it was too modest but because it was too ambitious. In Egypt's view, the Fez Plan was impracticable because Israel and the United States dismissed it. As an alternative, Egypt thought the Arabs should build upon the Reagan Plan—which had been announced, as we shall see in the next chapter, just as the Arab leaders gathered in Fez.

Manifestly, a peace plan on which all Arab states from Egypt to Libya and from Syria to Saudi Arabia can agree is impossible to draft. By default, then, the Fez Plan stands as *the* Arab peace plan. It encapsulates the Arabs' minimum demands. Mubarak's assertion that this minimum should be rejected because Israel and the United States do not like it is strange. Whenever in history has the recovery of a people's rights been thought to depend upon the goodwill of those who took the rights by force in the first place? What has been taken by force is never recovered except by force. If the Arabs are serious in their support of the Fez Plan as the minimum acceptable settlement, they must be ready to fight to achieve it.

The Reagan Plan

On 2 September 1982, as the Arab leaders met for the second time in Fez, President Reagan announced the thinking of his own administration on the best path to peace in the Middle East. The proposals he outlined became known, inevitably, as the Reagan Plan. It had five main points:

One: The United States will not support the establishment of an independent Palestinian state on the West Bank and Gaza, nor will it support the annexation of permanent control of those areas by Israel. It is the firm view of the United States that self-government by the Palestinians of the West Bank and Gaza in association with Jordan offers the best chance for a durable, just, and lasting peace.

Two: As outlined in the Camp David accords, there must be a five-year period of transition—to begin after free elections for a self-governing Palestinian authority—to prove to the Palestinians that they can run their own affairs and that such Palestinian autonomy poses no threat to Israel's security.

Three: The immediate adoption of a freeze on the construction of settlements by Israel during the transition period.

Four: When the border is negotiated between Jordan and Israel, the view of the United States on the extent to which Israel should be asked to give up territory will be heavily influenced by the degree of true peace and normalisation of relations and by the security arrangements offered in return.

Five: Jerusalem should remain undivided; but its final status should be decided through negotiation.

President Reagan ended his statement of these principles by adding: "And, make no mistake, the United States will oppose any proposal—from any party and at any point in the negotiating process—that threatens the security of Israel. America's commitment to the security of Israel is iron-clad. And, I might add, so is mine. . . ."

It is hard to conceive of a settlement more detrimental to Arab interests than this Reagan Plan. Reagan knows that the Arabs have no card to play at the negotiating table other than the recognition of Israel. Yet he summons them to direct negotiation with Israel without at the same time demanding any prior commitment by Israel to withdraw from the Arab territories occupied since 1967. Yet that has to be the price of peace. Without this commitment by Israel, though, the Arabs' agreement to sit down with her gives Israel de facto what she wants—and for what? Even if the negotiations then fail to find an overall political settlement, Israel would still have got what she wanted, while the Arabs would have surrendered the only card in their hands.

And just what territory does the United States think Israel should give up as the price for peace? On this the Reagan Plan is most eloquently silent. It nowhere mentions Israeli withdrawal from the Golan Heights. It does not even specify withdrawal from all of the West Bank and Gaza. That too is to be left to negotiation. But negotiation is a process of give-and-take. What are the Arabs to give? To recover sovereignty over some parts of their territory, are others to be surrendered to the aggressor? That is, of course, precisely what the Americans have in mind. That is what they constructed in the Camp David agreement, what they blessed in the 17 May 1983 agreement between Israel and Lebanon—the "bargain" later rejected by the Lebanese. President Reagan wants to force the same unequal settlement on the rest of the Arab world.

The plan calls for a freeze on the construction of Israeli settlements during the transition years; but it nowhere mentions what is to be the future of those settlements under the new regime—that strange hybrid of Palestinian autonomy in association with Jordan. We know what Israel's answer to that question is: Shamir's article in *Foreign Affairs* in Spring 1982 (described in Chapter One) answered that. Does Reagan approve or disapprove of those Israeli plans?

Some parts of the plan simply defy analysis. Take the question of the border between Jordan and Israel. This should depend, we are told, upon "normalisation" and "security arrangements." But how can matters as precise as borders hinge upon concepts as vague and ambiguous as those? Does Reagan seriously expect the Israelis ever to accept that they have adequate "security arrangements"? And who is to judge?

In his anxiety to appease Israel, President Reagan even ignored established American policy. The future of Jerusalem, he declared, should be "decided through negotiation." But even the United States has supported resolutions in the United Nations calling for Jerusalem's international status to be recognised and protected. Did nobody bother to tell Reagan that?

I see no difference between the Reagan Plan and the Israeli Plan as outlined in that Shamir article in *Foreign Affairs*. Shamir at least spelled out what Israel perceives as its right to retain land on the West Bank and in Gaza. The Reagan Plan maintains a coy silence on the point, but implicitly accepts the Israeli case by its failure to insist on the dismantling of existing Israeli settlements—a point so fundamental to the Arabs that it featured in the Fahd as well as the Fez Plan.

Finally, the Reagan Plan has as one of its objectives to draw the Arabs into negotiation with Israel outside the auspices of the United Nations. Thus isolated from their friends, the Arabs would be the more susceptible to American pressure. The oddity of it all—perhaps, rather, an indication of the blinkers through which the United States views the Middle East—is that President Reagan should for a moment have believed that the Arabs could accept a "peace plan" so biased at every point in Israel's favour.

The Brezhnev Plan

On 15 September 1982, President Brezhnev announced the Soviet Plan for a Middle East settlement. It stood in marked contrast to President Reagan's of two weeks earlier. The Brezhnez Plan has six main points:

One: The principle of the inadmissibility of the seizure of foreign lands by means of acts of aggression must be observed. This dictates that all the territories occupied by Israel since 1967—the Golan Heights, the West Bank of the River Jordan, the Gaza Strip, and the lands of Lebanon—must be returned to the Arabs. The borders between Israel and its Arab neighbours must be declared inviolable.

Two: The inalienable right of the Arab people of Palestine to self-determination, to the creation of their own independent state in the land of Palestine, which must be free of Israeli occupation—the West Bank of the River Jordan and the Gaza Strip—must be ensured by practicable measures. The Palestinian refugees must be granted the chance, envisaged in decisions of the United Nations, to return to their homes or to receive appropriate compensation for the property they have been forced to abandon.

Three: The eastern section of Jerusalem, occupied by Israel in 1967 and containing one of the principal Moslem holy shrines, must be returned to the Arabs and become an integral part of the Palestinian state. The free access of all believers to the holy shrines of three religions must be ensured throughout Jerusalem.

Four: The right of all states in the area to a safe and independent existence and development must be ensured; and this, of course, has to be fully and strictly reciprocal because it is impossible to ensure the security of some people while breaching the security of others.

Five: The state of war between Israel and the Arab states must be ended and peace established. This requires that all parties to the conflict, including Israel and the Palestinian State, commit themselves to a mutual respect for each other's sovereignty, independence, and territorial integrity, and agree to resolve any disputes which may arise between them by peaceful means, through negotiation.

Six: International guarantees of this settlement must be drawn up and adopted; the role of guarantors could be assumed by, for example, the permanent members of the United Nations Security Council or by the Security Council as a whole.

Brezhnev concluded his speech announcing these proposals by saying: "Such a comprehensive, just, and lasting settlement can only be drawn up and implemented by collective effort, with the participation of all parties concerned—including, certainly, the PLO, the sole legitimate representative of the Arab people of Palestine."

By any criteria, the Brezhnev Plan pays greater regard to Arab interests than does the Reagan Plan. The single point of substance on which the Brezhnev Plan was silent was the future of the Israeli settle- . ments in the occupied Arab territories. However, a subsequent statement by the Soviet government declared that it supported the Fez Plan on this issue—in other words, called for their dismantling.

The European Plan (The Venice Declaration)

On 13 June 1980 the nine countries of the European Economic Community, after a summit meeting in Venice, issued the following statement on the Middle East:

One: The heads of state and ministers of foreign affairs...agreed that the growing tensions affecting this region constitute a serious danger and render a comprehensive solution to the Israeli-Arab conflict more necessary and pressing than ever.

Two: The nine member-states of the European Community consider that the traditional ties and common interests which link Europe to the Middle East oblige them to play a special role and now require them to work in a more concrete way towards peace.

Three: All the countries in the area are entitled to live in peace within secure, recognised, and guaranteed borders.

Four: A just solution must be found to the Palestinian problem, which is not simply one of the refugees.

Five: The achievement of these objectives requires the involvement and support of all parties concerned in the peace settlement...and the PLO, which will have to be associated with the negotiations.

Six: The Nine stress that they will not accept any unilateral initiative designed to change the status of Jerusalem, and that any agreement on the city's status should guarantee freedom of access for everyone to the holy places.

Seven: The Nine stress the need for Israel to put an end to the territorial occupation which it has maintained since the conflict of 1967, as it has done for part of the Sinai. They are deeply concerned that the Israeli settlements constitute a serious obstacle to the peace process in the Middle East....

Eight: Concerned as they are to put an end to violence, the Nine consider that only the renunciation of force or the threatened use of force by all parties can create a climate of confidence in the area...

Nine: The Nine have decided to make the necessary contacts with all parties concerned.

If the Reagan Plan had demonstrated the fundamental American disregard for the Arabs, the European Plan showed with humiliating clarity the inability of Europe to take any decision displeasing to the United States. Before the Venice summit, Western European ministers had distanced themselves from the Camp David process and had discussed independent initiatives on the Palestinian issue, including the possibility of tabling a new United Nations resolution to amend Resolution 242. President Carter vowed to veto any such move. Put in their place, the heads of government of the EEC contented themselves in Venice with adopting this catalogue of limping banalities.

The Venice Declaration set a new record in bashfulness: it was silent on every single issue in dispute between the Arabs and Israel. It "considered" some things, was "concerned" by others, and "stressed" what remained. But at no point did the leaders of Western Europe dare to say how they thought these issues should be resolved. The Venice Declaration represents prudence taken to the point of paralysis. Still, it was a marginal advance on the Reagan Plan. First, it mentioned the PLO—while not, of course, daring to concede its undoubted status as the legitimate representative of the Palestinians. Second, it stated that Western Europe would not accept any unilateral initiative designed to change the status of Jerusalem—while not, of course, daring to refer to UN resolutions on the topic. Finally, the Europeans did grapple with the need to liberate the occupied territories, though only in characteristically ambiguous terms: what does "put an end to the territorial occupation" entail, precisely?

The Venice Declaration, as it became known, provoked nothing but anger from the PLO. In a statement on 15 June 1980, the PLO said, among other things: "In its sum total, the statement is largely a clear response to US will and pressures, which are based on an attempt to impose US hegemony upon the Arab region and to liquidate the Palestinian issue in the interests of US imperialism and Zionism, and in perpetuation of the course charted by the Camp David design and by the parties to those designs. The statement is also a clear attempt to draw some Arab states into the Camp David designs. . . . From the beginning, the PLO has entertained no illusions about the scope for a European role, given the fact that this role has so far been associated with US strategy. The PLO welcomes the fact of the European move. However, it calls on the European states to take a more independent stance and to free themselves from the pressures and blackmail of US policy. At the same time the PLO affirms that it is confident that the Arab nation will not be deluded by any attempts to peddle the Camp David designs and the autonomy conspiracy."

The Only Course Open To the Arabs

What Do the Israelis Want?

In his lecture at Stanford in April 1984, Professor Simpson said: "Nahum Goldman, former president of the World Jewish Congress and former president of the World Zionist Organisation, gives us a rare glimpse of the true convictions of Israeli leaders. Goldman records conversations he had with Israel's first prime minister, David Ben-Gurion. This is Ben-Gurion speaking: 'Why should the Arabs make peace? If I were an Arab leader I would never come to terms with Israel. That is natural. We have taken their country. Sure, God promised it to us, but what does that matter to them? Our God is not theirs. We came from Israel, that's true, but 2000 years ago—and what's that to them? There has been anti-Semitism, the Nazis, Hitler, Auschwitz, but was that their fault? They see only one thing. We have come here and stolen their country. Why should they accept that?'"

What Ben-Gurion said is what every true Arab says or thinks. Those who airily talk of a negotiated solution to the Arab-Israeli dispute simply ignore the facts. What are the Arabs to negotiate? The return of the Arab lands that Israel occupies? Israel will never agree—we know that. Or are we to subscribe to the Reagan Plan and discuss the ceding of yet more land to Israel? This the Arabs will never accept. There are many points of bitter discord between Israel and the Arabs, but all derive from a single, fundamental dispute over a land to which both claim historic and religious right. In such a dispute, there can be no negotiated compromise: there can only be victory or defeat. Up to the present, neither side can claim victory: neither party has crushed the will of the other. The Israelis have certainly won many of the battles; but the Arabs have won a few, and the war continues, and no end is in sight. Like the Crusades to which it bears a painful resemblance, the struggle could last for generations to come.

I laid out in Chapter Five the political options available in the international arena. Never mind, for the moment, whether any is acceptable to the Arabs. The fact is that Israel has rejected them all. Even the Reagan Plan the Israelis rejected. Why? Because it dared to suggest, in the vaguest and most ambiguous terms, that the West Bank and Gaza might achieve some measure of autonomy, albeit "in association with" Jordan. So what settlement do the Israelis want? They have never publicly said. They have presented no plan. Instead, they have called on the Arabs to negotiate, promising merely that everything could be discussed at the negotiating table. At the same time, on the ground in the West Bank and in what they tell their own people and their allies, they make it clearer with every passing day that they have no intention of giving up what they have gained. Certainly, the Israelis are sincere in wanting negotiation. But that does not mean they want a settlement. The Israelis want negotiations because they would dampen the heat of what is fast becoming an explosive situation in the Middle East. Negotiations can be dragged out indefinitely—20 years or more. For why should the Israelis make haste? They occupy the lands. Besides, after 20 years of talking, the Arabs would entirely have forgotten that there ever was a military option. The present unstable status quo would have become the permanent reality, lodged in place by the dead weight of words wasted round the negotiating table.

Can any Arab seriously doubt that this is Israel's strategy? As a British politician once remarked: "Why look in a crystal ball when you can read the book?" The Arabs have no need to wait for an official Israeli plan to be presented. All they have to do is to read the Israelis' own books, their press, their debates in the Knesset—and then to turn from their words to their deeds: their history of aggression, their continuing threat to the Arab world, their disregard for the human rights of the Arabs already under their control, their contempt for what the American founding fathers called "a decent respect to the opinions of mankind," as represented by countless resolutions of the United Nations. Part of my purpose in this book has been to set out what can be demonstrated about the real intentions of the Israelis. The best that is on offer to the Arabs as a political solution is Foreign Minister Shamir's plan as laid out in that 1982 *Foreign Af-*

fairs article, described in Chapter One. But no Arab leader, in my view, could or would ever accept that plan; and certainly no Arab leader should accept it. Which brings us back to where we started. There is no political solution possible in this dispute.

If that is so, the Arabs are left with only one choice: the military option. Right now, perhaps, they are unable to exercise it—not, at any rate, with sufficient impetus to win back their occupied lands. Very well, let them wait. Let them wait for years, if necessary—and all the while, prepare. If this generation of Arabs cannot recover its lost lands, their sons will one day do it for them. If not their sons, their grandsons. The strategic truth is that the Arabs possess the winning weapon: time is on their side. This is so obvious, so fundamental, that Israel and its allies try desperately to disguise it. But how can a nation of perhaps four million people by the end of this century hope to dominate an Arab people by then numbering 275 million? Does anyone seriously believe that a billion Moslems around the world will indefinitely tolerate Israel's occupation of one of their most holy shrines? Confronting this prospect, Israel's only hope is to survive tomorrow as it survives today: by manipulating the rivalries which divide the Arab world. But that is a strategy built upon sand. Soon the present generation of Arab leaders will pass; and one day not too distant, the Arab peoples will learn to concentrate on what unites rather than divides them. The prospect must terrify Israel. For how can Israel hope to confront an Arab world at last united? With technology? Right now, certainly, Israel has the edge in technology; but that too will pass. The disparity in resources dictates it.

For the moment, the Arabs may have no choice but to accept the status quo. Very well, let them accept it. That is better than signing a peace treaty on terms dictated by Israel. The status quo leaves Israel in possession of the Arab lands; but it also leaves open the prospect of Arab military action to liberate those lands. Any peace treaty negotiated now would also leave Israel in possession of Arab lands; but it would at the same time debar the Arabs from ever taking action to recover them. It follows that the Arabs have nothing to lose by rejecting the prospect of negotiation.

A Pan-Arab Responsibility

The Arabs spent $49 billion on defence in 1984. Year by year, as table nine shows, the total defence budget of the Arab world has tended to increase, until it would now be more than sufficient for the task confronting the Arabs if only it were rationally spent. If the Arabs, with a combined defence budget of $49 billion a year, cannot defeat Israel, with an annual defence budget of just $8 billion, the only possible conclusion is that there is something very wrong with the way the Arabs are spending their money. My own views as to what must be corrected I have already given; but ultimately the remedies lie in the hands of the Arab people themselves—those who govern, and those who are governed.

Together the Arabs could be strong; divided, they are weak. Slogans about pan-Arab responsibility for the struggle against Israel will remain mere words until the Arabs take energetic steps to bring real unity to their effort. Three steps would transform the situation: One: Every Arab country should allot to defence a certain percentage of its GNP related to its per capita income. The allotments could range from three per cent of GNP in the poorer countries to 25 per cent among the rich nations.

Two: An Arab unified command must be created, along the lines of the NATO or Warsaw Pact commands.

Three: Every Arab country must then dedicate a certain proportion of its armed forces to the struggle against Israel. These forces can be deployed in the Arab front-line states or they can remain in their own homelands. What matters is that they should be under the control of the Arab Unified Command and free from local interference. As a modest start, I would propose that each Arab country assign only 25 per cent of its forces to this unified command.

The Syrian Rock

In any future war between Israel and the Arabs, the theatre of conflict will be one or more of the front-line states, those Arab countries bordering Israel: Egypt, Lebanon, Jordan, Syria. In fact, the choice of arena is for the present narrowed still further. Egypt is excluded so long as it adheres to the Camp David Treaty. Lebanon has never posed a threat to Israel, save when the PLO was stationed in the south of the country. When the PLO was finally expelled from those bases in August 1982, Lebanon once again ceased to be a threat to Israel. Moreover, Lebanon's internal problems are such that Arabs should not expect it to play a significant external role for years to come. The most that can be hoped is that Lebanon will not fall under Israeli domination, and that its territory can somehow be denied to Israel as the route for a flanking attack upon Syria. Jordan, with its small army and its non-existent air defence, would be easy pickings for the Israeli military monster

By elimination, Syria emerges as the only base for the continuing Arab confrontation with Israel. Short of all-out war, Syria's armed forces are already strong enough to deter any Israeli attempt to disarm them. Geographically, Syria is strategically placed to be the springboard for an Arab attempt to recover the lost lands. Syria, in other words, is the rock stemming the tide of Israeli hegemony in the Middle East. The current military balance between Syria and Israel is by no means in Syria's favour, but at least Syria is strong enough already to have achieved a certain blocking function. But that is not the strength needed for positive action: action, for example, to force Israel to return the Golan Heights to Syria or the other occupied territories to their rightful owners. That is why Syria is bending every effort to achieve a true balance of power with Israel. Yet even that, while it will augment Syria's function as a deterrent, will still not give Syria the power actively to challenge Israel—not unless the rest of the Arab world stands at Syria's side.

The Deployment of Arab Troops

The Arabs possess 2899 combat aircraft—1969 of these being front-line aircraft—and 17,331 main battle tanks. Israel has only 830 combat aircraft and 3960 tanks. Those figures suggest that, to command the margin needed for victory, the Arabs would need to deploy against Israel about half the forces they have. But could such numbers of weapons actually be deployed around the borders of Israel, or anywhere within the territories of the front-line states?

Deployment, I have to admit, would not be an easy task; but it need not be impossible. It could be done in two phases.

Phase One: Syria has to reach a balance of forces with Israel.

Phase Two: Egypt has to return to the Arab fold after abrogating the Camp David Treaty. Iraq has likewise to return after extricating itself from the futile war with Iran. Egyptian and Iraqi troops could then be deployed against Israel.

Phase One would have to be completed before Phase Two could commence, since Israel would scarcely remain indifferent to the movement of Arab troops from their homelands to forward bases in the front-line states. The automatic Israeli response, indeed, would be to contemplate a pre-emptive strike. But so long as Syria's forces are already as strong as Israel's before Phase Two commences, there is a fair probability that Israel would not risk pre-emption. The Arab forces could settle at their forward bases unmolested.

Iraq, Syria, and Egypt have the largest and most effective armed forces in the Arab world. Libya has more arms and equipment than Egypt, but its lack of cadres, trained personnel, and experienced field commanders, especially commanders of major units, sharply reduces the value of its forces. To fight Israel with a good prospect of success, the Arabs need a superiority of two-to-one over Israel in arms and equipment—most particularly in combat aircraft and tanks. If we postulate that Syria has contrived, during Phase One, to deploy forces equivalent to those of Israel, then the task facing the rest of the Arab world is to deploy, during Phase Two, forces which are in aggregate equal again to Israel's. But the participation of Egypt and Iraq is vital to this second phase. Without their participation, the other Arab countries simply could not deploy field formations and combat aircraft to match the size and sophistication of Israel's.

What does the arithmetic look like? By 1988, Israel will possess about 948 combat aircraft and some 4533 tanks. Will Syria be able to deploy equivalent forces by then? And will the other Arab nations, combined, be able to field similar forces? To the first question, the answer is probably yes. To the second, the answer is that it cannot be achieved so long as Egypt continues to honour the Camp David agreement and so long as Iraq wastes its strength in a stalemated war with Iran. What the arithmetic demonstrates, however, is that given courageous political decisions by the Arabs, the task is by no means impossible. The future is on our side.

A People's War

Some Arab intellectuals seemingly believe that the way to victory over Israel is through what they call a "people's war"—by which they mean, in practice, the sacrifice of countless Arab lives in a World War One assault on Israel's frontiers. The Arabs number about 190 million, they say, while the Israelis are only three and a half million. Suppose they kill a million Arabs for every 50,000 Israelis killed: the ratio would still favour the Arabs. The Arabs could accept, on this line of reasoning, the loss of perhaps two million lives. But the Israelis would find the loss of 100,000 in exchange intolerable. Some variants of this line of thought actually call for the Israelis to occupy Cairo or Damascus, to be picked off then at every street corner. The Arab nation as a whole—and especially its cities—would thus become a quagmire big enough to swallow the Zionist entity.

At heart, this argument reflects disillusion with the Arabs' regular armed forces. They have been fighting Israel for 35 years with little to show for it. Perhaps a "people's war" modeled somehow on Algeria and Vietnam might prove more successful. But, while I respect the impulse behind this argument, I think its advocates exaggerate what such an approach could achieve against Israel. My own view is that a people's war might serve as the catalyst of a war fought by regular forces; I do not think it can ever be a substitute. The conflicts in Algeria and Vietnam cannot, in my view, be replicated in the Arab-Israeli arena for six main reasons:

One: The absence of a unified command. In Algeria all fighters were under the leadership of the *Fronte de Liberation Nationale* (FLN). When some guerrillas in the early days displayed other tendencies, the FLN accorded first priority to the task of liquidating them—precisely so that, in the struggle against the French, everyone would be under one command and following one ideology. Similarly, the people's struggle in Vietnam was under one leadership with one ideology. But how could Arabs divided among 21 countries with 21 leaders wage such a unified struggle?

Two: During the Algerian struggle, other Arab countries did not meddle in the Algerians' internal affairs. Relations with the FLN were limited to supplying money, arms, and equipment—though most Arab countries were too poor even to offer those. Today, however, some Arab countries command great wealth, and use it to advance their own views within the PLO. It is an open secret that each faction of the PLO has a "special relationship" with one or more Arab countries. It is equally plain that some of those countries use the PLO factions more to advance their own quarrels with other Arabs than to concert the struggle against Israel. In this anarchy, how could a people's war be directed?

Three: As for the Arabs' ability to tolerate casualties, it is correct in strictly demographic terms that losses of, say two or even three million might be bearable—but only if those losses fell evenly on the whole Arab world. Distributed like that, the losses would amount to no more than 1.5 per cent of the population of each Arab country. But will they in fact fall so equally? If the bulk of the casualities were to be suffered by one or two front-line states, they would be as intolerable as Israel's losses would be.

Four: During the Algerian struggle, the FLN guerrillas used bases in Tunisia and Morocco from which to launch their attacks and to which they returned after their missions. France never attacked those bases. In Vietnam, the guerrillas had bases in China; the United States never attacked those either. Israel would observe no such restraint. Any Arab country from which guerrillas move to attack Israeli people or property inside or outside Israel is held responsible for that attack, and the Israeli reprisals are not confined to strikes against the guerrilla bases themselves. That is why all Arab countries enforce strict controls upon PLO personnel based in their territory: they fear being dragged into a war for which they are not prepared. If Israel does that against the PLO, how much more savagely would it take reprisals to deter a people's war?

Five: Much has been written about the cruelty of the French in their struggle in Algeria. The fact is that the Israelis are prepared to do far worse. Rightly or wrongly, the Israelis believe that Palestine is the land promised them by God. Having been, as they believe, exiled once, they have no intention of going into exile a second time. To defend what they believe to be their right, the Israelis are prepared to do anything.

With brutality towards everyone and the torture of some, the Israelis could, in my view, hope to break the civilian population in the areas from which the guerrillas would have to operate. The guerrillas would be betrayed. The people's war would have failed.

Six: Except for very small areas, the terrain around Israel's borders is unsuitable for guerrilla warfare. In Algeria and Vietnam, mountains and forests both provided sanctuary and served as the best theatres for guerrilla operations. Such conditions do not exist around Israel.

As I have already said, I do not exclude a people's war; but I foresee it only as one element in the total struggle against Israel. It must run in parallel with more traditional and conventional warfare. As we prepare our soldiers for regular combat, the people must also be prepared for the irregular skirmishes of a people's war—and, most importantly, trained not to act until they are directed. Sporadic guerrilla actions need not cease while this training goes on. On the contrary, selected guerrilla activities would keep the conflict uppermost in the people's minds, and also serve to identify and train the cadres who must lead the people's war when the day comes.

Conclusions

One: Israel will never return the Arab lands on a golden platter. What was taken by force can be recovered only by force. Those Arabs who live in hopes of retrieving the occupied territories through negotiation are deluding themselves and those who listen to them. Without military strength to back it, the political option for the Arabs is merely the path to further concessions and to the ultimate acceptance of American and Israeli hegemony in the region.

Two: The United States has as its main objective in the Middle East the enforcement of American hegemony over the nations and peoples of the region, in order to control and exploit its raw materials and preserve it as captive market for American manufactured goods. Israel is America's principal instrument to this end. It follows that American-Israeli cooperation in every field—and American military, political, and economic support for Israel—is not an aberration of American domestic politics but a long-term programme to further America's strategic interests.

Three: To deceive its Arab allies, the United States talks with calculated ambiguity about the settlement it wants. "Israel's right to live within secure borders" is just such a phrase. What does it mean? What are secure borders? Who is to judge them secure? Is Israel to be allowed to draw its boundaries wherever it chooses in the name of this security? And how far will the United States go to guarantee Israel's security? Will it keep Israel securely in control of the occupied Arab territories? Or will it guarantee Israel's security only within its pre-1967 borders? These ambiguities the US has no intention of clarifying, because puzzling over them serves usefully to distract people from America's real objectives in the region.

Four: American-manufactured arms and equipment can never be used against Israel. The US takes great pains to ensure this. It demands a contractual pledge from the buyer; US control of maintenance and the supply of spares; the removal of the most sophisticated equipment so as to make a weapon supplied to the Arabs deliberately inferior to the same system in Israel; and, if necessary, direct American participation in the operating of the weapon system. The final sanction is an Israeli pre-emptive strike, mounted of course with American approval.

Five: The continuation of the Iraq-Iran war serves US interests. The spectre of the war spreading to their territories will persuade the Gulf States, or so America hopes, to allow US bases on their soil.

Six: The Soviet Union needs to comprehend that, in rejecting American hegemony, the Arabs equally reject any other hegemony. The Soviet Union is an invaluable ally in the Arabs' struggle to recover their lost territories and to repel American hegemony. And the Arabs accept that the waning of American influence in the area will be to the Soviets' benefit. But the Arabs' long-term objective must be a policy in world affairs of positive neutrality.

Seven: The resurgence of Islamic militancy has further still to rise. It will be a major factor in shaping the future of the region.

Eight: The armed might of the Arab people will never be fully mobilised against Israel until the Arabs are united in a single political entity; and this will not come about in the foreseeable future. The best that can be hoped is to give some meaning to what are currently empty slogans about pan-Arab responsibility by the Arab nations agreeing, first, to devote specified percentages of their GNP to defence according to their wealth; and, second, assigning an agreed proportion of their forces to a unified Arab command for permanent deployment against Israel.

Nine: Human rights are routinely violated in virtually all Arab states. Until Arab citizens have the right to take complaints of such violations to some international tribunal, there can be no hope of permanent improvement. Unless there is reform, however, and the rights of the Arab people respected, the people will never be motivated to defeat Israel, no matter how sophisticated the weaponry put into their hands.

Ten: The military option offers the only realistic chance the Arabs have of recovering their lost lands. To advocate this does not mean that the Arabs must go to war in a month or even a year. It means that the Arabs must begin to prepare themselves physically, materially, and spiritually to that end. It means that the Arabs must mobilise all their resources. The Arabs possess all the elements necessary for victory over Israel. If the present scene is one of Arab impotence, also it is certain that in time the Arabs will rid themselves of the social and political causes of that weakness. What matters is that the Arabs must not despair, and, in despairing, abandon their dreams, settling for a false peace and continued humiliation. The Arabs must not discard the military option. The future is on their side.

References

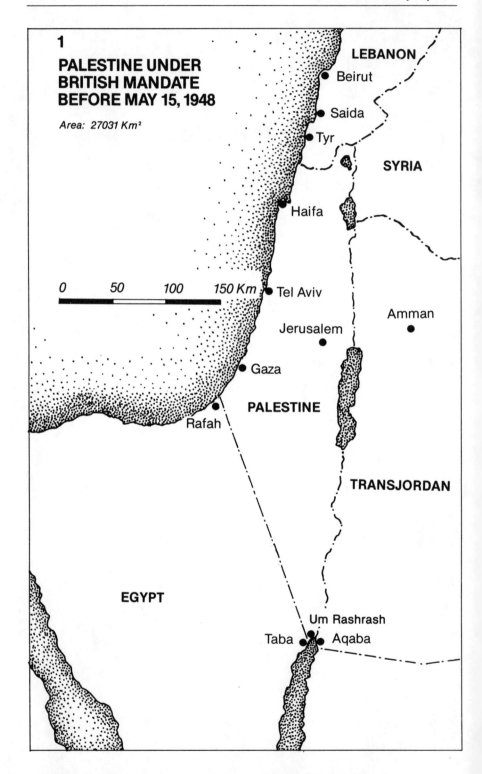

1

**PALESTINE UNDER
BRITISH MANDATE
BEFORE MAY 15, 1948**

Area: 27031 Km²

LEBANON

● Beirut

● Saida

● Tyr

SYRIA

● Haifa

0   50   100   150 Km   ● Tel Aviv

Amman
●

Jerusalem
●

● Gaza

PALESTINE

●
Rafah

TRANSJORDAN

EGYPT

Um Rashrash
Taba ●● Aqaba

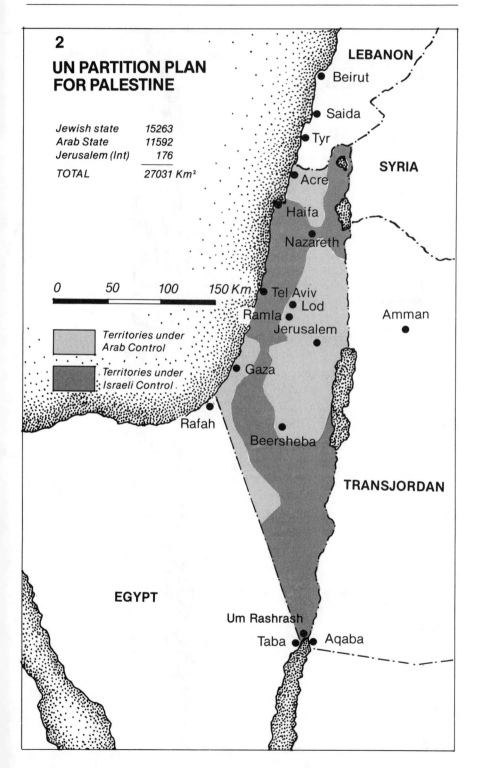

2

UN PARTITION PLAN
FOR PALESTINE

Jewish state	*15263*
Arab State	*11592*
Jerusalem (Int)	*176*
TOTAL	*27031 Km²*

LEBANON

Beirut

Saida

Tyr

SYRIA

Acre

Haifa

Nazareth

0   50   100   150 Km.

Tel Aviv

Lod

Ramla

Amman

Jerusalem

Territories under
Arab Control

Territories under
Israeli Control

Gaza

Rafah

Beersheba

TRANSJORDAN

EGYPT

Um Rashrash

Taba   Aqaba

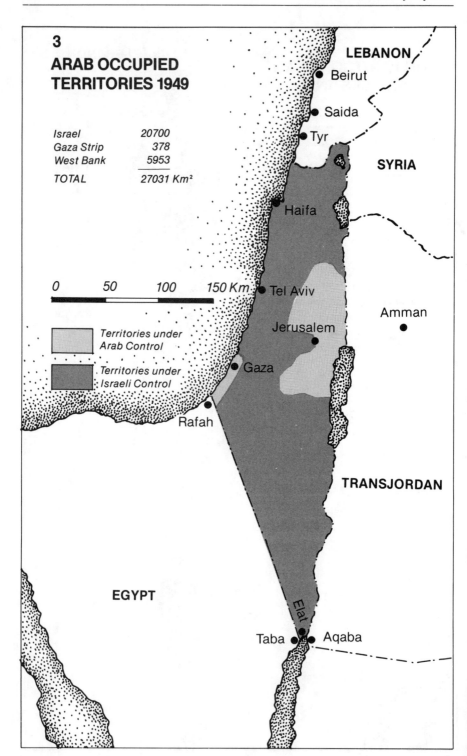

3

**ARAB OCCUPIED
TERRITORIES 1949**

Israel	*20700*
Gaza Strip	*378*
West Bank	*5953*
TOTAL	*27031 Km²*

0   50   100   150 Km

Territories under
Arab Control

Territories under
Israeli Control

LEBANON

● Beirut

● Saida

● Tyr

SYRIA

● Haifa

● Tel Aviv

Amman
●

Jerusalem
●

● Gaza

● Rafah

TRANSJORDAN

EGYPT

Elat

Taba ●● Aqaba

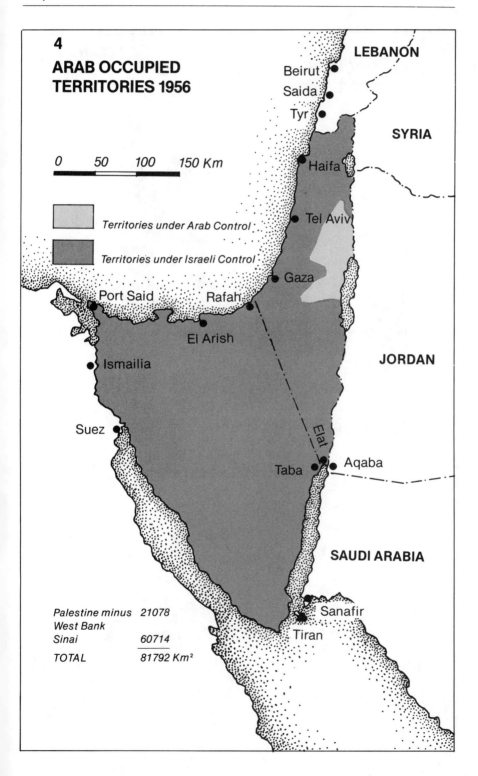

4

ARAB OCCUPIED TERRITORIES 1956

0   50   100   150 Km

Territories under Arab Control

Territories under Israeli Control

LEBANON

Beirut
Saida
Tyr

SYRIA

Haifa

Tel Aviv

Gaza

Port Said   Rafah

El Arish

JORDAN

Ismailia

Suez

Elat

Taba   Aqaba

SAUDI ARABIA

Sanafir

Tiran

Palestine minus West Bank	21078
Sinai	60714
TOTAL	81792 Km²

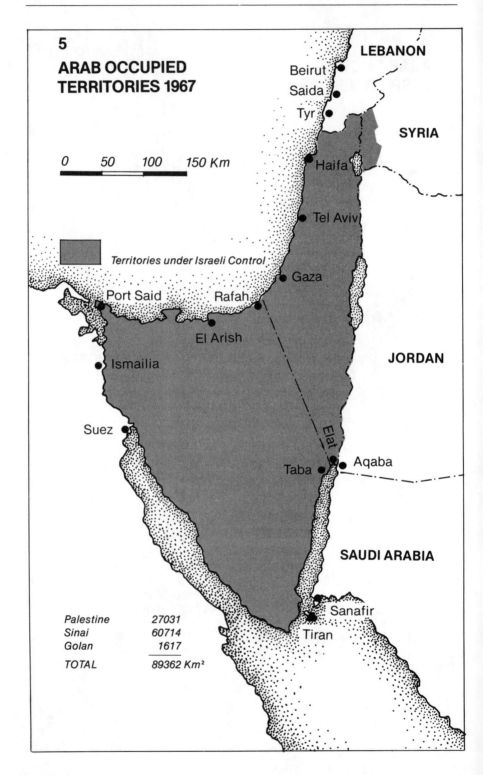

5

**ARAB OCCUPIED
TERRITORIES 1967**

0   50   100   150 Km

☐ *Territories under Israeli Control*

LEBANON

Beirut
Saida
Tyr

SYRIA

Haifa

Tel Aviv

Gaza

Port Said   Rafah

El Arish

Ismailia

JORDAN

Suez

Elat

Taba ● ● Aqaba

SAUDI ARABIA

Sanafir

Tiran

Palestine	27031
Sinai	60714
Golan	1617
TOTAL	89362 Km²

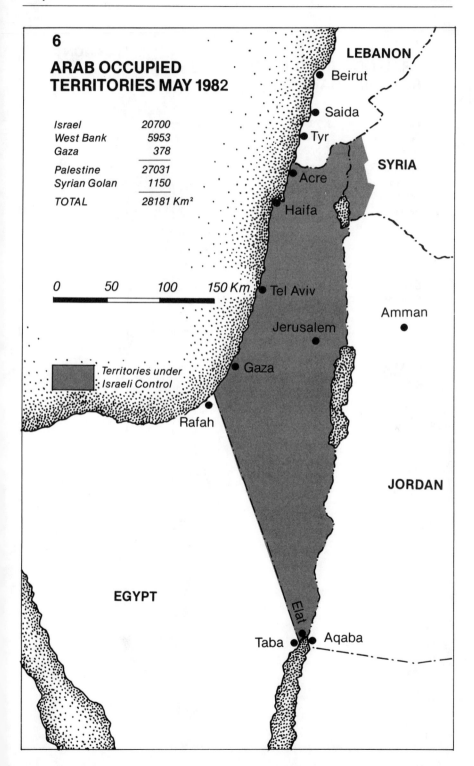

6

ARAB OCCUPIED TERRITORIES MAY 1982

Israel	20700
West Bank	5953
Gaza	378
Palestine	27031
Syrian Golan	1150
TOTAL	28181 Km²

LEBANON

● Beirut

● Saida

● Tyr

SYRIA

● Acre

● Haifa

0   50   100   150 Km.

● Tel Aviv

Amman
●

Jerusalem
●

Territories under
Israeli Control

● Gaza

● Rafah

JORDAN

EGYPT

Elat

Taba ● ● Aqaba

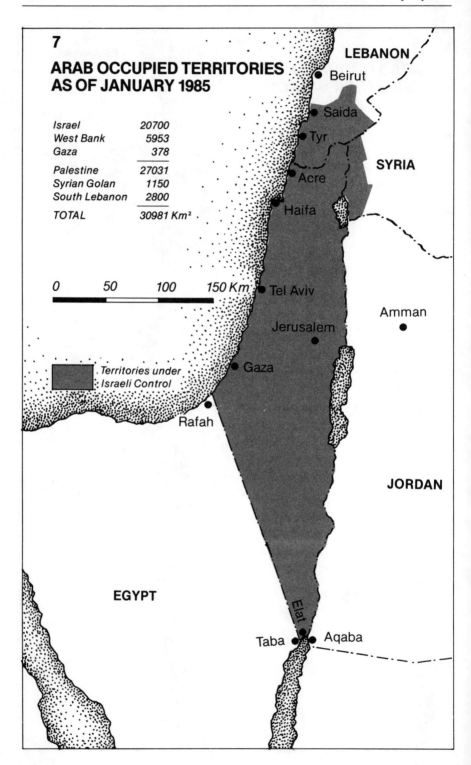

7

ARAB OCCUPIED TERRITORIES AS OF JANUARY 1985

Israel	20700
West Bank	5953
Gaza	378
Palestine	27031
Syrian Golan	1150
South Lebanon	2800
TOTAL	30981 Km²

0   50   100   150 Km

Territories under Israeli Control

LEBANON

Beirut

Saida

Tyr

SYRIA

Acre

Haifa

Tel Aviv

Amman

Jerusalem

Gaza

Rafah

JORDAN

EGYPT

Elat

Taba   Aqaba

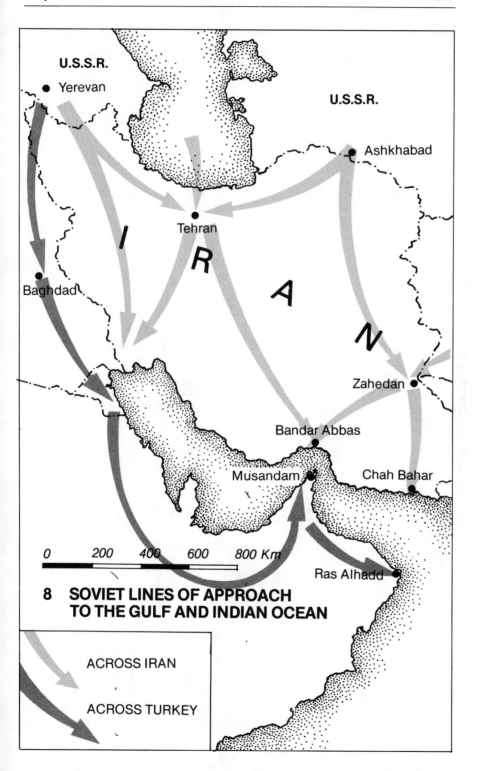

**8   SOVIET LINES OF APPROACH
TO THE GULF AND INDIAN OCEAN**

ACROSS IRAN

ACROSS TURKEY

Table 1
Combat aircraft in service in the Arab Air Forces 1973

Serial No.	Country	Western Origin		Soviet Origin		Chinese Origin		Total		Total Combat ac.
		L1	L2	L1	L2	L1	L2	L1	L2	
1	Algeria	—	—	35	120	—	—	35	120	155
2	Bahrain	—	—	—	—	—	—	—	—	—
3	Egypt	—	—	210	210	—	—	210	210	420
4	Iraq	—	36	90	98	—	—	90	134	224
5	Jordan	20	32	—	—	—	—	20	32	52
6	Kuwait	12	8	—	—	—	—	12	8	20
7	Lebanon	10	8	—	—	—	—	10	8	18
8	Libya	65	9	—	—	—	—	65	9	74
9	Morocco	—	24	—	—	—	—	—	24	24
10	Oman	—	—	—	—	—	—	—	—	—
11	Qatar	—	4	—	—	—	—	—	4	4
12	Saudi Arabia	35	—	—	—	—	—	35	—	35
13	Sudan	—	—	20	—	—	17	20	17	37
14	Syria	—	—	200	126	—	—	200	126	326
15	Tunisia	—	—	—	—	—	—	—	—	—
16	United Arab Emirates	—	12	—	—	—	—	—	12	12
17	Yemen (North)	—	—	—	28	—	—	—	28	28
18	Yemen (South)	—	—	—	15	—	—	—	15	15
19	Mauritania	—	—	—	—	—	—	—	—	—
20	Somalia	—	—	—	19	—	—	—	19	19
21	Djibouti	—	—	—	—	—	—	—	—	—
22	Total	142	133	555	616	—	17	697	766	1463

NB
Magister (W.O.), Mig 15 (S.O.), and what is equivalent or inferior, are not included.

Table 1/A
Combat aircraft (W.O.) in service in the Arab Air Forces 1973

Serial No.	Country	L 1						L 2		Total
		Mirage V	Mirage III	F-104	Lightning	Subtotal	F-5	Hunter	Subtotal	Total Combat ac.
1	Algeria	—	—	—	—	—	—	—	—	—
2	Bahrain	—	—	—	—	—	—	—	—	—
3	Egypt	—	—	—	—	—	—	36	36	36
4	Iraq	—	—	20	—	20	—	32	32	52
5	Jordan	—	—	—	12	12	—	8	8	20
6	Kuwait	—	10	—	—	10	—	8	8	18
7	Lebanon	30	35	—	—	65	9	—	9	74
8	Libya	—	—	—	—	—	24	—	24	24
9	Morocco	—	—	—	—	—	—	—	—	—
10	Oman	—	—	—	—	—	—	4	4	4
11	Qatar	—	—	—	35	35	—	—	—	35
12	Saudi Arabia	—	—	—	—	—	—	—	—	—
13	Sudan	—	—	—	—	—	—	—	—	—
14	Syria	—	—	—	—	—	—	12	12	12
15	Tunisia	—	—	—	—	—	—	—	—	—
16	United Arab Emirates	—	—	—	—	—	—	—	—	—
17	Yemen (North)	—	—	—	—	—	—	—	—	—
18	Yemen (South)	—	—	—	—	—	—	—	—	—
19	Mauritania	—	—	—	—	—	—	—	—	—
20	Somalia	—	—	—	—	—	—	—	—	—
21	Djibouti	—	—	—	—	—	—	—	—	—
22	Total	30	45	20	47	142	33	100	133	275

NB
Magister, and what is equivalent or inferior, are not included.

Table 1/B
Combat aircraft (S.O.) in service in the Arab Air Forces 1973

Serial No.	Country	L 1		L 2					Total
		Mig-21	Sub-Total	Mig-17	SU-7	TU-16	IL-28	Sub-Total	Total Combat ac.
1	Algeria	35	35	70	20	—	30	120	155
2	Bahrain	—	—	—	—	—	—	—	—
3	Egypt	210	210	100	80	25	5	210	420
4	Iraq	90	90	30	60	8	—	98	188
5	Jordan	—	—	—	—	—	—	—	—
6	Kuwait	—	—	—	—	—	—	—	—
7	Lebanon	—	—	—	—	—	—	—	—
8	Libya	—	—	—	—	—	—	—	—
9	Morocco	—	—	—	—	—	—	—	—
10	Oman	—	—	—	—	—	—	—	—
11	Qatar	—	—	—	—	—	—	—	—
12	Saudi Arabia	—	—	—	—	—	—	—	—
13	Sudan	20	20	—	—	—	—	—	20
14	Syria	200	200	80	30	—	16	126	326
15	Tunisia	—	—	—	—	—	—	—	—
16	United Arab Emirates	—	—	—	—	—	—	—	—
17	Yemen (North)	—	—	12	—	—	16	28	28
18	Yemen (South)	—	—	15	—	—	—	15	15
19	Mauritania	—	—	—	—	—	—	—	—
20	Somalia	—	—	19	—	—	—	19	19
21	Djibouti	—	—	—	—	—	—	—	—
22	Total	555	555	326	190	33	67	616	1171

NB
Mig-15, and what is equivalent or inferior, are not included.

Table 2
Main battle tanks in service in the Arab Armed Forces 1973

Serial No.	Country	W.O.	S.O.	C.O.	Total
1	Algeria	—	400	—	400
2	Bahrain	—	—	—	—
3	Egypt	—	1880	—	1880
4	Iraq	—	990	—	990
5	Jordan	440	—	—	440
6	Kuwait	100	—	—	100
7	Lebanon	60	—	—	60
8	Libya	6	215	—	221
9	Morocco	—	120	—	120
10	Oman	—	—	—	—
11	Qatar	—	—	—	—
12	Saudi Arabia	25	—	—	25
13	Sudan	130	—	20	150
14	Syria	—	1170	—	1170
15	Tunisia	—	—	—	—
16	United Arab Emirates	—	—	—	—
17	Yemen (North)	—	30	—	30
18	Yemen (South)	—	50	—	50
19	Mauritania	—	—	—	—
20	Somalia	—	150	—	150
21	Djibouti	—	—	—	—
22	Total	761	5005	20	5786

NB
Light tanks such as AMX-13 (French), M-41 (American), and T-76 (Soviet), are not included.

212

Table 3
Combat aircraft in service in the Arab Air Forces 1978

Serial No.	Country	W.O. L1	W.O. L2	S.O. L1	S.O. L2	C.O. L1	C.O. L2	Total L1	Total L2	Total Combat ac.
1	Algeria	—	—	90	74	—	—	90	74	164
2	Bahrain	—	—	—	—	—	—	—	—	—
3	Egypt	46	—	228	188	—	—	274	188	462
4	Iraq	—	20	225	82	—	—	225	102	327
5	Jordan	20	56	—	—	—	—	20	56	76
6	Kuwait	20	20	—	—	—	—	20	20	40
7	Lebanon	—	—	—	—	—	—	—	—	—
8	Libya	110	—	29	12	—	—	139	12	151
9	Morocco	—	39	—	—	—	—	—	39	39
10	Oman	—	24	—	—	—	—	—	24	24
11	Qatar	—	3	—	—	—	—	—	3	3
12	Saudi Arabia	32	100	—	—	—	—	32	100	132
13	Sudan	—	—	10	—	—	12	10	12	22
14	Syria	—	—	282	110	—	—	282	110	392
15	Tunisia	—	—	—	—	—	—	—	—	—
16	United Arab Emirates	32	7	—	—	—	—	32	7	39
17	Yemen (North)	—	—	—	26	—	—	—	26	26
18	Yemen (South)	—	—	12	22	—	—	12	22	34
19	Mauritania	—	—	—	—	—	—	—	—	—
20	Somalia	—	—	7	18	—	—	7	18	25
21	Djibouti	—	—	—	—	—	—	—	—	—
22	Total	260	269	883	532	—	12	1143	813	1956

NB
Magister (W.O.), Mig-15 (S.O.), and what is equivalent or inferior, are not included.

Table 3/A

Combat aircraft (W.O.) in service in the Arab Air Forces 1978

Serial No.	Country	L 1					L 2					Total Combat ac.
		Mirage F-1	Mirage V	F-104	Lightning	Subtotal	Jaguar	F-5	A-4	Hunter	Subtotal	
1	Algeria	—	—	—	—	—	—	—	—	—	—	—
2	Bahrain	—	—	—	—	—	—	—	—	—	—	—
3	Egypt	—	46	—	—	46	—	—	—	—	—	46
4	Iraq	—	—	20	—	20	—	—	—	—	—	20
5	Jordan	20	—	—	—	20	—	56	—	—	56	76
6	Kuwait	—	—	—	—	—	—	—	20	20	40	40
7	Lebanon	—	—	—	—	—	—	—	—	—	—	—
8	Libya	110	—	—	—	110	—	—	—	—	—	110
9	Morocco	—	—	—	—	—	—	39	—	—	39	39
10	Oman	—	—	—	—	—	12	—	—	12	24	24
11	Qatar	—	—	—	—	—	—	—	—	3	3	3
12	Saudi Arabia	—	—	—	32	32	—	100	—	—	100	132
13	Sudan	—	—	—	—	—	—	—	—	—	—	—
14	Syria	—	—	—	—	—	—	—	—	—	—	—
15	Tunisia	—	—	—	—	—	—	—	—	—	—	—
16	United Arab Emirates	32	—	—	—	32	—	—	—	7	7	39
17	Yemen (North)	—	—	—	—	—	—	—	—	—	—	—
18	Yemen (South)	—	—	—	—	—	—	—	—	—	—	—
19	Mauritania	—	—	—	—	—	—	—	—	—	—	—
20	Somalia	—	—	—	—	—	—	—	—	—	—	—
21	Djibouti	—	—	—	—	—	—	—	—	—	—	—
22	Total	162	46	20	32	260	12	195	20	42	269	529

NB
Magister, and what is equivalent or inferior, are not included.

Table 3/B
Combat aircraft (S.O.) in service in the Arab Air Forces 1978

Serial No.	Country	L 1				
		Mig-25	Mig-23	Mig-21	SU-20	Subtotal
1	Algeria	—	—	90	—	90
2	Bahrain	—	—	—	—	—
3	Egypt	108	21	80	19	228
4	Iraq	—	80	115	30	225
5	Jordan	—	—	—	—	—
6	Kuwait	—	—	—	—	—
7	Lebanon	—	—	—	—	—
8	Libya	—	—	29	—	29
9	Morocco	—	—	—	—	—
10	Oman	—	—	—	—	—
11	Qatar	—	—	—	—	—
12	Saudi Arabia	—	—	—	—	—
13	Sudan	—	—	10	—	10
14	Syria	—	50	220	12	282
15	Tunisia	—	—	—	—	—
16	United Arab Emirates	—	—	—	—	—
17	Yemen (North)	—	—	—	—	—
18	Yemen (South)	—	—	12	—	12
19	Mauritania	—	—	—	—	—
20	Somalia	—	—	7	—	7
21	Djibouti	—	—	—	—	—
22	Total	108	151	563	61	883

NB
Mig-15, and what is equivalent or inferior, are not included.

| | L | 2 | | | | Total |
Mig-17	SU-7	TU-16	TU-22	IL-28	Subtotal	Combat ac.
30	20	—	—	24	74	164
—	—	—	—	—	—	—
90	70	23	—	5	188	416
—	60	—	12	10	82	307
—	—	—	—	—	—	—
—	—	—	—	—	—	—
—	—	—	—	—	—	—
—	—	—	12	—	12	41
—	—	—	—	—	—	—
—	—	—	—	—	—	—
—	—	—	—	—	—	—
—	—	—	—	—	—	—
—	—	—	—	—	—	10
50	60	—	—	—	110	392
—	—	—	—	—	—	—
—	—	—	—	—	—	—
12	—	—	—	14	26	26
15	—	—	—	7	22	34
—	—	—	—	—	—	—
15	—	—	—	3	18	25
—	—	—	—	—	—	—
212	210	23	24	63	532	1415

Table 4
Main battle tanks in service in the Arab Armed Forces 1978

Serial No.	Country	W.O.	S.O.	C.O.	Total
1	Algeria	—	350	—	350
2	Bahrain	—	—	—	—
3	Egypt	—	1600	—	1600
4	Iraq	100	1800	—	1900
5	Jordan	500	—	—	500
6	Kuwait	124	—	—	124
7	Lebanon	—	—	—	—
8	Libya	—	2000	—	2000
9	Morocco	90	—	—	90
10	Oman	—	—	—	—
11	Qatar	12	—	—	12
12	Saudi Arabia	325	—	—	325
13	Sudan	—	130	30	160
14	Syria	—	2500	—	2500
15	Tunisia	—	—	—	—
16	United Arab Emirates	—	—	—	—
17	Yemen (North)	—	220	—	220
18	Yemen (South)	—	260	—	260
19	Mauritania	—	—	—	—
20	Somalia	—	80	—	80
21	Djibouti	—	—	—	—
22	Total	1151	8940	30	10121

NB
Light tanks, such as AMX-13 (French), M-41 (American), and T-76 (Soviet) are not included

Table 5
Combat aircraft in service in the Arab Air Forces 1983

Serial No.	Country	W.O.		S.O.		C.O.		Total		Total Combat ac.
		L1	L2	L1	L2	L1	L2	L1	L2	
1	Algeria	—	—	189	80	—	—	189	80	269
2	Bahrain	—	—	—	—	—	—	—	—	—
3	Egypt	89	12	12	125	—	44	101	181	282
4	Iraq	37	—	162	12	70	40	269	52	321
5	Jordan	23	80	—	—	—	—	23	80	103
6	Kuwait	19	30	—	—	—	—	19	30	49
7	Lebanon	—	—	—	—	—	—	—	—	—
8	Libya	111	—	385	9	—	—	496	9	505
9	Morocco	41	57	—	—	—	—	41	57	98
10	Oman	—	19	—	—	—	—	—	19	19
11	Qatar	—	8	—	—	—	—	—	8	8
12	Saudi Arabia	65	105	—	—	—	—	65	105	170
13	Sudan	—	4	8	—	—	19	8	23	31
14	Syria	—	—	354	103	—	—	354	103	457
15	Tunisia	—	—	—	—	—	—	—	—	—
16	United Arab Emirates	30	3	—	—	—	—	30	3	33
17	Yemen (North)	—	10	55	10	—	—	55	20	75
18	Yemen (South)	—	—	73	40	—	—	73	40	113
19	Mauritania	—	—	—	—	—	—	—	—	—
20	Somalia	—	—	7	9	—	30	7	39	46
21	Djibouti	—	—	—	—	—	—	—	—	—
22	Total	415	328	1245	388	70	133	1730	849	2579

NB

The 230 Chinese-built aircraft are distributed as: F-7 (replica of Soviet Mig-21): 70 Iraq; F-6 (replica of Soviet Mig-19): 44 Egypt, 40 Iraq, 9 Sudan, 30 Somalia; F-5 (replica of Soviet Mig-17): 10 Sudan.

Table 5/A

Combat aircraft (W.O.) in service in the Arab Air Forces 1983

Ser. no.	Country	L 1									L 2			Total Combat ac.
		F-15	F-16	Mirage F-1	Mirage V	Light-ning	Sub-Total	Jaguar	F-5	A-4	Alfajet	AEW	Sub-Total	
1	Algeria	—	—	—	—	—	—	—	—	—	—	—	—	—
2	Bahrain	—	—	—	—	—	—	—	—	—	—	—	—	—
3	Egypt	—	24	—	65	—	89	—	—	—	10	2	12	101
4	Iraq	—	—	37	—	—	37	—	—	—	—	—	—	37
5	Jordan	—	—	23	—	—	23	—	80	—	—	—	80	103
6	Kuwait	—	—	19	—	—	19	—	—	30	—	—	30	49
7	Lebanon	—	—	—	—	—	—	—	—	—	—	—	—	—
8	Libya	—	—	46	65	—	111	—	—	—	—	—	—	111
9	Morocco	—	—	41	—	—	41	—	35	—	22	—	57	98
10	Oman	—	—	—	—	—	—	19	—	—	—	—	19	19
11	Qatar	—	—	—	—	—	—	—	—	—	8	—	8	8
12	Saudi Arabia	48	—	—	—	17	65	—	105	—	—	—	105	170
13	Sudan	—	—	—	—	—	—	—	4	—	—	—	4	4
14	Syria	—	—	—	—	—	—	—	—	—	—	—	—	—
15	Tunisia	—	—	—	—	—	—	—	—	—	—	—	—	—
16	United Arab Emirates	—	—	—	30	—	30	—	—	—	3	—	3	33
17	Yemen (North)	—	—	—	—	—	—	—	10	—	—	—	10	10
18	Yemen (South)	—	—	—	—	—	—	—	—	—	—	—	—	—
19	Mauritania	—	—	—	—	—	—	—	—	—	—	—	—	—
20	Somalia	—	—	—	—	—	—	—	—	—	—	—	—	—
21	Djibouti	—	—	—	—	—	—	—	—	—	—	—	—	—
22	Total	48	24	166	160	17	415	19	234	30	43	2	328	743

NB

1—Aircraft assigned for non-advanced training are not included.

2—Aircraft assigned for advanced training such as Mig-21, Mirage-5, F-16, etc., are included.

3—With the exception of Lightning, all aircarft more than thirty years of age have been excluded.

Table 5/B
Combat aircraft (S.O.) in service in the Arab Air Forces 1983

Ser. No.	Country	L 1									L 2			Total Combat ac.
		Mig-25	Mig-23	Mig-21	SU-17 SU-20 SU-22	Sub-Total	Mig-19	Mig-17	SU-7	TU-16	TU-22	IL-28	Sub-Total	
1	Algeria	22	40	95	32	189	8	60	–	–	–	12	80	269
2	Bahrain	–	–	–	–	–	–	–	–	–	–	–	–	–
3	Egypt	–	–	12	–	12	–	50	56	14	–	5	125	137
4	Iraq	22	70	–	70	162	–	–	–	–	7	5	12	174
5	Jordan	–	–	–	–	–	–	–	–	–	–	–	–	–
6	Kuwait	–	–	–	–	–	–	–	–	–	–	–	–	–
7	Lebanon	–	–	–	–	–	–	–	–	–	–	–	–	–
8	Libya	55	175	55	100	385	–	–	–	–	9	–	9	394
9	Morocco	–	–	–	–	–	–	–	–	–	–	–	–	–
10	Oman	–	–	–	–	–	–	–	–	–	–	–	–	–
11	Qatar	–	–	–	–	–	–	–	–	–	–	–	–	–
12	Saudi Arabia	–	–	–	–	–	–	–	–	–	–	–	–	–
13	Sudan	–	–	8	–	8	–	–	–	–	–	–	–	8
14	Syria	24	90	200	40	354	–	85	18	–	–	–	103	457
15	Tunisia	–	–	–	–	–	–	–	–	–	–	–	–	–
16	United Arab Emirates	–	–	–	–	–	–	–	–	–	–	–	–	–
17	Yemen (North)	–	–	40	15	55	–	10	–	–	–	–	10	65
18	Yemen (South)	–	–	48	25	73	–	30	–	–	–	10	40	113
19	Mauritania	–	–	–	–	–	–	–	–	–	–	–	–	–
20	Somalia	–	–	7	–	7	–	9	–	–	–	–	9	16
21	Djibouti	–	–	–	–	–	–	–	–	–	–	–	–	–
22	Total	123	375	458	282	1245	8	244	74	14	16	32	388	1633

NB

1—Aircraft assigned for non-advanced training are not included.

2—With the exception of IL-28, all aircraft which are more than thirty years of age have been excluded.

3—Five super-Etendard hired from France by Iraq late 1983 are not included.

Table 6
Main battle tanks in service in the Arab Armed Forces 1983

Serial No.	Country	Tanks (W.O.)						
		AMX-30	M-47 M-48	M-60	Cen-turion	Vickers	Chief-tain	Khalid
1	Algeria	—	—	—	—	—	—	—
2	Bahrain	—	—	—	—	—	—	—
3	Egypt	—	—	250	—	—	—	—
4	Iraq	—	—	—	—	—	—	—
5	Jordan	—	350	—	200	—	—	30
6	Kuwait	—	—	—	10	70	160	—
7	Lebanon	—	54	—	—	—	—	—
8	Libya	—	—	—	—	—	—	—
9	Morocco	—	120	—	—	—	—	—
10	Oman	—	—	6	—	—	12	—
11	Qatar	24	—	—	—	—	—	—
12	Saudi Arabia	300	—	150	—	—	—	—
13	Sudan	—	—	20	—	—	—	—
14	Syria	—	—	—	—	—	—	—
15	Tunisia	—	14	—	—	—	—	—
16	United Arab Emirates	100	—	—	—	—	—	—
17	Yemen (North)	—	—	64	—	—	—	—
18	Yemen (South)	—	—	—	—	—	—	—
19	Mauritania	—	—	—	—	—	—	—
20	Somalia	—	—	—	40	—	—	—
21	Djibouti	—	—	—	—	—	—	—
22	Total	424	538	490	250	70	172	30

NB

1—Light tanks such as AMX-13 (French), M-41 (American), T-76 (Soviet), are not included.

2—M/TR-77 is made by Romania. It is a replica of the Soviet tank T-55. Egypt got 200 tanks of that type in 1982.

3—T-59 is a replica of the Soviet tank T-54.

4—T-69 is a replica of the Soviet tank T-55.

5—Khalid is the same as Chieftain, with minor modifications.

OF-40	Sub-Total	T-59 T-69	T-34	T-54 T-55	M/TR-77	T-62	T-72	Sub-Total	Total
	Chinese Tanks			Tanks (S.O.)					
—	—	—	—	400	—	200	30	630	630
—	—	—	—	—	—	—	—	—	—
—	250	—	—	860	200	600	—	1660	1910
—	—	260	—	2100	—	—	—	2100	2360
—	580	—	—	—	—	—	—	—	580
—	240	—	—	—	—	—	—	—	240
—	54	—	—	—	—	—	—	—	54
100	100	—	—	2600	—	—	200	2800	2900
—	120	—	—	15	--	—	—	15	135
—	18	—	—	—	—	—	—	—	18
—	24	—	—	—	—	—	—	—	24
—	450	—	—	—	—	—	—	—	450
—	20	—	17	123	—	—	—	140	160
—	—	—	—	2200	—	1100	900	4200	4200
—	14	—	—	—	—	—	—	—	14
18	118	—	—	—	—	—	—	—	118
—	64	—	150	500	—	—	—	650	714
—	—	—	—	450	—	—	—	450	450
—	—	—	—	—	—	—	—	—	—
—	40	—	—	100	—	—	—	100	140
—	—	—	—	—	—	—	—	—	—
118	2092	260	167	9348	200	1900	1130	12745	15097

222

Table 7
Fighting ships in service in the Arab Navies 1983

	Algeria	Bahrain	Egypt	Iraq	Jordan	Kuwait	Lebanon	Libya	Morocco
Fleet submarine									
Patrol submarine	1		12					6	
Mini submarine								2	
Destroyer			5						
Frigate	2		5					1	1
Corvette	3							7	
FAC-M	18		24	12				23	4
FAC-T	8		16	6					
FAC-G		2	14						2
Large Patrol Craft	6		12	5				9	4
Mine Layer									
Mine Sweeper (Ocean)	2		10	2				4	
Mine Sweeper (Coastal)									1
Mine Sweeper (Inshore)			2	3					
Assault ship									
LST								2	
LCT	1		3	4				5	
LCU			13			6			
Light Transport ship									3
Hydrofoil & ACV			3						
Miscellaneous	35	2	77	12	9	47	4	10	15
Personnel	8,000	300	20,000	4,250	300	500	250	6,500	6,000
Total fighting ships	76	4	196	44	9	53	4	69	30

NB
Police Crafts and Coastal Crafts are included in Miscellaneous.

Oman	Qatar	Saudi Arabia	Sudan	Syria	Tunisia	United Arab Emirates	Yemen (North)	Yemen (South)	Mauritania	Somalia	Djibouti	Total
											.	19
												2
												5
			2	1								12
		4						1				15
3	2	9		18	3	6	2	6		2		132
		3		8			4	2		8		55
4	2		6		2							32
	6	1	6	1	1	6		2				59
												—
				1				1				20
		4		2	2							9
												5
												—
								1				3
		2						3		1		19
6		4	1									30
1												4
												3
5	36	10	3	2	14	5	6	11	8	9	3	323
2,000	700	2,500	2,000	2,500	3,500	1,500	550	1,000	320	550	20	63,240
19	46	35	18	34	23	17	12	27	8	20	3	747

Table 7/A
Fighting ships in service in the Arab Navies 1983
According to origin

Serial No.	Country	Submarine S.O.	Submarine W.O.	Destroyer S.O.	Destroyer W.O.	Frigate S.O.	Frigate W.O.	Corvette S.O.	Corvette W.O.	FAC-M S.O.	FAC-M W.O.	FAC-T S.O.	FAC-T W.O.	FAC-G S.O.	FAC-G W.O.	Total S.O.	Total W.O.
1	Algeria	1	—	—	—	2	—	3	—	18	—	8	—	—	—	32	—
2	Bahrain	—	—	—	—	—	—	—	—	—	—	—	—	—	2	—	2
3	Egypt	12	—	4	1	—	5	—	—	18	6	16	—	14	—	64	12
4	Iraq	—	—	—	—	—	—	—	—	12	—	6	—	—	—	18	—
5	Jordan	—	—	—	—	—	—	—	—	—	—	—	—	—	—	—	—
6	Kuwait	—	—	—	—	—	—	—	—	—	—	—	—	—	—	—	—
7	Lebanon	—	—	—	—	—	—	—	—	—	—	—	—	—	—	—	—
8	Libya	6	—	—	—	—	1	2	5	12	11	—	—	—	—	20	17
9	Morocco	—	—	—	—	—	1	—	—	—	4	—	—	—	2	—	7
10	Oman	—	—	—	—	—	—	—	—	—	3	—	—	—	4	—	7
11	Qatar	—	—	—	—	—	—	—	—	—	2	—	—	—	2	—	4
12	Saudi Arabia	—	—	—	—	—	—	—	4	—	9	—	3	—	—	—	16
13	Sudan	—	—	—	—	—	—	—	—	—	—	—	—	6	—	6	—
14	Syria	—	—	—	—	2	—	—	—	18	—	8	—	—	—	28	—
15	Tunisia	—	—	—	—	—	1	—	—	—	3	—	—	—	2	—	6
16	United Arab Emirates	—	—	—	—	—	—	—	—	—	6	—	—	—	—	—	6
17	Yemen (North)	—	—	—	—	—	—	—	—	2	—	4	—	—	—	6	—
18	Yemen (South)	—	—	—	—	—	—	1	—	6	—	2	—	—	—	9	—
19	Mauritania	—	—	—	—	—	—	—	—	—	—	—	—	—	—	—	—
20	Somalia	—	—	—	—	—	—	—	—	2	—	8	—	—	—	10	—
21	Djibouti	—	—	—	—	—	—	—	—	—	—	—	—	—	—	—	—
22	Total	19	—	4	1	4	8	6	9	88	44	52	3	20	12	193	77

Table 8
Arab Armed Forces strengths & cost per soldier 1973, 1978, 1983 (in dollars)

Serial No.	Country	1973		1978		1983	
		Strength	Cost per soldier	Strength	Cost per soldier	Strength	Cost per soldier
1	Algeria	63,000	2,317	78,800	7,970	140,000	6,055
2	Bahrain	1,100	–	2,300	–	2,700	93,778
3	Egypt	400,000	6,892	395,000	4,015	447,000	4,698
4	Iraq	101,800	8,222	212,000	9,377	517,250	14,929
5	Jordan	72,850	2,018	67,850	4,569	72,800	6,393
6	Kuwait	10,000	–	12,000	84,833	12,000	125,887
7	Lebanon	15,250	6,122	7,800	21,410	27,000	17,841
8	Libya	25,000	5,800	37,000	11,865	73,000	9,715
9	Morocco	56,000	3,500	89,000	8,685	144,000	9,222
10	Oman	9,600	8,073	19,200	39,948	23,550	75,244
11	Qatar	2,200	–	4,000	15,250	6,000	27,666
12	Saudi Arabia	42,500	34,776	58,500	177,008	51,500	430,431
13	Sudan	38,600	2,953	52,100	3,858	58,000	4,043
14	Syria	132,000	3,068	227,500	5,336	222,500	11,452
15	Tunisia	24,000	1,196	22,200	8,333	28,500	4,158
16	United Arab Emirates	11,150	–	25,900	30,116	49,000	59,490
17	Yemen (North)	20,900	622	38,000	3,789	21,550	24,450
18	Yemen (South)	9,500	1,632	20,900	4,163	25,000	6,376
19	Mauritania	–	–	12,450	–	8,470	7,320
20	Somalia	17,300	659	51,500	485	62,550	2,037
21	Djibouti	–	–	–	–	2,700	1,074
22	Total	1,052,750	6,269	1,434,000	14,609	1,995,470	23,079

NB
During 1973, Egypt mobilised 800,000 and Syria mobilised 350,000. Hence the Armed Forces Strength during the October War reached 1,200,000 in Egypt, and about 500,000 in Syria.

Table 9

Defence expenditure in the Arab Countries 1973, 1978, 1983

Serial No.	Country	1973			1978			1983		
		in millions of dollars	per capita in dollars	% GNP	in millions of dollars	per capita in dollars	% GNP	in millions of dollars	per capita in dollars	% GNP
1	Algeria	146	9	2.7	628	34	6.2	847.7	41	2.0
2	Bahrain	–	–	–	–	–	–	253.2	633	5.6
3	Egypt	2,757	77	36.8	1,586	40	11.9	2,100.0	46	7.1
4	Iraq	837	83	23.9	1,988	159	12.2	7,722.0	540	24.3
5	Jordan	147	57	21.4	310	104	23.8	465.4	188	12.0
6	Kuwait	–	–	–	1,018	878	8.5	1,561.0	1,077	7.7
7	Lebanon	75	25	3.9	167	55	5.8	481.7	166	12.2
8	Libya	145	67	3.1	439	159	2.4	709.2	222	2.2
9	Morocco	196	12	4.4	773	42	8.1	1,328.0	63	8.9
10	Oman	77.5	109	–	767	916	30.7	1,772.0	1,827	28.5
11	Qatar	–	–	–	61	298	2.5	166.0	638	2.4
12	Saudi Arabia	1,478	176	29.4	10,355	1,151	18.7	21,952.0	2,195	14.4
13	Sudan	114	7	6.0	201	11	4.6	234.5	11	2.6
14	Syria	405	60	21.0	1,214	150	18.7	2,548.0	277	15.8
15	Tunisia	28.7	5	1.4	185	30	3.7	118.5	18	1.5
16	United Arab Emirates	–	–	–	780	891	10.8	2,915.0	2,580	8.9
17	Yemen (North)	13	2	2.8	144	20	12.0	526.9	73	18.6
18	Yemen (South)	15.5	1	11.0	87	48	38.8	159.4	80	15.1
19	Mauritania	–	–	–	–	–	–	62.0	36	8.7
20	Somalia	11.4	4	6.3	25	7	5.9	127.4	32	7.3
21	Djibouti	–	–	–	–	–	–	2.9	9.2	0.8
22	Subtotal	6,446.1	47.1	16.1	20,728	133	12.2	46,052.8	261	10.9

23	Assumed figure to cover the countries whose defence budgets were not available	153.9	—	—	222	—	—	—	—	—
24	Total	6,600	47.7	15.0	20,950	133	12.2	46,052.8	261	10.9

NB

1—Population in all Arab Countries in 1973—after excluding Bahrain, Kuwait, Oman, Qatar, United Arab Emirates, and Mauritania—was 136.913 million; the defence expenditure was 6.4461 billion dollars, and the GNP was 40.008 billion dollars.

2—Population in all Arab Countries in 1978—after excluding Bahrain and Mauritania—was 156.117 million; the defence expenditure was 20.728 billion dollars; and the GNP was 169.649 billion dollars.

Table 10
Population, GNP, and per capita income in the Arab Countries 1973, 1978, 1983

Serial No.	Country	1973			1978			1983		
		Population in millions	GNP in millions of dollars	per capita income in dollars	Population in millions	GNP in millions of dollars	per capita income in dollars	Population in millions	GNP in millions of dollars	per capita income in dollars
1	Algeria	15.700	5,500	350	18.420	10,100	548	20.600	41,707	2,025
2	Bahrain	0.233	–	–	0.345	1,700	4,928	0.400	4,516	11,290
3	Egypt	35.700	7,500	210	39.760	13,300	334	46.000	29,614	644
4	Iraq	10.142	3,500	345	12.470	16,300	1,307	14.300	31,832	2,226
5	Jordan	2.560	686	270	2.970	1,300	438	2.470	3,878	1,570
6	Kuwait	0.957	3,630	3,793	1.160	12,000	10,345	1.450	20,215	13,941
7	Lebanon	3.009	1,880	625	3.060	2,900	948	2.900	3,941	1,359
8	Libya	2.160	4,590	2,125	2.760	18,500	6,703	3.200	33,050	10,328
9	Morocco	16.300	4,460	274	18.590	9,500	511	21.000	14,984	714
10	Oman	0.710	–	–	0.837	2,500	2,987	0.970	6,219	6,411
11	Qatar	0.089	280	3,146	0.205	2,400	11,707	0.260	6,839	26,304
12	Saudi Arabia	8.400	5,200	619	9.000	55,400	6,156	10.000	152,207	15,221
13	Sudan	17.000	1,900	112	19.120	4,400	230	20.500	9,160	447
14	Syria	6.775	1,930	285	8.110	6,500	801	9.200	16,158	1,756
15	Tunisia	5.500	2,080	378	6.250	5,000	800	6.700	8,084	1,207
16	United Arab Emirates	0.164	–	–	0.875	7,700	8,800	1.130	32,610	28,858
17	Yemen (North)	7.000	460	66	7.270	1,200	165	7.200	2,838	394
18	Yemen (South)	1.560	140	90	1.830	224	122	2.000	1,055	527
19	Mauritania	1.360	214	157	1.430	300	210	1.700	715	420
20	Somalia	3.000	182	61	3.430	425	124	4.000	1,753	438
21	Djibouti	–	–	–	–	–	–	0.315	357	1,133
22	Total	138.319	44,132	322	157.892	171,649	1,087	176.295	421,732	2,392

229

Table 11

The ratio of personnel under arms, number of main battle tanks and first line combat aircraft per each 100,000 persons of the population in the Arab Countries

Serial No.	Country	1973 Regular soldier	1973 Tank	1973 Combat ac L 1	1978 Regular soldier	1978 Tank	1978 Combat ac L 1	1983 Regular soldier	1983 Tank	1983 Combat ac L 1
1	Algeria	401.27	2.54	0.22	427.79	1.90	0.48	679.61	3.05	0.91
2	Bahrain	472.1	–	–	666.66	–	–	675.00	–	–
3	Egypt	1,120.44	5.26	0.58	993.46	4.02	0.68	971.73	4.15	0.21
4	Iraq	1,003.74	9.76	0.88	1,700.08	15.23	1.80	3,617.13	16.50	1.88
5	Jordan	2,845.70	17.18	0.78	2,284.51	16.83	0.67	2,947.36	23.48	0.93
6	Kuwait	1,044.90	10.44	1.25	1,034.48	10.68	1.72	855.17	16.55	1.31
7	Lebanon	506.81	1.99	0.33	254.90	–	–	931.03	1.86	–
8	Libya	1,157.40	10.23	3.00	1,340.57	72.46	5.03	2,281.25	90.62	15.50
9	Morocco	343.55	0.73	–	478.75	0.48	–	685.71	00.64	0.19
10	Oman	1,352.11	–	–	2,293.90	–	–	2,427.83	1.85	–
11	Qatar	2,471.91	–	–	1,951.21	5.85	–	2,307.69	9.23	–
12	Saudi Arabia	505.95	0.29	0.41	650.00	3.61	0.35	515.00	4.50	0.65
13	Sudan	227.05	0.88	0.11	272.48	0.83	0.05	282.92	0.78	0.03
14	Syria	1,948.33	17.26	2.95	2,805.17	30.82	3.47	2,418.47	45.65	3.84
15	Tunisia	436.36	–	–	355.20	–	–	425.37	0.2	–
16	United Arab Emirates	6,798.78	–	–	2,960.00	–	3.65	4,336.28	10.44	2.65
17	Yemen (North)	298.57	0.42	–	522.69	3.02	–	299.30	9.91	0.90
18	Yemen (South)	608.97	3.20	–	1,142.07	14.20	0.65	1,250.00	22.50	3.65
19	Mauritania	–	–	–	870.62	–	–	498.23	–	–
20	Somalia	576.66	5.00	–	1,501.45	2.33	0.20	1,563.75	3.50	0.17
21	Djibouti	–	–	–	–	–	–	857.14	–	–
22	average in all Arab countries	761.102	4.18	0.50	908.21	6.41	0.72	1,131.89	8.56	0.98

Table 12
Israeli Armed Forces strength and main weapons 1973, 1978, 1983

	Armed Forces Strength				First Line Combat aircraft						Second Line Combat ac			Total Combat ac.	Total MBTs
Year	Population in millions	Regular	Reserve	Total after mobilisation	F-15	F-16	F-4	Mirage III	Barak/ Kfir	Sub-total	A-4	AEW ECM	Sub-total		
73	3.180	115,000	285,000	400,000	—	—	101	35	24	160	160	2	162	322	1700
78	3.730	164,000	286,000	450,000	25	—	182	30	50	287	250	6	256	543	3,000
83	4.100	172,000	328,000	500,000	60	147	144	—	260	611	203	16	219	830	3,960

NB

—Non-advanced training aircraft are not included.

—Liaison aircraft are also not included although they were up to 76 light aircraft in 1983.

—Approximately 90–100 Combat aircraft are stored (about 10–12 percent of the Combat aircraft in service).

—Although AEW and ECM aircraft are used in the early stages of the battle, they are mentioned within the second line Combat aircraft, because of their low speed and their need for protection.

—Full mobilisation is complete within seven days.

—In December 1983, the Israeli tank strength included 1100 centurion, 650 M-48, 1320 M-60, 440 T54/T55, 150 T62, 300 Merkava.

Table 13
Israeli defence budget 1973, 1978, 1983

	GNP		Defence budget			Soldiers, Tanks, Combat ac L1, for each 100,000 of the population				
						Armed Forces Strength				Combat ac
Year	millions of dollars	per capita income	millions of dollars	dollars per capita	% of GNP	regular	reserve	Total	Tanks	L 1
73	6,850	2,054	1,474	464	21.52	3,616	8,962	12,578	53.4	5.0
78	14,200	3,807	3,310	887	23.31	4,397	7,667	12,064	80.4	7.7
83	21,770	5,310	6,461	1,576	29.68	4,195	8,000	12,195	96.6	14.9

NB

The costs of the occupation of Lebanon are included in 1983 defence budget and officially estimated to be 1.5–2.0 billion dollars.

Table 14
Increases in Armed Forces in the Arab Countries & Israel between 1973–1983

Serial No.	Country	% increase between 73–78 in				% increase between 78–83 in			
		Population	Armed Forces Strength	Tanks	Combat ac L1	Population	Armed Forces Strength	Tanks	Combat ac L1
1	Algeria	17.32	25.08	-12.50	157.14	11.83	77.66	80.00	110.00
2	Bahrain	48.06	109.09	—	—	15.94	17.39	—	—
3	Egypt	11.37	-1.25	-14.90	30.47	15.69	13.16	19.37	-63.13
4	Iraq	22.95	109.90	91.91	150.00	14.67	143.98	24.21	19.55
5	Jordan	16.01	93.14	13.64	—	-16.84	7.29	16.00	15.00
6	Kuwait	21.21	20.00	24.00	66.66	25.00	3.33	93.55	-5.00
7	Lebanon	1.69	-51.15	—	—	-5.33	246.15	—	—
8	Libya	27.77	48.00	804.98	113.85	15.94	97.29	45.00	256.83
9	Morocco	14.04	58.92	-25.00	—	12.96	61.79	50.00	—
10	Oman	17.89	100.00	—	—	15.89	22.66	—	—
11	Qatar	130.34	81.82	—	—	26.83	50.00	100.00	—
12	Saudi Arabia	7.14	37.65	1,200.00	-8.60	11.11	-11.97	38.46	103.12
13	Sudan	12.47	34.97	6.66	-50.00	7.22	11.32	—	-20.00
14	Syria	19.70	72.35	113.67	35.00	13.44	2.20	68.00	25.53
15	Tunisia	13.64	-7.50	—	—	7.20	28.38	—	—
16	United Arab Emirates	433.54	32.29	—	—	29.14	89.19	—	-6.25
17	Yemen (North)	3.86	81.82	633.33	—	-00.96	43.29	224.55	—
18	Yemen (South)	17.31	120.00	420.00	—	9.29	19.62	73.08	508.33
19	Mauritania	5.15	—	—	—	18.88	-31.97	—	—
20	Somalia	14.33	197.69	-64.66	—	16.62	21.46	75.00	—
21	Djibouti	—	—	—	—	—	—	—	—
22	Total Arab countries	14.15	36.21	74.92	63.99	11.65	39.15	49.16	51.36
23	Israel	17.29	12.5	76.47	79.37	9.92	11.11	32.00	112.89

Table 15
**Combat aircraft expected to stay in service or to enter service
in the Arab & Israeli Air Forces between 1984–1993**

Ser. no.	Model	Combat aircraft Name	Contractors	Country of origin	Span m.	Length m.	Max T.O. weight/ Kg
1	—	Super Etendard	Dassault-Breuguet	France	9.60	14.31	11,500
2	—	Mirage F-1	Dassault-Breuguet	France	8.40	15.00	15,200
3	—	Mirage 5	Dassault-Breuguet	France	8.22	15.55	13,700
4	—	Mirage 2000	Dassault-Breuguet	France	9.00	14.35	16,500
5	—	Mirage 4000	Dassault-Breuguet	France	12.00	18.70	—
6	F-4E	Phantom	McDonnell-Douglas	U.S.A.	11.77	19.20	28,030
7	F-5E	Tiger II	Northrop	U.S.A.	8.13	14.68	11,193
8	F-15C	Eagle	McDonnell-Douglas	U.S.A.	13.05	19.43	30,875
9	F-16A	Fighting Falcon	General Dynamics	U.S.A.	9.45	14.52	16,057
10	E-2C	Hawkeye	Grumman	U.S.A.	24.56	17.55	23,503
11	E-3A	Sentry	Boeing	U.S.A.	44.42	46.61	147,420
12	SR-71	Blackbird	Lockheed	U.S.A.	16.95	32.74	—
13	A-12	—	Lockheed	U.S.A.	17.37	31.09	54,430
14	—	Alphajet	Dassault-Breuguet Dornier	Inter-national	9.11	13.23	7,500
15	—	Jaguar	BAe/Dassault-Breuguet	Inter-national	8.69	16.83	15,700
16	—	Tornado	Aeritalia/BAe/MBB	Inter-national	13.90 8.60	16.70	27,215

Crew	Weapons	Max speed Mach	Operational range/Km	Remarks
1	Two 30 mm guns 2100 kg bombs and missiles	1.0	650	Entered service 1978 production ended 1983
1	Two 30 mm guns 4000 kg bombs and missiles	2.2	650	Range with 2000 kg payload
1	Two 30 mm guns 4000 kg bombs and missiles	2.2	650	Range with 1000 kg payload
1	Two 30 mm guns 4000 kg bombs and missiles	2.3	1,110	Range with 2000 kg + 2 air to air missiles
1	Two 30 mm guns 8000 kg bombs and missiles	2.3	1,850	Range with external tanks and a reconnaissance pod
2	2750 kg bombs and missiles	2.2	640	
1	Two 30 mm guns 3175 kg bombs and missiles	1.63	445	Range with 500 kg payload
1	One 20 mm gun 7527 kg bombs and missiles	2.5	1,500	
1	One 20 mm gun 5420 kg bombs and missiles	+ 2.0	925	
5	AEW	598 Km	—	endurance 3–4 h without refueling
17	AWACS	853 Km	—	endurance 6h without refueling
2	Strategic Reconnaissance	3.0	—	
1	Strategic Reconnaissance	+ 3.0	—	range up to 5555 Km
2	One 30 mm gun 2500 kg bombs and missiles	0.85	425	
1	Two 30 mm guns 4535 kg bombs and missiles	1.6	537	
2	Two 27 mm guns 8165 kg bombs and missiles	2.2	740	

234

Table 15 continued

Ser. no.	Model	Name	Contractors	Country of origin	Span m.	Length m.	Max T.O. weight/ Kg
		Combat aircraft					
17	—	Kfir	Israel aircraft industry	Israel	8.22	15.65	14,700
18	—	Lavi	Israel aircraft industry	Israel	8.71	14.39	17,010
19	SU-7	Fitter-A	Sukhoi	USSR	8.93	17.37	13,500
20	SU-17 SU-20 SU-22	Fitter-C	Sukhoi	USSR	10.60 14.00	18.75	17,770
21	SU-24	Fencer-A	Sukhoi	USSR	10.30 17.25	21.29	39,700
22	MIG-21 MF	Fishbed	Mikoyan	USSR	7.15	15.76	9,400
23	MIG-23	Flogger-B	Mikoyan	USSR	8.17 14.25	16.80	21,100
24	MIG-25	Foxbat	Mikoyan	USSR	13.95	23.82	36,200
25	Mig-29	Ram L	The Mig-29 is likely to have a true dual role, air combat/attack capability similar to that of F-16 and F/A-18. Its max T.O. weight is said to be 17,000 Kg, and its max speed 2.8 mach.				
26	TU-16	Badger	Tupolev	USSR	32.93	34.80	72,000
27	TU-22	Blinder	Tupolev	USSR	27.70	40.53	83,900
28	TU-22M	Backfire	Tupolev	USSR	34.45	40.23	122,500
29	TU-126	Moss	Tupolev	USSR	51.20	55.20	170,000

Crew	Weapons	Max speed Mach	Operational range/Km	Remarks
1	Two 30 mm guns 4295 kg bombs and missiles	2.3	768	—Development of Mirage 5 —Range is estimated on the basis of ground attack mission with 1540 kg bombs and missiles
1	Two air to air missiles Eight bombs each 340 kg	1.85	452	—Designed mainly for ground attack missions. —Range is estimated on the basis of low flying with the mentioned payload —It will replace A4 and Kfir.
1	Two 30 mm guns 1500 kg bombs and missiles	1.2	250	
2–1	Two 30 mm guns 3500 kg bombs and missiles	2.17	360	Range with 2000 kg external weight
2	Two 20 mm guns 8000 kg bombs and missiles	+2.0	322	Swing wing attack aircraft
1	Two 23 mm guns 2000 kg bombs and missiles	2.02	370	
1	Two 23 mm guns 4500 kg bombs and missiles	2.35	900	Swing wing interceptor, and strike aircraft
1	Air to Air missiles	3.2	—	Production ended 1978
6	9000 kg bombs and missiles	992 Km	2,900	
3	5500 kg bombs and missiles	1.4	3,100	
4	12,000 kg bombs and missiles	2.0	5,470	
12	AWACS	850 km	12,550	endurance 19 h without refueling

236

Table 16
Tanks expected to stay in service or to enter service
in the Arab and Israeli Armed Forces 1984–1993

Serial no.	Name	Country of origin	Length m.	Width m.	Height m.	Combat weight (tons)	Crew	Engine	Weapons	Remarks
1	AMX-40	France	6.90	3.3	2.38	43.1	4	1100 hp D	One 120 mm One 20 mm CA One 7.62 mm AA	
2	Leopard 2	W. Germany	7.72	3.7	2.79	55.0	4	1500 hp MF	One 120 mm One 20 mm CA One 7.62 mm AA	
3	Merkava-2	Israel	7.45	3.7	2.64	60.0	4	900 hp D	One 105 mm One 7.62 mm CA Two 7.62 mm AA	
4	Merkava-3	Israel	—	—	—	—	4	1200 hp D	One 120 mm One 7.62 mm CA Two 7.62 mm AA	
5	OF-40	Italy	6.89	3.51	2.68	43.0	4	830 hp MF	One 105 mm One 7.62 mm CA One 7.62 mm AA	
6	T-80	USSR	7.00	3.50	2.30	45.0	3	750 hp D	One 125 mm One 7.62 mm CA One 14.5 mm AA	

									Armament
7	T-72	USSR	6.90	3.49	2.37	41.0	3	750 hp D	One 125 mm One 7.62 mm CA One 12.7 mm AA
8	T-64	USSR	6.40	3.38	2.30	38.0	3	750 hp D	One 125 mm One 7.62 mm CA One 12.7 mm AA
9	T-62	USSR	6.63	3.30	2.395	40.0	4	580 hp D	One 115 mm One 7.62 mm CA One 12.7 mm AA
10	T-55	USSR	6.45	3.27	2.40	36.0	4	580 hp D	One 100 m One 7.62 mm CA One 12.7 mm AA
11	T-54	USSR	6.45	3.27	2.40	36.0	4	520 hp D	One 100 mm One 7.62 mm CA One 12.7 mm AA
12	Challenger	UK	8.39	3.52	2.89	62.10	4	1200 hp D	One 120 mm One 7.62 mm CA One 7.62 mm AA
13	Chieftain 900	UK	7.62	3.51	2.44	56.0	4	900 hp D	One 120 mm One 7.62 mm CA One 7.62 mm AA
14	M1 Abrams	U.S.A.	7.92	3.66	2.38	54.4	4	1500 hp T	One 105 mm One 7.62 mm CA One 127 mm AA One 7.62 mm AA
15	M60 A1	U.S.A.	6.95	3.63	3.27	49.0	4	750 hp D	One 105 mm One 7.62 mm CA One 12.7 mm AA

Table 17: Fighting ships expected to stay in service or to enter service in the Arab Navies between 1984-1993

Submarines

Serial no.	Submarine		Displacement (tons)		Dimensions (meters)		
	Class	Country of origin	surfaced	dived	length	width	draught
1	Foxtrot (Patrol)	USSR	1,950	2,500	91.5	8.0	6.1
2	Romeo (Patrol)	USSR	1,400	1,800	76.8	7.3	5.5
3	Whisky (Patrol)	USSR	1,080	1,350	76.0	6.5	4.9

Destroyers

Serial no.	Fighting Ship		Displacement (tons)		Dimensions (meters)		
	Class	Country of origin	standard	full load	length	width	draught
4	Skory	USSR	2,240	3,080	120.5	11.8	4.6
5	Z	U.K.	1,730	2,575	110.6	10.9	4.9

Weapons	Main machinery hp	Speed (knots)		Range (miles)	Comple-ment	In service in
		surfaced	dived			
Six 533 mm torpedo tubes Four 406 mm torpedo tubes 22 torpedoes carried	6,000 hp D 6,000 hp E	18	16	20,000	75	Libya
Eight 533 mm torpedo tubes 18 torpedoes carried	4,000 hp D 4,000 hp E	17	14	16,000	54	Algeria, Egypt
Four 533 mm torpedo tubes Two 406 mm torpedo tubes 14 torpedoes carried	4,000 hp D 2,700 hp E	18	14	13,000	54	Egypt

Weapons			Main machinery hp	Speed (knots)	Range (miles)	Comple-ment	In service in
A/S	SAM	guns					
Two SS-N2 Two DCTs Four DC racks Two 16 barreled RBU 2500 Fifteen 533 mm torpedo tubes 80 mines		Four 130 mm Two 85 mm Six 37 mm	60,000-T	33	3,900	280	Egypt
Four DCTs		Four 115 mm Six 40 mm	40,000-T	31	2,800	186	Egypt

Table 17 continued

Frigates

| Serial no. | Fighting Ship | | Displacement (tons) | | Dimensions (meters) | | |
	Class	Country of origin	standard	full load	length	width	draught
6	Koni	USSR	1,700	1,900	95.0	12.8	4.2
7	Grisha III	USSR	950	1,200	72.0	10.0	3.7
8	Petya	USSR	950	1,160	81.8	9.1	3.2
9	Lupo	Italy	2,208	2,500	113.2	11.3	3.7
10	Descubietra	Spain	1,233	1,479	88.8	10.4	3.8
11	Vosper MK-7	U.K.	1,360	1,780	101.5	11.7	3.4
12	Black Swan	U.K.	1,490	1,925	91.2	11.4	2.6
13	River	U.K.	1,490	2,216	91.9	11.1	4.3
14	Hunt	U.K.	1,000	1,490	85.4	8.8	2.3
15[1,2]	Oliver Hazard Perry	U.S.A.	2,750	3,585	135.6	13.7	5.7

[1]Cost per ship in the FY 1980 programme 200 million dollars.
[2]Equipped with satellite communications capabilities, and SLQ 32 electronic warfare system.

Weapons			Main machinery hp	Speed (knots)	Range (miles)	Complement	In service in
A/S	SAM	guns					
Two 12 barreled RBU 6000	Four SA-N4 launchers	Four 76 mm	18,000-T	27	1,800	110	Algeria
Two DC racks 20 mines	Twenty SA-N4 missiles	Four 30 mm	12,000-D				
Four 533 mm torpedo tubes	Four SA-N4 launchers	Two 57 mm	24,000-T	30	4,500	80	
Two RBU 6000 Two DC racks 18 mines	Twenty SA-N4 missiles	One 30 mm	16,000-D				
Four RBU 6000 Two DC racks Three 533 mm torpedo tubes 22 mines		Four 76 mm	30,000-T	32	450	98	Syria
1 Helicopter 8 Otomat 2 Rocket launchers 6 US MK 32 torpedo tubes	8 launchers 32 Aspide missiles	One 127 mm Four 40 mm	34,400-T 7,800-D	35 21	5,000	185	
Two 375 mm torpedo tubes Six US MK 32 torpedo tubes		One 76 mm Two 40 mm	16,000-D	25.5	4,100	116	Egypt, Morocco
Four Otomat Six 244 mm torpedo tubes	4 Aspide	One 114 mm Two 40 mm Two 35 mm	46,400-T 3,500-D	37.5	5,700	—	Libya
Two DCTs Two DC racks		Six 102 mm Four 37 mm Two 20 mm	3,600-T	19	4,500	180	Egypt
Four DCTs		One 102 mm Four 37 mm Six 20 mm	5,500-T	18	7,700	110	Egypt
Two DCTs		Four 102 mm Two 27 mm Two 25 mm	19,000-T	25	2,000	133	Egypt
Two Helicopters LAMPS One launcher capable of firing SAM Standard MR and SSM Harpoon 40 missiles (Harpoon and Standard)		One 76 mm One 20 mm	40,000-T	29	4,500	185	

Table 17 continued

Corvettes

Serial no.	Fighting Ship		Displacement (tons)		Dimensions (meters)		
	Class	Country of origin	standard	full load	length	width	draught
16	Nanuchka III	USSR	—	770	59.3	12.6	2.4
17	Assad	Italy	—	685	62.3	9.3	2.5
18	Badr	U.S.A.	732	815	74.7	9.6	2.7

Weapons			Main machinery hp	Speed (knots)	Range (miles)	Comple-ment	In service in
A/S	SAM	guns					
Six SS-N9	Four SA-N4 launchers	Two 57 mm	24,000-D	32	2,500	70	Algeria, Libya
		One 76 mm					
	20 SA-N4	One 30 mm					
One Heli-copter	4 launchers	One 67 mm	24,000-D	37	4,400	54	Libya
4 Otomat	16 Aspide missiles	Two 35 mm					
Six 244 torpedo tubes							
16 mines							
Eight SSM Harpoon		One 76 mm	23,000-T	30	4,000	58	Saudi Arabia
		One 20 mm	4,000-D	20			
Six MK 32 torpedo tubes		Two 40 mm grenade launcher					

244

Table 17 continued

FACs (M)

Serial no.	Fighting Ship Class	Country of origin	Displacement (tons) standard	full load	Dimensions (meters) length	width	draught
19	OSA	USSR	165	210	39.0	7.8	1.8
20	Komar	USSR	68	75	26.8	6.2	1.5
21	La Combattante	France	—	311	49.0	7.1	2.0
22	Susa	France	95	114	30.5	7.8	2.1
23	Type 45	W. Germany	—	255	44.9	7.0	2.3
24	Lazaga	Spain	—	410	57.4	7.6	2.7
25	Province	U.K.	311	363	56.7	8.2	2.4
26	Ramadan	Egypt + U.K.	—	207	52.0	7.6	2.3
27	October	Egypt + U.K.	—	82	25.5	6.1	1.3
28[1]	PHM	U.S.A.	—	239	44.3	8.6	2.3
29	Al-Siddik	U.S.A.	—	384	58.1	8.1	2.0

[1] Italian and German design. To be used by NATO navies.

	Weapons		Main machinery hp	Speed (knots)	Range (miles)	Comple-ment	In service in
A/S	SAM	guns					
Four SS-N2C		Four 30 mm	12,000-D	40	800	30	Algeria, Egypt, Iraq, Libya, Syria, North Yemen, South Yemen, Somalia
Two SS-N2		Two 25 mm	4,800-D	40	400	19	Algeria, Egypt, Syria
Four Otomat		One 76 mm Two 40 mm	18,000-D	39	1,600	27	Libya, Qatar, Tunisia
Eight SS-12		Two 40 mm	12,750-D	54	—	20	Libya
Four Exocet		One 76 mm One 40 mm	14,400-D	38	—	40	Bahrain, Libya, United Arab Emirates
Four Exocet		One 76 mm One 40 mm One 20 mm	8,000-D	36	3,000	41	Morocco
Six Exocet		One 76 mm Two 40 mm	18,200-D	40	—	40	Oman
Four Otomat		One 76 mm Two 40 mm	17,150-D	40	2,000	40	Egypt
Two Otomat		Four 40 mm	4,500-D	40	400	20	Egypt
Four Harpoon		One 76 mm	18,000-T	48	700	21	
Four Harpoon		One 76 mm One 81 mm mortar Two 20 mm	23,000-T 4,000-D	38 15.5	—	38	Saudi Arabia

Table 17 continued

FACs (T)

Serial no.	Fighting Ship		Displacement (tons)		Dimensions (meters)		
	Class	Country of origin	standard	full load	length	width	draught
30	Shershen	USSR	145	165	34.7	6.7	1.5
31	P-6	USSR	64	73	26.0	6.1	1.5
32	P-4	USSR	22	25	19.0	3.3	1.0
33	Type 143	W. Germany	—	391	57.5	7.6	2.5
34	Jaguar	W. Germany	160	190	42.5	7.0	2.4

FACs (G)

Serial no.	Fighting Ship		Displacement (tons)		Dimensions (meters)		
	Class	Country of origin	standard	full load	length	width	draught
35	P R-72	France	375	455	57.5	7.6	2.1
36	Type 38	W. Germany	—	188	38.5	7.0	2.2
37	Sar 33	Turkey	—	170	33.0	8.6	3.0

Weapons			Main machinery hp	Speed (knots)	Range (miles)	Comple-ment	In service in
A/S	SAM	guns					
Four 533 mm torpedo tubes Two DC racks 6 mines		Four 30 mm	12,000-D	45	850	23	Egypt
Four 533 mm torpedo tubes 12 DCs		Two 25 mm	4,800-D	41	600	15	Egypt, Iraq, South Yemen, Somalia
Two 533 mm torpedo tubes 8 barreled 122 mm rocket launchers		Two 14.5 mm	2,400-D	42	410	12	Egypt, Syria, North Yemen
Two 533 mm torpedo tubes wire guided		Two 76 mm	16,000-D	35	1,300	40	
Four 533 mm torpedo tubes		Two 40 mm	12,000-D	42	—	33	Saudi Arabia

Weapons			Main machinery hp	Speed (knots)	Range (miles)	Comple-ment	In service in
A/S	SAM	guns					
		One 76 mm One 40 mm	11,040-D	28	2,500	53	Morocco
		Two 40 mm One rocket launcher	9,000-D	32	1,100	—	Bahrain
		One 40 mm	12,000-D	40	450	23	Qatar

Table 17 continued

Large Patrol Craft

Serial no.	Fighting Ship		Displacement (tons)		Dimensions (meters)		
	Class	Country of origin	standard	full load	length	width	draught
38[1]	Babochka	USSR	—	400	50.0	10.2	2.0
39	Poti	USSR	—	400	60.0	8.0	2.0
40	Stenika	USSR	170	210	39.0	7.8	1.8
41	SO-1	USSR	170	215	42.0	6.0	1.8
42	Vosper	U.K.	120	—	33.5	6.4	1.6
43	Garian	U.K.	120	159	32.3	6.5	1.7
44	Asheville	U.S.A.	225	235	50.1	7.3	2.9
45	High Point (PCH)	U.S.A.	—	110	35.0	9.4	1.8

[1]Hydrofoil.

Minesweepers (Ocean)

Serial no.	Fighting Ship		Displacement (tons)		Dimensions (meters)		
	Class	Country of origin	standard	full load	length	width	draught
46	Natya	USSR	—	765	61.0	10.0	3.5
47	Yurka	USSR	—	550	52.0	8.8	2.6
48	T-43	USSR	500	600	60.0	8.4	2.1
49[1]	Eridan	France + Holland + Belgium	510	544	49.1	8.9	2.5
50[2]	MSH	U.S.A.	—	470	45.7	6.1	2.7
51[3]	Aggressive	U.S.A.	620	735	52.4	11.0	4.2

[1]Entered service 1979.
[2]Four ships planned 1986–88.
[3]Design based on the lessons of the Korean War 1950–53. In service in many NATO navies.

Weapons			Main machinery hp	Speed (knots)	Range (miles)	Complement	In service in
A/S	SAM	guns					
Eight 533 mm torpedo tubes		Two 30 mm	36,000-T	50	—	45	
Four 533 mm torpedo tubes Two RBU 6000		Two 57 mm	30,000-T 8,000-D	37	500	80	
Four 406 mm torpedo tubes Two DC racks		Four 30 mm	12,000-D	36	500	30	
Two 406 mm torpedo tubes		Two 25 mm	7,500-D	28	350	31	Algeria, Egypt Iraq
		Two 20 mm	6,250-D	27	1,800	25	Qatar, United Arab Emirates
		One 40 mm One 20 mm	2,200-D	24	1,500	22	Libya
		One 76 mm One 40 mm Four 12.7 mm	13,300-T 1,450-D	40 16	325	24	
		One 40 mm	6,200-T 600-D	48 12	—	13	

Weapons			Main machinery hp	Speed (knots)	Range (miles)	Complement	In service in
A/S	SAM	guns					
Two RBU 1200 five barreled mortars 10 mines	Two SA-N-S launchers 16 missiles	Four 30 mm Four 25 mm	8,000-D	20	1,800	50	Libya
10 mines		Four 30 mm	4,000-D	18	1,100	45	Egypt
Two DCTs 16 mines		Four 37 mm Four 25 mm	2,200-D	15	3,000	65	Algeria, Egypt, Iraq, Syria
		One 20 mm	2,280-D	15	3,000	45	
		One 127 mm	—	—	—	45	
			2,280-D	14	3,000	76	

Table 17 continued

Minesweepers (Coastal/Inshore)

Serial no.	Fighting Ship		Displacement (tons)		Dimensions (meters)		
	Class	Country of origin	standard	full load	length	width	draught
52	Sonya (coastal)	USSR	—	460	49.0	8.8	2.0
53	Vanya (coastal)	USSR	200	260	40.0	7.3	1.8
54	Yevgenya (inshore)	USSR	—	90	26.0	6.1	1.5
55	Olya (inshore)	USSR	50	60	24.5	4.5	1.4
56[1]	Troika (coastal)	W. Germany	—	463	47.1	8.3	2.8
57[2]	Hunt (coastal)	U.K.	615	725	57.6	10.0	2.6
58[3]	Ton (coastal)	U.K.	360	440	46.3	8.5	2.5
59	MSC 322 (coastal)	U.S.A.	320	470	46.6	8.2	2.5
60	Adjutant (coastal)	U.S.A.	—	375	43.8	8.2	2.5
61[4]	MSB (inshore)	U.S.A.	30	39	17.4	4.7	1.2

[1] Entered service 1981.
[2] Entered service 1980, cost 40 million dollars.
[3] Production started 1953. Stopped 1960.
[4] They were used extensively in Vietnam for river minesweeping operations.

Weapons			Main machinery hp	Speed (knots)	Range (miles)	Comple-ment	In service in
A/S	SAM	guns					
Two DCTs 5 mines		Two 30 mm Two 25 mm	2,400-D	18.0	—	43	
12 mines		Two 30 mm Two 25 mm	2,200-D	16.0	1,400	30	Syria
		One twin 25 mm	850-D	11.0	300	10	Iraq
		One twin 25 mm	600-D	18.0	500	15	
		One 40 mm	4,000-D	16.5	850	43	
		One 40 mm	3,800-D	16.0	1,500	45	
		One 40 mm	2,500-D	15.0	2,500	29	
		Two 20 mm	1,200-D	13.0	—	39	Saudi Arabia
		Two 20 mm	1,200-D	13.0	2,500	38	Saudi Arabia, Tunisia
			600-D	12.0	—	6	

Table 17 continued

LPD—LST—LCT

| Serial no. | Fighting Ship | | | Displacement (tons) | | Dimensions (meters) | | |
	Class	Country of origin		standard	full load	length	width	draught
62[1]	Ivan Rogov—LPD	USSR		—	13,000	159.0	24.5	6.5
63	Ropucha—LST	USSR		3,450	4,400	113.0	14.5	3.6
64	Alligator—LST	USSR		3,400	4,500	114.0	15.5	4.5
65[2]	Polnochny—LCT	USSR		700	1,150	82.0	10.0	1.8
66[3]	Ondatra—LCT	USSR		—	145	24.0	6.0	1.5
67[4]	PS 700—LST	France		—	2,800	99.5	15.6	2.4
68	C-107—LCT	Turkey		280	600	56.0	11.6	1.3
69[5]	De Soto Country—LST	U.K.		4,164	7,100	135.6	18.9	5.3

[1]Can carry a battalion of naval infantry (522) with up to 40 tanks.
[2]Can carry 6 tanks.
[3]Can carry one tank.
[4]Can carry one alouette, 11 tanks, and 240 troops.
[5]Can carry a batallion of marines (634) with 23 tanks.

A/S	Weapons SAM & AA guns	Guns	Main machinery hp	Speed (knots)	Range (miles)	Comple-ment	In service in
4 Hormone Helicopter	Two SA-N-4 20 missiles	Two 76 mm Four 30 mm One RL BM-21	45,000-T	14.0	12,500	400	
	Sixteen SA-N-5 32 missiles SA-N-5	Four 57 mm	10,000-D	18.0	3,500	95	
	Six SA-N-5 24 missiles SA-N-5 Two RL Four 25 mm guns	Two 57 mm	9,000-D	18.0	1,100	100	
	Eight SA-N-5 16 missiles SA-N-5	Four 30 mm One 140 mm RL	5,000-D	18.0	900	40	Algeria, Egypt, Libya
		Diesel					
		Six 40 mm	4,000-D	15.4		35	Libya
		Two 20 mm	900-D	8.5	600	15	Libya
		Six 76 mm	13,700-D	16.5		188	

Table 17 continued

LCU & Light Transport Ships

| Serial no. | Fighting Ship | | Displacement (tons) | | Dimensions (meters) | | |
	Class	Country of origin	standard	full load	length	width	draught
70[1]	Vydra—LCU	USSR	425	600	54.8	8.1	2.0
71[2]	SMB-1—LCU	USSR	180	340	48.5	6.5	2.0
72[3]	Batral	France	750	1,330	80.0	13.0	2.4

[1]Can carry 250 tons of military equipment and stores.
[2]Can carry 150 tons of military equipment and stores.
[3]Can carry one company (138) with 12 vehicles, and one helicopter.

	Weapons		Main machinery hp	Speed (knots)	Range (miles)	Comple-ment	In service in
A/S	SAM	Guns					
			800-D	11			Egypt
			600-D	10		16	Egypt
		Two 40 mm	3,600-D	16	4,500	47	Morocco
		One 81 mm mortar					
		Two 12.7 mm					

Table 18: Fighting ships expected to stay in service or to enter service in the Israeli Navies between 1984–1993

Serial no.	Fighting ship			Displacement (tons)			
	Type	Class	Country of origin	standard	full load	surfaced	dived
1	Patrol submarine	Vickers 206	U.K.			420	600
2	Frigate	SAAR-5	Israel		1,000		
3	FAC-M	SAAR-4.5	Israel	488.0			
4	FAC-M	SAAR-4	Israel	415.0	450		
5	FAC-M	SAAR-2	France	220.0	250		
6	FAC-M	SAAR-2	France	220.0	250		
7	FAC-M (Hydrofoil)	Flagstaff 2	U.S.A.	105.0			
8	FAC-M	Dvora	Israel		47		
9	Landing Ship	LSM-1	U.S.A.		1,095		
10	LCT	ASH	Israel	400.0	730		
11	LCT	LC	Israel	182.0	230		
12	Landing craft	LCM	U.S.A.	22.0	62		
13	Landing craft	LCAC	U.S.A.	87.5	170		

N.B.

1—Within the coming ten years, it is expected that Israel will have some submarines about 1,000-tons, with a range of about 5,000 miles, a speed of about 30 knots per hour, and a complement of about 50.

2—Some SAAR-2 carry five Gabriel missiles, together with four 533 mm torpedo tubes. We did not include this class within the FAC-T, because surface to surface missiles are the main weapons of that craft.

3—The Israeli Navy has 4 Seascan 1124 N MR aircraft. This figure will be 7 by 1988.

Dimensions (meters)				Main	Speed (knots)		Range	Comple-
length	width	draught	Weapons	machinery hp	surfaced	dived	miles	ment
45.0	4.7	3.7	Eight 533 mm torpedo tubes	2,000-D 1,800-E	11.0	17		22
77.2	8.8	4.2	One helicopter 8 Harpoon 4 Gabriel Two 76 mm OTO Melara guns Four 30 mm guns Three 375 mm anti-submarine Bofors RL Six 533 mm torpedo tubes	24,000-T 4,000-D	42.0 25.0		4,500	45
61.7	7.6	2.5	One Helicopter 4 Harpoon 4 Gabriel Two 30 mm guns Two 20 mm guns Four 12.7 mm MG	8,280-D	31.0			53
58.0	7.8	2.4	4 Harpoon 5 Gabriel Two 76 mm guns Two 20 mm guns	10,680-D	32.0		1,650	45
45.0	7.0	2.5	2 Gabriel One 40 mm gun	13,500-D	32.0		1,000	40
45.0	7.0	2.5	6 Gabriel One 76 mm OTO Melara gun					
25.6	7.3	1.6	4 Harpoon 2 Gabriel Two 30 mm guns	5,400-T	52.0		1,000	
21.6	5.5	1.8	2 Gabriel Two 20 mm guns Two MGs	5,440-D	36.0		700	10
62.1	10.5	2.2	Four 20 mm guns	2,800-D	12.5			70
62.7	10.0	1.8	Two 20 mm guns	1,900-D	10.5			20
36.6	7.1	1.4	Two 20 mm guns	1,280-D	10.0			12
15.3	4.3	1.0		450-D	11.0			
26.8	13.1		Can carry one tank and four Jeeps	12,280-T	47.0		300	4

Table 19
Weapons expected to stay in service or to enter service
in the Arab and Israeli Navies 1984–1993

Surface-to-surface missiles

Ser. No.	Designa-tion	Name	Country of origin	Dimensions/cm			Weight (kg)	
				length	diameter	span	total	warhead
1	MM-38	Exocet 38	France	521	35	100	735	165
2	MM-40	Exocet 40	France	578	35	113	850	165
3	SS-12		France	189			75	29.9
4		Gabriel	Israel	381	34	135	560	150
5		Otomat	Inter-national	446	46	135	770	210
6		Otomat MK2	Inter-national	481			700	60
7		Kormoran	W. Germany	439			603	158.7
8	SS-N-2C	Styx C	USSR	625	75	275	2,313	453
9	SS-N-3B	Shaddock	USSR	1,280			4,490	998
10	SS-N-9	Siren	USSR	914				499
11	SS-N-12		USSR					
12	CL-234	Sea Skua	U.K.	250	25	72	113	20.4
13	84/1C	Harpoon	U.S.A.	457	34	83	519	
14		16-inch guided projectile	U.S.A.	370	40.6		1,179	263
15		8-inch guided projectile	U.S.A.	230	20.3		211.6	61
16		5-inch guided projectile	U.S.A.	154	12.7		47.5	13.5

Surface-to-surface missiles

Guidance	Range (km)	Speed (mach)	In service in	Remarks
Inertial + active radar	42	0.9	Oman	
Inertial + active radar	70	0.9	Iraq, Morocco, Oman, Qatar, United Arab Emirates	
Wire	8		Libya	
Autopilot/ command + IR or radar	36	0.7	Israel	
Autopilot + active radar	70	0.9	Egypt, Libya	
Autopilot + active radar	185	0.9	Egypt, Libya	Midcourse guidance by Helicopter AB 212, SH 3D
Inertial, active radar, passive radar homing	39	0.95		
Radio command + IR or active radar homing	83	0.9	Algeria, Egypt, Iraq, Libya, Syria, North Yemen, South Yemen	Arab countries have A and B models, the range of both are only 46 km.
Radio command + IR or active radar homing	450	1.4		
Radio command + IR or active radar homing	130	0.9		
Radio command + IR or active radar homing	555	2.5	Libya	
Programmed, semi-active radar homing	15	0.9		
Active radar	110		Saudi Arabia, Israel	
Semi-active laser homing, proportional navigation	67			These projectiles are equipped with a rocket motor to increase their range, and with a semi-active laser seeker. After being fired by a ship's gun, the laser seeker receives the reflected energy from the designator laser (marked by friendly troops) and automatically homes into the target.
Semi-active laser homing, proportional navigation	44			
Semi-active laser homing, proportional navigation	24			

Table 19 continued

Surface-to-air missiles

Ser. No.	Designa- tion	Name	Country of origin	Dimensions/cm			Weight (kg)	
				length	diameter	span	total	warhead
1	R 440	Crotale Navale	France	289	15	54	84	15
2		Barak	Israel	240	15		90	
3		Albatros/ Aspide	Italy	370	20	80	220	
4	SA-N-4		USSR	320				12.5
5	SA-N-5		USSR	145			14.5	
6	SA-N-6		USSR	700				
7	SA-N-7		USSR					
8	CF-299	Sea Dart	U.K.	436			450	
9	PX-430	Sea Wolf	U.K.	198			80	
10		Seacat	U.K.	149			62.5	
11		Sea Sparrow (MK 57)	U.S.A.	366	20	102	200	
12	RIM 66B	Standard (MR)	U.S.A.	457	31		590	
13		SM-1 (ER)	U.S.A.	823	31		1,060	
14		Terrier	U.S.A.	800	31		1,400	

Surface-to-air missiles

Guidance	Range (km)	Speed (mach)	In service in	Remarks
Radio command	18	0.9 1.2	Saudi Arabia	
Semi-active radar	10			
Semi-active radar	18		Libya	
	11	2.0	Algeria, Libya	Can be used also against ships.
	10	1.5		Naval version of SAM-7.
	77	3.0		Anti-missile. Entered service 1979.
	28	3.0		Naval version of SAM-11.
Semi-active radar	74			
Radio command or TV	5.5	2.0		
Radio command or TV	6			Can be used also against ships.
Semi-active radar	25			
Semi-active radar	18			
Semi-active radar	55			Gradually replacing Terrier.
Beam rider	35			

Table 19 continued

Torpedoes

Ser. No.	Designa-tion	Name	Country of origin	Dimensions (cm)		Weight (kg)		Guidance	Range (km)	Carried by	Anti	Remarks
				length	diameter	total	explo-sives					
1	A-244		Italy	270	32.4			Active/passive acoustic homing		Ships, aircraft	Ships	
2	533 mm		USSR	500	53.3					Ships, aircraft, submarines	Ships	
3	406 mm		USSR	500	40.6					Aircraft, ships, submarines	Ships	
4	MK-24	Tigerfish	U.K.	646	53.5	1,550		Wire, plus active/passive acoustic homing	32	Ships, submarines	Submarines	
5	MK-44		U.S.A.	260	32.4	196.4		Active acoustic homing		Aircraft, ships	Submarines	
6	MK-46		U.S.A.	260	32.4	257		Active acoustic homing		Aircraft, ships, helicopters	Submarines	

Guns

Serial No.	Calibre (mm)	Country of origin	Number of barrels	Elevation degrees	Rate of fire per barrel per minute	Weight of shell/kg (explosive charge)	Range km surface/height	Range km AA slant	Associated radar
1	130	USSR	2	40	10	27.0	24	8	
2	130	USSR	2	50	15	27.0	28	13	Sun Visor, Egg Cup, Wasp Head
3	114	U.K.	1	55	25	21.0	22		
4	102	U.K.	1	30	15	16.0	11		
5	100	France	1	80	60	13.5	13/7		DRBC 32
6	100	USSR	1	80	15	13.5	18/11	6	Sun Visor
7	85	USSR	2	75	15	9.5	9/6	6	
8	76	U.K.	2	90	90	7.0	17		
9	76	Italy	1	85	85	6.0	8/5		
10	76	USSR	2	85	60	6.0	15/10	6	Owl Screech, Hawk Screech
11	76	Sweden	1	30	30	5.9	13	6	
12	57	USSR	4/2	85	120	2.8	9/6	6	Hawk Screech
13	40	Sweden	4/2	85	260	2.4	9/6	4	
14	37	USSR	2/1	80	130	0.7	8/5	3	
15	30	Switzerland	2	80	650	0.36	10	3	
16	30	USSR	2	80	500			2.5	Drum Tilt
17	20	Switzerland	1	85	800	0.24		1	

Table 20
Anti-tank guided missiles expected to stay in service or to enter service in the Arab and Israeli armed forces 1984–1993

Serial No.	Designation	Country of origin	Dimensions (cm)		
			length	diameter	span
1	ADATS	International	205	15.2	
2	HOT	International	128	14.0	31
3	PICKET	Israel	76	8.1	
4	AT-1 (Snapper)	USSR	113	14.0	75
5	AT-2 (Swatter)	USSR	116	13.2	66
6	AT-3 (Sagger)	USSR	86	12.0	47
7	AT-5 (Spandrel)	USSR	102	13.5	
8	AT-6 (Spiral)		Still under development. It is believed to have the same characteristics of the ADATS.		
9	Swingfire	U.K.	107	17.0	37
10	Shillelag (MGM-51)	U.S.A.	114	15.2	
11	TOW (BGM-71)	U.S.A.	117.0	15.2	
12	Copperhead (M-712)	U.S.A.	137.2	15.5	

| Weight (kg) | | | | | |
total	warhead	Range (m)	Penetra-tion (mm)	Guidance	Remarks
51.0	12.0	8,000	900	Laser	Also to be used as SAM, its speed mach 3 plus, max height up to 5000 m. associated with a radar that can detect air targets and ground targets up to 20 km.
21.0	6.0	4,000	800	Wire	Max speed 250 m per second. Flight duration 17 seconds to reach 4000 m
4.2		500		Gyro	
22.0	5.5	500–2,300	380	Wire	Speed 90 m per second
29.4		500–3,500	500	Wire	Speed 150 m per second
11.3		500–3,000	400	Wire	Speed 120 m per second
12.0		4,000	500	Wire	Speed 200 m per second
				Wire	
34.0		4,000		Wire	
27.0		4,500		Infrared Laser	Cannon-launched (155 mm howitzer). Some of its warheads to be guided with IR, Others to be guided with laser.
18.0	3.6	65–3,750		Wire	Speed 278 m per second
63.5	4.6	16,000		Laser	Cannon-launched (155 mm howitzer). Its warhead to be guided with laser.

Table 21

Tactical land-based surface-to-surface missiles expected to stay in service, or to enter service in the Arab and Israeli armed forces 1984–1993

Serial No.	Designation	Country of origin	Dimensions (cm)			Weight (kg)		Range (km)	Speed (mach)	Guidance	Remarks
			length	calibre	span	total	warhead				
1	Frog-7	USSR	900	55		2,000	HE/nuclear	60		Unguided	
2	SS-1B (Scud A)	USSR	1,050	85		4,500	HE/nuclear	80–150		Radio command	
3	SS-1C (Scud B)	USSR	1,125	85		6,300	HE/nuclear	160–270		Simplified inertial	
4	SS-12	USSR	1,125	100		6,800	HE/nuclear	800		Inertial	
5	SS-21	USSR	944	46			HE/nuclear	120			Replacement for Frog-7
6	SS-22	USSR					HE/nuclear	900			Replacement for SS-12
7	SS-23	USSR					HE/nuclear				Still under development
8	Lance (MGM-52)	U.S.A.	614	56		1,500	HE/nuclear	120	3	Simplified inertial	
9	Lance II	U.S.A.								Inertial	It uses a solid rocket motor giving three times the present range of Lance (120 km), greater payload, and lower cost. It also uses an advanced inertial guidance system which produced accuracy five times better than the standard Lance.

Table 22

**Coastal defence missiles expected to stay in service,
or to enter service in the Arab and Israeli armed forces 1984–1993**

Serial No.	Designation	Country of origin	Dimensions (cm)			Weight (kg)		Range (km)	Speed (mach)	Remarks
			length	calibre	span	total	warhead			
1	Exocet 40	France	578	35	113	850	165	70	0.9	
2	Otomat	International								Range capability 180 km. The basic coastal defence Otomat system normally consists of one or more battery. Each battery is composed of one command group (four vehicles) and two to four firing groups. Each firing group consists of one firing vehicle with two missiles, and one reload vehicle with another two missiles. A stretch of 340 km of coastline can be covered by ten batteries. It employs a naval helicopter equipped with over-the-horizon guidance facilities for engaging distant targets of more than 60 km. Guidance is by autopilot plus active radar homing.
3	Sepal (SSC-1B)	USSR								It is the land-based version of the shipboard surface-to-surface missile shaddock. Guidance is by radio command with active radar homing. Range capability in the order of 450 km, but midcourse guidance by aircraft or helicopter would be necessary for each long mission. Each coastal defence battalion is equipped with between 15 and 18 missiles (inclusive of reloads).

Table 23
Surface-to-air missiles expected to stay in service
or to enter service in the Arab and Israeli Air Forces 1984–1993

Serial No.	Designation	Country of origin	Dimensions (cm)			Weight (kg)	
			length	diameter	span	total	warhead
1	Crotate	France	294	16	54	80	15
2	Shahine Sica (TSE 5100)	France					14
3	Low Strike	Israel	—	—	—	—	—
4	Barak 1	Israel				90	
5	Aspide	Italy	370	20	100	220	35
6	SA-2 (Guideline)	USSR	1,070	70	—	2,300	130
7	SA-3 (Goa)	USSR	670	60	—	636	—
8	SA-4 (Ganef)	USSR	880	90	260		
9	SA-5 (Gammon)	USSR	1,650	100	—	10,000	—
10	SA-6 (Gainful)	USSR	620	33	124	550	40
11	SA-7 (Grail)	USSR	129	—	—	9.5	—
12	SA-8 (Gecko)	USSR	320	21	60	190	—
13	SA-9 (Gaskin)	USSR	200	12	—	30	—
14	SA-11	USSR	—	—	—	—	—
15	SA-13	USSR					

Range (km)	Ceiling (meters)	Speed (mach)	Guidance	Remarks
8.5	5,000	2.3	Radio command	It covers 8 km in 16 seconds. Typical target speed 1.2 mach and altitude between 15 and 5000 m. Reaction time 6 seconds from first detection to missile launch. Minimum range 500 m.
10.0	5,000	2.3	Radio command	A version of Crotale fitted on an AMX-30 chassis. Made by France for Saudi Arabia.
—	—	—	Semi-active radar	It was first revealed in mid 1983. It is capable of locating identifying and engaging low flying aircraft targets by day or night and under adverse weather conditions.
10.0	—	—	Semi-active radar	It was first revealed in the 1983 Paris show. It is claimed to be effective against Sea-skimming missiles, aircraft, and other anti-ship threats. A vertical launch unit containing up to 8 missiles weighing 1300 kg can be fitted anywhere on the vessel. Its radar- and fire-control gear accounts for another 1300 kg. A complete defence system consists of four launch units with 32 missiles $(4 \times 1300 + 1300 = 6500$ kg).
10.0			Semi-active radar	
40–50	18,000	3.5	Radio command	
25–30	13,000	2.0	Radio command	
70	24,000	2.5	Radio command	
300	29,000			
60	18,000	2.8	Radio command + radar homing	
9–10	4,000		IR homing	Man-portable.
8–16	6,000	2.0	Radio command	
8	5,000	1.5	IR homing	
28		3.0		Engages targets flying at altitudes between 30 meters and 14,000 meters. Minimum range 300 m.
7.5				Still under development. Engages targets flying between 50 meters and 10,000 meters. It is expected to replace SAM-9.

Table 23 continued

Serial No.	Designation	Country of origin	Dimensions (cm)			Weight (kg)	
			length	diameter	span	total	warhead
16	Improved Hawk	U.S.A.	503	36	122	639	
17	Nike Hercules (MIM-14B)	U.S.A.	1,210	80	—	4,858	
18	Patriot (MIM-104)	U.S.A.	530	41	—		
19	Stinger (FIM-92A)	U.S.A.	152	7	—	15.8	

Range (km)	Ceiling (meters)	Speed (mach)	Guidance	Remarks
40	16,000		Semi-active radar	Engages targets flying at altitudes between 30 meters and 16,000 m.
140	45,000		Radio command	
				Patriot is an advanced guided weapon system intended as a replacement for the Hawk and Nike Hercules systems. Its production started in 1981, and it is expected to be completed by 1985.
			IR homing	Man-portable, entered service 1980.

Table 24
Air-to-surface missiles expected to stay in service
or to enter service in the Arab and Israeli Air Forces 1984–1993

Serial No.	Designation	Country of origin	Dimensions (cm)			Weight (kg)	
			length	diameter	span	total	warhead
1	Exocet (AM 39)	France	470	35	110	655	165
2	Otomat	International (France, Italy)	440	46	119	600	200
3	Gabriel	Israel	385	43	110	600	150
4	Kitchen (AS-4)	USSR	1,130	95			
5	Kelt (AS-5)	USSR	859	430	—	—	160
6	Kingfish (AS-6)	USSR	1,050	—	250	—	—
7	Kerry (AS-7)	USSR	—	—	—	350	100
8	AS-9	USSR	—	—	—	—	—
9	AS-10	USSR	—	—	—	—	—
10	Shrike (AGM-45A)	U.S.A.	305	20	91	117	—
11	Standard Arm (AGM-78)	U.S.A.	450	34	—	635	—
12	HARM (AGM-88A)	U.S.A.	416	25	113	360	66
13	Maverick (AGM-65)	U.S.A.	246	30	71	209	59
14	Harpoon (AGM-84A)	U.S.A.	384	34	91	522	230
15	Hellfire	U.S.A.	178	18	33	43	—
16	Walleye I (AGM-62A)	U.S.A.	344	33	116	499	385
17	Paveway (GBU-10)	U.S.A.	900 kg bomb fitted with a laser seeker				
18	Paveway (GBU-12)	U.S.A.	225 kg bomb fitted with a laser seeker				
19	Wasp (mini missile)	U.S.A.	137	25	51	—	45

Range (km)	Guidance	Remarks
50–70	Inertial + radar homing	
60–80	Inertial + radar homing	
60	Inertial (plus optional command update midcourse), active radar and-homing	The system provides all-weather, day and night anti-ship capability against targets ranging from small fast patrol boats to destroyers and larger ships. The Gabriel MK III A/S is an active homing, sea-skimming missile, with fire-and-forget, and fire-and-update models.
300	Inertial + active radar homing	Carried by TU-22 and other Soviet bombers.
180	Auto-pilot + active radar homing	Carried by TU-16.
220	Inertial + active radar homing	Carried by TU-16 and other Soviet bombers. Its speed is 3 mach.
10		Carried by SU-24 and other Soviet fighter bombers.
80–90		Carried by SU-19.
40		Still under development.
12–16	Anti-radiation homing	Designed to destroy SAM battalions.
25	Passive radar homing	Designed to destroy SAM battalions.
20	Anti-radiation homing	To destroy all kinds of radars. It is intended as a replacement to Shrike and Standard Arm.
45	TV, Laser homing, IR homing	Designed for a wide variety of missions, and to be carried by many combat aircraft.
110	Radar homing	Designed to destroy ships.
	Laser homing	
12	TV	Walleye II is 907 kg, and is designed for the destruction of large semi-hard targets such as bridges, air base facilities and ships.
	Laser	
	Laser	
		This is the most advanced of the WAAM concepts, and entails loading miniature missiles, each with its own new technology seeker, into cluster bomb containers. Normally 10 WASP in each container.

Table 25

Air to air missiles expected to stay in service, or to enter service in the Arab and Israeli Armed Forces 1984–1993

Ser. No.	Desig-nation	Country of origin	Dimensions (cm)			Weight (kg)		range (km)	guidance	speed (mach)	Remarks
			length	diameter	span	total	warhead				
1	R-530	France	328	26	110	195	27	18	Radar & IR versions	3.0	
2	Super 530	France	354	26	90	250	30	36	Radar	4–5	
3	R-550 (Magic)	France	280	16	65	91	—	10	IR	—	
4	AMRAM (AIM-120A)	International	365	18	53	148			Inertial + radar homing		
5	Python-3	Israel	300	16	—	120	11	15	IR	—	
6	Atoll (AA-2)	USSR	280	12	53	—	—	15	IR	—	
7	Anab (AA-3)	USSR	360	28	130	—	—	16	Radar & IR versions		

#	Name	Country							Guidance	
8	Ash (AA-5)	USSR	530	30	130	—	—	30	Radar & IR versions	
9	Acrid (AA-6)	USSR	629	30	—	750	100	37	Radar & IR versions	2.2
10	Apex (AA-7)	USSR	420	24	105	350	40	35	Radar & IR versions	
11	Aphid (AA-8)	USSR	210	13		54	8	8	IR	
12	Phoenix (Aim 54A)	U.S.A.	396	38	91	380		110–165	Radar	—
13	Sidewinder (Aim 9M)	U.S.A.	287	13	61	86		18	Semi-active radar & IR versions	2.0
14	Sparrow (Aim 7F)	U.S.A.	365	20	100	200	30	25	Semi-active radar	

NB

AMRAM air to air missile have been ordered by USA and NATO countries. Production started 1984. It could be carried by F-4, F-14, F-15, F-16, F-18 and all other Western combat aircraft. It is intended to replace Sparrow. The design calls for an all-weather, all-aspect, radar-guided missile, capable of engaging numerically superior aircraft forces before they come within visual range. Simultaneous launches of up to eight missiles at multiple targets will also be possible by AMRAM.

Table 26
Guns expected to stay in service, or to enter service in the Arab and Israeli Armed Forces 1984–1993

Self-propelled Artillery

Serial No.	Model	Country of origin	Type	Calibre (mm)	Combat weight (kg)	Shell weight (kg)	Range (meter)	Type of ammunition	Engine hp/type
1	GCT	France	Gun	155	42,000	43.20	23,500	NATO	720-D
2	SP-70	International	Howitzer	155		43.40	24,000	NATO	
3	L-33	Israel	Gun/Howitzer	155	41,500	43.70	21,000	NATO	460-D
4	Palmaria	Italy	Howitzer	155	46,000	43.50	24,000	HE	
5	M-1973	USSR	Gun/Howitzer	152	23,000	43.50	18,500	HE-HERAP	520-D
6	M-110 A2	U.S.A.	Howitzer	203	28,350	92.53	21,300	HE—chemical—nuclear	405-D
7	M-107	U.S.A.	Gun	175	28,168	66.78	32,700	HE	405-D
8	M-109 A2	U.S.A.	Howitzer	155	23,786	42.91	18,100	NATO	405-D

Self-propelled Anti-aircraft Guns

Ser. No.	Model	Country of origin	Type	Calibre (mm)	Combat weight	Shell weight (kg)	Muzzle velocity m/sec	Type of ammunition	Engine hp/type
1	Dragon	International	Twin	30	31,000	0.36	1,000	AP-HEI	720-D
2	ZSU-57-2	USSR	Twin	57	28,100	2.81	1,000	FRAG-APC	520-D
3	ZSU-23-4	USSR	Quad	23	19,000	0.19	970	API, HEI	280-D
4	M-162	U.S.A.	Rotary	20	12,310	0.10	1,030	HE-AP	215-D
5	Vulcan Commando	U.S.A.	Rotary	20	10,206	0.10	1,030	HE-AP	202-D

Towed Artillery

Serial No.	Model	Country of origin	Type	Calibre (mm)	Length of barrel (m)	Combat weight (kg)	Shell weight (kg)	Range (m)	Type of ammunition
1	TR	France	Gun	155	6.200	10,000	43.40	24,000	NATO
2	FH-70	International	Howitzer	155	6.022	9,300	43.40	24,000	NATO
3	M-71	Israel	Gun/ Howitzer	155	6.045	9,200	43.40	23,500	NATO
4	M-68	Israel	Gun/ Howitzer	155	5.180	8.500	43.70	21,000	NATO
5	Model 56	Italy	Howitzer	105	1.478	1,290	21.06	10,575	NATO
6	S-23	USSR	Gun	180	8.800	21,450	84.09	30,400	HE, HERAP
7	D-20	USSR	Gun/ Howitzer	152.4	5.195	5,650	43.51	17,410	HE, CP, AP-T
8	M-46	USSR	Gun	130	7.600	7,700	33.40	27,150	HE, APC-T
9	D-74	USSR	Gun	122	6.450	5,500	27.30	24,000	HE, APC-T
10	D-30	USSR	Howitzer	122	4.875	3,150	27.30	15,400	HE, HEAP
11	T-12	USSR	ATK Gun	100	8.484	3,000	09.50	8,500	HEAT, APFSDS
12	SD-44	USSR	Gun	85	4.693	2,250	09.60	15,650	HE, AP-T, HEAT, HVAP-T
13	ZIS-3	USSR	Gun	76	3.455	1,116	06.20	13,920	HE, AP-T, HEAT, HVAP-T
14	CH-26	USSR	ATK Gun	57	4.070	1,250	03.75	6,700	HE, AP, HVAP
15	M-115	U.S.A.	Howitzer	203	5.142	13,471	92.53	16,800	HE, chemical, nuclear ARP, SALP, SADARM
16	M-198	U.S.A.	Howitzer	155	6.096	7,076	42.91	24,000	NATO
17	M-59	U.S.A.	Gun	155	7.036	12,600	43.40	22,000	HE, AP
18	M-114	U.S.A.	Howitzer	155	3.778	5,760	42.91	14,600	NATO
19	M-101	U.S.A.	Howitzer	105	2.574	2,030	21.06	11,270	NATO

Towed Anti-aircraft Guns

Table 26 continued

Serial No.	Model	Country of origin	Type	Calibre (mm)	Combat weight (kg)	Shell weight (kg)	Vertical range (m)	Type of ammunition	Rate of fire (rpm)
1	Cerbere	France	Twin	20	1,513	0.12	2,000	HEI, APDS, API	900
2	ADS	W. Germany	Twin	20	1,640	0.12	2,000	HEI, APDS, API	1,000
3	TCM-20	Israel	Quad	20	1,350	0.125	4,500	APT, HEIT	1,000
4	Breda (40 L 70)	Italy	Twin	40	9,900	0.96	8,700	AP, PREFRAG	600
5	S-60	USSR	Single	57	4,500	2.85	6,000	FRAG, APC	120
6	ZU-23	USSR	Twin	23	950	0.19	5,100	HEI, API	1,000
7	ZPU-2	USSR	Twin	14.5	621	0.064	5,000	API	600
8	ZPU-4	USSR	Quad	14.5	1,810	0.064	5,000	API	1,200
9	M-1	U.S.A.	Single	40	2,656	0.9	4,660	HE, HEI, AP	120
10	Vulcan (M-167)	U.S.A.	Six barrels	20	1,565	0.103	1,200	APT, HEIT	3,000

NB
Israel claims that TCM-20 is credited with shooting down 60 percent of the aircraft downed by ground air defences during the October War 1973.

Table 27
Expected increase in the population, and in the Armed Forces in Israel until 1993

Year	Population (million)	Strength of the Armed Forces	Regular Forces				Reserve Forces						Total after mobilisation
			Army	Navy	Air Force	Subtotal	Army	Navy	Air Force	mis.	Subtotal		
83	4.100	500,000	135,000	9,000	28,000	172,000	315,000	1,000	9,000	3,000	328,000	Army	450,000
												Navy	10,000
												AF	37,000
												Mis.	3,000
												Total	500,000
88	4.510	563,750	152,212	10,148	31,287	193,647	355,163	1,128	10,429	3,383	370,103	Army	507,376
												Navy	11,276
												AF	41,716
												Mis.	3,382
												Total	563,750
93	4.961	620,125	167,434	11,162	34,417	213,011	390,678	1,240	11,472	3,722	620,125	Army	558,112
												Navy	12,402
												AF	45,889
												Mis.	3,722
												Total	620,125

NB

1— Population of Israel at the end of 1983 was 4.1 million (3.3 Jews, 0.7 Israeli Arabs, 0.1 Arabs living in Jerusalem). There are other 1,225,000 Arab population living under Israeli occupation, 750,000 of them live in the West Bank. Other 450,000 live in Gaza strip.

2— Israeli population was increasing in the past at an almost constant rate of 10 percent every 5 years.

3— Statistics show that Israel mobilises about 12.5 percent of its population in its armed forces (the highest in the world).

4— The strength of the Israeli armed forces personnel is distributed among the services as follows: 90 percent for the Army, 7.4 percent for the Air Force, 2 percent for the Navy, and 0.6 percent for miscellaneous jobs.

5— The army keeps only 30 percent of its full strength constantly under arms, and calls the other 70 percent when fully mobilised. The navy keeps 90 percent constantly under arms, while the Air Force keeps only 75 percent of its personnel constantly under arms.

Table 28

Expected increase in the main weapons in the Israeli Armed Forces to 1993

Year	Expected increase in the population	Expected increase in the Armed Forces	In the Army		In the Navy		In the Air Force		
			Troops	Max tanks to be manned	Troops	Max navy units to be manned	Troops	Max combat aircraft to be manned	Miscellaneous
88	410,000	63,750	57,376	573	1,276	24	4,716	118	382
93	451,000	56,375	50,736	507	1,126	23	4,173	104	340
Total	861,000	120,125	108,112	1,080	2,402	47	8,889	222	722

NB

1—Statistics show that the Israeli army is having one MBT for each 113 soldiers of its strength. For the future I calculated one MBT for each increase of 100 soldier in the Army strength.

2—Statistics show that the Israeli Air Force keeps 44 persons for each combat aircraft in service. For the future I calculated one combat aircraft for each increase of 40 persons in the Air Force strength.

3—The expected increase in the strength of the Israeli Navy up till 1993 (about 2400), would suffice to create the new following units:
3 submarines, 4 corvette, 20 FAC-M, 20 LCAC. All these units would need approximately 1300 men at sea and 1100 on shore.

Table 29
Main battle tanks expected to stay in service,
or to enter service in the Israeli Armed Forces 1984–93

Designation	83	88	93	Remarks
Centurion	1,100	1,100	1,100	
M-48	650	650	650	
M-60	1,320	1,320	1,320	
T-54/T-55	440	440	440	
T-62	150	150	150	
Merkava	300	540	780	
M-1	—	333	600	
Total	3,960	4,533	5,040	

NB

1—The Israeli tank Mercava is in production between 40 and 50 per year.

2—In 1983 Israel had 33 Armoured brigade. This figure will reach 37 by 1988, and 42 by 1993.

Table 30
Combat aircraft expected to stay in service,
or to enter service in the Israeli Air Force 1984–93

Designation	83	88	93	Remarks
F-15	60	80	100	
F-16	147	240	300	
F-4	144	142	140	
Kfir	260	260	260	
Command, warning and ECM	16	20	26	
A-4	203	124	—	
Lavi	—	80	220	
SR-71	—	2	4	
A-12	—	—	2	
Total	830	948	1,052	

Table 31
Fighting ships expected to stay in service,
or to enter service, in the Israeli Navy 1984–93

Serial No.	Type	Class	83	88	93
1	Patrol submarine (420 ton)	Vickers 206	3	3	3
2	Patrol submarine (1000 ton)		—	2	3
3	Corvette	SAAR-5	—	2	4
4	FAC-M (Hydrofoil)	Flagstaff	2	7	12
5	FAC-M	SAAR-4	8	13	18
6	FAC-M	SAAR-2	12	12	12
7	FAC-M	Dvora	2	2	2
8	Landing craft air cushion vehicle	JEFF		10	20
9	Landing ship medium	LSM	1	1	1
10	Landing craft tank	Ash	3	3	3
11	Landing craft tank	LC	3	3	3
12	Landing craft mechanised	LCM	3	3	3
13	Miscellaneous ships		40	40	40
14	Total number of ships		77	101	124
15	Navy strength		10,000	11,276	12,402

NB
The Israeli Navy deploy 4 Seascan 1124 N for reconnaissance and patrol missions.
By 1988 the figured deployed is expected to be seven aircraft.

Table 32
Strategic offensive arms in possession of USA and USSR December 1983

| Category | Strategic (over 5500 km range) | | | | | |
| | U.S.A. | | | USSR | | |
	num-ber	war-heads	mega-ton	num-ber	war-heads	mega-ton
ICBMs	1,045	2,145	1,734.0	1,398	5,654	4,351.6
SLBMs	568	5,152	468.8	980	2,688	760.8
Heavy bombers	272			143		
Subtotal	1,885	7,297	2,202.8	2,521	8,342	5,112.4
Land-based						
Sea-launched						
Air-launched						
Subtotal						
Total	1,885	7,297	2,202.8	2,521	8,342	5,112.4

Table 32 continued

| Intermediate (1000–5500 km range) | | | | | | Total | | | | | |
| USA | | | USSR | | | USA | | | USSR | | |
num-ber	war-heads	mega-ton	num-ber	war-heads	mega-ton	num-ber	war-heads	mega-ton	num-ber	war-heads	mega-ton
						1,045	2,145	1,734.0	1,398	5,654	4,351.6
						568	5,152	468.8	980	2,688	760.8
						272			143		
						1,885	7,297	2,202.8	2,521	8,342	5,112.4
149	149	46.5	599	1,320	401	149	149	46.5	599	1,320	401.0
44	44	8.8				44	44	8.8			
200	200	40.0				200	200	40.0			
393	393	95.3	599	1,320	401	393	393	95.3	599	1,320	401.0
393	393	95.3	599	1,320	401	2,278	7,690	2,298.1	3,120	9,662	5,513.4

Table 33
Destructive capacity aimed at major nuclear Powers

Aimed by	Aimed at							
	U.S.A.	Eastern block	W. Europe	U.K.	France	China	Reserve	Total
U.S.A.		2,202.8						2,202.8
USSR	2,202.8		95.3	38.4	117.6	200	2,859.3	5,513.4
W. Europe		95.3						95.3
U.K.		38.4						38.4
France		117.6						117.6
China		200.0						200.0
Total	2,202.8	2,654.1	95.3	38.4	117.6	200	2,859.3	8,167.5

NB

1—Major nuclear powers possess strategic and intermediate missiles with 8,167.5 megaton destructive capacity.

2—Tactical nuclear warheads are not included in this table. The destructive capacity of nuclear tactical warhead is 234.7 megatons for NATO countries, and 856.6 megatons for Warsaw countries.

3—Hence total destructive nuclear capacity in both blocks is 9,258.8 megatons.

Table 34
Tactical nuclear weapons deployed by NATO December 1983

Designation	Number	Destructive capacity (kiloton)		Remarks
		Per warhead	Total	
Pershing A	72	1	72	SSM
Honest John	54	1	54	SSM
Pluton	42	10	420	SSM
Lance	92	1	92	SSM
AGM-69A	1,140	200	228,000	ASM
M-110 shell	587	1	587	203 mm Howitzer
M-109 shell	2,740	2	5,480	155 mm Howitzer
Total	4,727	—	234,705	

Table 35
Tactical nuclear weapons deployed by Warsaw Pact, December 1983

Category	Designation	Number	Destructive capacity (kiloton)	
			Per warhead	Total
Land-based	Scud-A	440	1	440
	Scud-B	570	1	570
	SS-21	620	200	124,000
	SS-12	120	200	24,000
	SS-22	100	500	5,000
	Sepal	100	1	100
	Subtotal	1,950	—	154,110
Sea-launched	SS-N-3	316	350	110,600
	SS-N-7	144	200	28,800
	SS-N-9	154	200	30,800
	SS-N-12	80	350	28,000
	SS-N-14	288	?	100,800
	SS-N-19	44	?	15,400
	SS-N-22	20	?	7,000
	Subtotal	1,046	—	321,400
Air-launched	AS-2	90	1	90
	AS-3	70	1,000	70,000
	AS-4	645	200	129,000
	AS-6	880	200	176,000
	Subtotal	1,685	—	375,090
	Total	4,681	—	850,600

NB
It is believed that the Soviet Union has nuclear shells for its 180 mm howitzer, 152 mm howitzer, 203 mm howitzer, and 240 mm mortar. But the number and the yield of these shells are not yet known. If we suppose that the yield of these shells is similar to that of NATO, this will add another 6 megatons, bringing the total destructive capacity of the Warsaw Pact tactical warheads to 856.6 megatons.

Table 36
The Area of the Arab countries

Serial No.	Country	Area (square km)	Rank by area
1	Algeria	2,381,741	2
2	Bahrain	622	23
3	Egypt	1,001,449	6
4	Iraq	434,924	9
5	Jordan	91,787	16
6	Kuwait	17,818	20
7	Lebanon	10,400	22
8	Libya	1,759,540	4
9	Morocco	446,550	8
10	Oman	212,457	12
11	Qatar	11,437	21
12	Saudi Arabia	2,150,000	3
13	Sudan	2,505,800	1
14	Syria	185,180	14
15	Tunisia	163,610	15
16	United Arab Emirates	83,600	17
17	Yemen (North)	195,000	13
18	Yemen (South)	333,038	10
19	Mauritania	1,030,700	5
20	Somalia	637,700	7
21	Djibouti	23,200	19
22	Palestine	27,031	18
23	RASD	266,000	11
24	Total	13,969,584	—

Table 37
Ore production in the Arab world 1978

Country	Millions of Tons		Thousands of tons			
	Phosphate Phosphate Rock	Iron Ore	Lead B.M.	Zinc B.M.	Copper B.M.	Mag-nesium B.M.
Mauritania	—	8.971	—	—	2.8	—
Morocco	19.017	0.062	109.5	5.1	4.3	66
Algeria	0.997	3.780	1.6	4.0	0.4	—
Tunisia	3.713	0.339	8.2	7.4	—	—
Egypt	0.644	1.387	—	—	—	—
Jordan	2.320	—	—	—	—	—
Syria	0.747	—	—	—	—	—
Iraq	—	—	—	—	—	—
Sudan	—	—	—	—	—	—
Total Arab production	27.538	14.539	119.3	16.5	7.5	66
Ratio of Arab world production (in percent)	20	1.49	3.32	0.26	0.1	0.78

*Natural sulphur

B.M.: Bearing minerals

Source: Arab Organisation for Mineral Wealth, *Al Tharwa Al Madania,*
November 1, 1981.

Thousands of tons			Thousands of kg	Thousands of tons			
Cobalt B.M.	Chromium B.M.	Mercury	Silver	Coal	Fluorine	Pyrrhotite	Sulphur*
—	—	—	—	—	—	—	—
1.05	—	—	99.2	720	58.3	174	—
—	—	1.034	6.2	—	—	120	—
—	—	—	2.0	—	26.7	21	—
—	—	—	—	—	2.2	1	—
—	—	—	—	—	—	—	—
—	—	—	—	—	—	—	—
—	—	—	—	—	—	—	600
—	7.1	—	—	—	—	—	—
1.05	7.1	1.034	107.4	720	87.2	316	600
4.3	0.17	17	1	0.027	1.9	3.96	3.7

Table 38
Reserves and production of phosphate in Arab countries
1975 and 1979

	Millions of Tons	
Country	Proven Reserves 1975	Production in 1979
Algeria	642	1.10
Egypt	4,325	0.65
Iraq	1,760	—
Jordan	1,062	2.83
Morocco	57,000	20.32
Saudi Arabia	912	—
Syria	860	1.17
Tunisia	885	4.04
Arab total	66,446	30.21
World total	130,000	126.79
Ratio of Arab total to World total (in percent)	51	23.82

Source: Various publications of the Office Cherifien de Phosphate of Morocco
    in 1979.
—First Arab Energy Conference, Abu Dhabi, 1979.
—The British Sulphur Corporation Ltd. *Statistical Supplement,*
    July/August, 1980.

Table 39
Arab manufacturing industry: product and per capita share 1980–1981

Country	Output of manufacturing industry (million US$)		Per capita share of manufacturing industry (US$)	
	1980	1981	1980	1981
Algeria	4,222	4,039	213.6	197.7
Iraq	1,878	1,018	143.6	76.0
Subtotal	6,100	5,057	185.7	149.5
U.A.E.	1,131	1,364	1,413.8	1,604.7
Qatar	231	237	1,050.0	1,077.3
Kuwait	1,626	1,616	1,195.6	1,122.2
Saudi Arabia	5,033	5,748	601.3	666.1
Libya	821	995	275.5	319.9
Subtotal	8,842	9,960	644.0	699.0
Jordan	363	401	113.8	121.9
Bahrain	466	544	1,294.4	1,236.4
Tunisia	959	943	150.8	144.6
Syria	—	—	—	—
Oman	52	65	57.8	65.0
Lebanon	520	466	164.6	145.6
Egypt	2,717	3,084	64.7	72.1
Morocco	2,944	2,565	145.5	123.3
Subtotal	8,021	8,068	105.3	103.4
Sudan	432	438	23.1	22.8
Somalia	100	116	27.4	30.5
Mauritania	40	46	24.5	28.1
Yemen A.R.	144	169	24.3	26.4
P.D.R. Yemen	61	72	31.0	34.3
Djibouti	22	27	55.0	67.5
Subtotal	799	868	24.8	25.9
Total	23,762	23,953	153.3	150.02

Source: Arab League Report 1980–1981

Table 40
Development of Arab and world oil reserves 1978–1982
(Billions of Barrels at end of year)

Country	1978	1979	1980	1981	1982	1981/82 percent change	Years for depletion of reserves
U.A.E	31.3	29.4	30.4	32.2	32.4	0.6	72
Bahrain	0.3	0.2	0.2	0.2	0.2	—	12
Tunisia	2.3	2.2	1.6	1.7	1.9	11.8	49
Algeria	6.3	8.4	8.2	8.1	9.4	16.0	38
Saudi Arabia	168.9	166.5	168.0	167.8	165.3	−1.5	68
Syria	2.1	2.0	1.9	1.9	1.5	−21.1	23
Iraq	32.1	31.0	30.0	29.7	41.0	38.0	114
Qatar	4.0	3.8	3.6	3.4	3.4	—	28
Kuwait	69.4	68.5	68.2	67.7	67.1	−0.9	221
Libya	24.3	23.5	23.0	22.6	21.5	−4.9	58
Egypt	3.2	3.1	2.9	2.9	3.3	13.8	14
Oman	2.5	2.4	2.3	2.6	2.7	3.8	23
Arab countries	346.7	341.0	340.3	340.8	349.7	2.6	75
Non-Arab OPEC Countries	108.6	103.6	103.2	105.0	105.0	0.0	43.4

Country	1978	1979	1980	1981	1982	1981/82 percent change	Years for depletion of reserves
OPEC countries	444.9	434.6	434.5	436.5	447.8	2.6	67
UK	16.0	15.4	14.8	14.8	13.9	− 6.1	18
Norway	5.9	5.8	5.5	7.6	6.8	− 10.5	37
U.S.A.	28.5	26.5	26.4	29.8	29.8		8
Mexico	16.0	31.2	44.0	56.9	48.3	− 15.2	45
Canada	6.0	6.8	6.4	7.3	7.0	− 4.1	12
USSR	71.0	67.0	63.0	63.0	63.0		14
China	20.0	20.0	20.5	19.9	19.5	− 2.0	26
Total World	641.6	641.6	648.5	670.9	670.2	− 0.1	34
OAPEC %	53.6	52.8	52.1	50.4	51.8	1.4	
OPEC %	69.3	67.7	67.0	65.1	66.8	1.7	

Source: Joint Arab Economic Report 1983

Table 41
Development of Arab and world natural gas reserves 1978–1982

Country	1978	1979	1980	1981	1982	Percent change 81/82
U.A.E.	612	581	588	658	810	23.1
Bahrain	198	255	255	243	223	− 8.2
Tunisia	168	168	157	153	122	− 20.3
Algeria	2,974	3,738	3,724	3,707	3,152	− 15.0
Saudi Arabia	2,730	2,711	3,183	3,346	3,433	2.6
Syria	42	42	42	91	36	− 60.4
Iraq	787	778	777	773	816	5.6
Qatar	1,133	1,699	1,699	1,699	1,756	3.3
Kuwait	957	949	940	981	966	− 1.5
Libya	685	680	674	657	609	− 7.3
Egypt	85	85	84	83	203	144.0
Oman	56	56	56	76	76	—
Arab countries	10,427	11,742	12,179	12,467	12,202	2.1
Non-Arab OPEC	17,371	17,085	16,878	17,095	17,089	—

Country	1978	1979	1980	1981	1982	Percent change 81/82
OPEC	27,249	28,221	28,463	28,916	28,631	− 1.0
UK	765	708	702	736	720	− 2.2
Norway	680	665	1,209	1,398	1,643	17.5
U.S.A.	5,806	5,494	5,409	5,607	5,779	3.1
Mexico	906	1,671	1,827	2,134	2,149	0.7
Canada	1,671	2,421	2,472	2,546	2,748	7.9
USSR	25,772	25,488	26,052	32,848	35,127	6.9
China		708	694	691	844	22.1
Total world	70,858	72,874	74,724	82,441	85,652	3.9
OAPEC %	14.6	16.2	16.2	15.0	14.2	− 0.8
OPEC %	38.4	38.7	38.1	35.1	33.4	− 1.7

Source: Joint Arab Economic Report 1983

Table 42
Development of world oil production 1978–1982   (1,000 Barrels per day)

Country	1978	1979	1980	1981	1982
U.A.E.	1,829	1,829	1,710	1,502	1,229
Bahrain	55	51	48	46	45
Tunisia	103	115	116	118	106
Algeria	1,287	1,217	1,020	798	670
Saudi Arabia	8,301	9,533	9,900	9,808	6,697
Syria	171	166	158	166	175
Iraq	2,629	3,700	2,646	897	987
Qatar	487	508	472	415	330
Kuwait	2,129	2,496	1,658	1,130	833
Libya	1,983	2,029	1,827	1,109	1,017
Egypt	484	497	554	578	667
Oman	315	295	282	317	322
Arab countries	19,773	22,499	20,391	16,884	13,078
Non-Arab OPEC countries	11,350	9,834	7,644	6,830	6,635
OPEC	29,995	31,209	26,877	22,489	18,398
World production	60,142	63,185	59,740	55,886	54,572
Arab countries %	32.8	35.6	34.1	30.2	24.0
OPEC %	49.9	49.4	45.0	40.2	33.7

Source: Joint Arab Economic Report 1983

Table 43
Combat aircraft in service in the Arab and Israeli Air Forces 1984

Serial No.	Country	W.O.		S.O.		C.O.		Total		Total combat ac.
		L 1	L 2	L 1	L 2	L 1	L 2	L 1	L 2	
1	Algeria	—	—	180	80	—	—	180	80	260
2	Bahrain	—	—	—	—	—	—	—	—	—
3	Egypt	116	14	12	111	—	44	128	169	297
4	Iraq	49	—	360	115	—	—	409	155	564
5	Jordan	35	68	—	—	—	—	35	68	103
6	Kuwait	19	30	—	—	—	—	19	30	49
7	Lebanon	—	—	—	—	—	—	—	—	—
8	Libya	111	—	395	7	—	—	506	7	513
9	Morocco	40	62	—	—	—	—	40	62	102
10	Oman	—	20	—	—	—	—	—	20	20
11	Qatar	—	8	—	—	—	—	—	8	8
12	Saudi Arabia	79	109	—	—	—	—	79	109	188
13	Sudan	—	2	8	10	—	14	8	26	34
14	Syria	—	—	400	103	—	—	400	103	503
15	Tunisia	—	—	—	—	—	—	—	—	—
16	United Arab Emirates	30	3	—	—	—	—	30	3	33
17	Yemen (North)	—	11	55	10	—	—	55	21	76
18	Yemen (South)	—	—	73	30	—	—	73	30	103
19	Mauritania	—	—	—	—	—	—	—	—	—
20	Somalia	—	—	7	9	—	30	7	39	46
21	Djibouti	—	—	—	—	—	—	—	—	—
22	Total	479	327	1,490	515	—	88	1,969	930	2,899
23	Israel	—	—	—	—	—	—	611	219	830

NB

The 88 Chinese-built aircraft are distributed as:

F-5 (replica of Mig-17) 8, in Sudan

F-6 (replica of Mig-19): Egypt 44, Sudan 6, Somalia 30

Table 43A
Combat aircraft (W.O.) in service in the Arab Forces 1984

Serial No.	Country	L 1							L 2							Total combat ac.
		F-15	F-16	Mirage F-1	Mirage V	Light-ning	F-4	Sub-total	Jaguar	F-5	A-4	Alfa-jet	AEW	ELINT	Sub-total	
1	Algeria	—	—	—	—	—	—	—	—	—	—	—	—	—	—	—
2	Bahrain	—	—	—	—	—	—	—	—	—	—	—	—	—	—	—
3	Egypt	—	24	—	59	—	33	116	—	—	—	10	2	2	14	130
4	Iraq	—	—	49	—	—	—	49	—	—	—	—	—	—	—	49
5	Jordan	—	—	35	—	—	—	35	—	68	—	—	—	—	68	103
6	Kuwait	—	—	19	—	—	—	19	—	—	30	—	—	—	30	49
7	Lebanon	—	—	—	—	—	—	—	—	—	—	—	—	—	—	—
8	Libya	—	—	46	65	—	—	111	—	—	—	—	—	—	—	111
9	Morocco	—	—	40	—	—	—	40	—	38	—	24	—	—	62	102
10	Oman	—	—	—	—	—	—	—	20	—	—	—	—	—	20	20
11	Qatar	—	—	—	—	—	—	—	—	—	—	8	—	—	8	8
12	Saudi Arabia	62	—	—	—	17	—	79	—	105	—	—	4	—	109	188
13	Sudan	—	—	—	—	—	—	—	—	2	—	—	—	—	2	2
14	Syria	—	—	—	—	—	—	—	—	—	—	—	—	—	—	—
15	Tunisia	—	—	—	—	—	—	—	—	—	—	—	—	—	—	—
16	United Arab Emirates	—	—	—	30	—	—	30	—	—	—	3	—	—	3	33
17	Yemen (North)	—	—	—	—	—	—	—	—	11	—	—	—	—	11	11
18	Yemen (South)	—	—	—	—	—	—	—	—	—	—	—	—	—	—	—
19	Mauritania	—	—	—	—	—	—	—	—	—	—	—	—	—	—	—
20	Somalia	—	—	—	—	—	—	—	—	—	—	—	—	—	—	—
21	Djibouti	—	—	—	—	—	—	—	—	—	—	—	—	—	—	—
22	Total	62	24	189	154	17	33	479	20	224	30	45	6	2	327	806

Table 43B
Combat aircraft (S.O.) in service in the Arab Air Forces 1984

Serial No.	Country	L 1							L 2								Total combat ac.
		Mig 25	Mig 23	Mig 21	SU 17	SU 20	SU 22	Sub-total	Mig 19	Mig 17	SU 7	TU 16	TU 22	IL 28	Super Etendar	Sub-total	
1	Algeria	25	42	95	—	18	—	180	—	60	20	—	—	—	—	80	260
2	Bahrain	—	—	—	—	—	—	—	—	—	—	—	—	—	—	—	—
3	Egypt	—	—	12	—	—	—	12	—	50	56	—	—	5	—	111	123
4	Iraq	30	100	150	—	80	—	360	40	—	95	8	7	—	5	155	515
5	Jordan	—	—	—	—	—	—	—	—	—	—	—	—	—	—	—	—
6	Kuwait	—	—	—	—	—	—	—	—	—	—	—	—	—	—	—	—
7	Lebanon	—	—	—	—	—	—	—	—	—	—	—	—	—	—	—	—
8	Libya	55	185	55	—	80	20	395	—	—	—	—	7	—	—	7	402
9	Morocco	—	—	—	—	—	—	—	—	—	—	—	—	—	—	—	—
10	Oman	—	—	—	—	—	—	—	—	—	—	—	—	—	—	—	—
11	Qatar	—	—	—	—	—	—	—	—	—	—	—	—	—	—	—	—
12	Saudi Arabia	—	—	—	—	—	—	—	—	—	—	—	—	—	—	—	—
13	Sudan	—	—	8	—	—	—	8	—	10	—	—	—	—	—	10	18
14	Syria	50	110	200	—	40	—	400	—	85	18	—	—	—	—	103	503
15	Tunisia	—	—	—	—	—	—	—	—	—	—	—	—	—	—	—	—
16	United Arab Emirates	—	—	—	—	—	—	—	—	—	—	—	—	—	—	—	—
17	Yemen (North)	—	—	40	—	—	15	55	—	10	—	—	—	—	—	10	65
18	Yemen (South)	—	—	48	—	10	15	73	—	30	—	—	—	—	—	30	103
19	Mauritania	—	—	—	—	—	—	—	—	—	—	—	—	—	—	—	—
20	Somalia	—	—	7	—	—	—	7	—	9	—	—	—	—	—	9	16
21	Djibouti	—	—	—	—	—	—	—	—	—	—	—	—	—	—	—	—
22	Total	160	437	615	—	228	50	1,490	40	254	189	8	14	5	5	515	2005

Table 44
Main battle tanks in service in the Arab and Israeli Armed Forces 1984

Serial No.	Country	Tanks (W.O.)						
		AMX 30	M-47 M-48	M-60	Centur-ion	Vickers	Chief-tain	Khalid
1	Algeria	—	—	—	—	—	—	—
2	Bahrain	—	—	—	—	—	—	—
3	Egypt	—	—	350	—	—	—	—
4	Iraq	—	—	—	—	—	—	—
5	Jordan	—	150	200	200	—	—	200
6	Kuwait	—	—	—	10	70	160	—
7	Lebanon	—	—	—	—	—	—	—
8	Libya	—	—	—	—	—	—	—
9	Morocco	—	120	—	—	—	—	—
10	Oman	—	6	—	—	—	12	—
11	Qatar	24	—	—	—	—	—	—
12	Saudi Arabia	300	—	150	—	—	—	—
13	Sudan	—	—	20	—	—	—	—
14	Syria	—	—	—	—	—	—	—
15	Tunisia	—	14	—	—	—	—	—
16	United Arab Emirates	100	—	—	—	—	—	—
17	Yemen (North)	—	—	64	—	—	—	—
18	Yemen (South)	—	—	—	—	—	—	—
19	Mauritania	—	—	—	—	—	—	—
20	Somalia	—	100	—	40	—	—	—
21	Djibouti	—	—	—	—	—	—	—
22	Total	424	390	784	250	70	172	200
23	Israel	—	—	—	—	—	—	—

QF-40	Sub-total	Chinese Tanks T-59 T-69	T-34	Tanks (S.O.) T-54 T-55	M/TR 77	T-62	T-72	Sub-total	Total
—	—	—	—	300	—	300	100	700	700
—	—	—	—	—	—	—	—	—	—
—	350	—	—	800	—	600	—	1,400	1,750
—	—	260	—	2,500	60	1,000	1,000	4,560	4,820
—	750	—	—	—	—	—	—	—	750
—	240	—	—	—	—	—	—	—	240
—	—	—	—	—	—	—	—	—	—
—	—	—	—	1,900	—	600	300	2,800	2,800
—	120	—	—	—	—	—	—	—	120
—	18	—	—	—	—	—	—	—	18
—	24	—	—	—	—	—	—	—	24
—	450	—	—	—	—	—	—	—	450
—	20	—	—	53	—	—	—	53	73
—	—	—	—	1,800	—	1,200	1,100	4,100	4,100
—	14	—	—	—	—	—	—	—	14
18	118	—	—	—	—	—	—	—	118
—	64	—	100	500	—	—	—	600	664
—	—	—	—	350	—	100	—	450	450
—	—	—	—	—	—	—	—	—	—
—	140	—	55	45	—	—	—	100	240
—	—	—	—	—	—	—	—	—	—
18	2,308	260	155	8,248	60	3,800	2,500	14,763	17,331
—	—	—	—	—	—	—	—	—	3,960

Table 45
Defence in figures 1984

Serial No.	Country	Population in millions	GNP in $ millions	Defence budget $ millions
1	Algeria	21.700	44,924	877.046
2	Bahrain	00.400	4,617	253.191
3	Egypt	47.200	31,755	3,043.000
4	Iraq	14.900	34,600	10,296.000
5	Jordan	2.555	4,098	541.755
6	Kuwait	1.750	19,903	1,360.000
7	Lebanon	2.700	2,593	349.488
8	Libya	3.490	26,100	709.220
9	Morocco	23.350	14,697	1,097.000
10	Oman	1.000	7,600	1,960.000
11	Qatar	0.270	7,903	165.980
12	Saudi Arabia	10.000	119,967	21,952.000
13	Sudan	23.250	7,100	230.770
14	Syria	10.400	18,467	3,210.000
15	Tunisia	7.000	7,757	454.307
16	United Arab Emirates	1.300	34,978	1,867.000
17	Yemen (North)	7.500	3,208	526.904
18	Yemen (South)	2.200	923	159.409
19	Mauritania	1.800	717	67.326
20	Somalia	6.000	1,267	148.211
21	Djibouti	0.370	355	25.000
22	Arab total	189.135	393,529	49,293.607
23	Israel	4.200	24,015	8,000.000

NB
War costs in Lebanon estimated 1.5–2 billion dollars included in defence budget in Israel.

% Defence to GNP	Strength of armed forces	Income per capita in $	Defence expenditure per capita in $	Cost per soldier in $
1.95	130,000	2,070	40	4,646
5.48	2,800	11,542	633	90,425
9.58	460,000	673	64	6,615
29.76	642,500	2,322	691	16,025
13.22	76,300	1,604	212	7,100
6.83	12,500	11,373	777	108,800
13.48	20,300	960	129	17,216
2.72	73,000	7,479	203	9,715
7.46	144,000	629	47	7,618
25.79	21,500	7,600	1,960	91,163
2.10	6,000	29,270	615	27,663
18.30	51,500	11,997	2,195	426,252
3.25	58,000	305	10	3,979
17.38	362,000	1,776	309	8,867
5.86	35,100	1,108	65	12,943
5.34	43,000	26,906	1,436	43,419
16.42	36,550	428	70	14,416
17.27	27,500	420	72	5,797
9.39	8,470	398	37	7,949
11.70	62,550	211	25	2,369
7.04	2,700	959	68	9,259
12.53	2,276,270	2,081	261	21,655
33.31	500,000	5,718	1,905	16,000

Abbreviations

AA	anti aircraft
AAM	air-to-air missile
AAUG	Association of Arab-American University Graduates
AB	airborne
ABM	anti-ballistic missile
ac	aircraft
ACV	air cushion vehicle
AD	air defence
AEW	airborne early warning
armd	armoured
AFV	armoured fighting vehicle
AHRC	Arab Human Rights Committee
ALCM	air launched cruise missile
AP	armour piercing
APC	armoured personnel carrier
APC-T	armour piercing capped tracer
APDS	armour piercing discarding sabot
APFSDS	armour piercing fin established discarding sabot
AP-T	armour piercing tracer
API	armour piercing incendiary
ARM	anti-radiation missile
ARP	anti-radiation projectile
arty	artillery
A/S	anti-ship, anti-submarine
ASBM	air-to-surface ballistic missile
ASM	air-to-surface missile
ASW	anti-submarine warfare
ATGW	anti-tank guided weapon
ATK	anti-tank
AWACS	airborne warning and control system
bde	brigade
bn	battalion
bty	battery
CA	Coaxial
cdo	commando
CIA	Central Intelligence Agency
cm	centimetre
C.O	Chinese origin
COIN	counter-insurgency

coy	company
CP	command post; concrete piercing
CW	chemical warfare
D	diesel
DC	depth charge
DCT	depth charge thrower
div	division
E	electric
ECM	electronic counter measures
EEC	European Economic Community
ELINT	electronic intelligence
ER	extended range
ER	extended range guided projectile
FAC (G)	fast attack craft (gun)
FAC (M)	fast attack craft (missile)
FAC (P)	fast attack craft (patrol)
FAC (T)	fast attack craft (torpedo)
FFG	frigate, guided missile
FY	fiscal year
GDP	gross domestic product
GLCM	ground launched cruise missile
GNP	gross national product
GP	guided projectile
h	hour
HE	high explosive
HEAT	high explosive anti-tank
HEI	high explosive incendiary
HEIT	high explosive incendiary tracer
HERAP	high explosive rocket assisted projectile
HESH	high explosive squash head
hp-D	horse power, diesel
hp-E	horse power, electric
hp-P	horse power, petrol
hp-T	horse power, turbine
HVAP-T	high velocity armour piercing, tracer
IAEA	International Atomic Energy Agency
IAI	Israel Aircraft Industries
ICBM	inter-continental ballistic missile
IL	illyushin
Inf	infantry
IR	infra-red
IRBM	intermediate range ballistic missile
Kg	kilogram
Km	kilometre
Kt	kiloton (1000 tons TNT equivalent)
L1	first line

L2	second line
LC	landing craft
LCAC	landing craft air-cushion vehicle
LCA	landing craft assault
LCM	landing craft mechanised
LCT	landing craft, tank
LCU	landing craft utility
LCVP	landing craft vehicles and personnel
LPD	landing platform, dock
LSM	landing ship medium
LST	landing ship, tank
m	metre
MAD	mutual assured destruction
MARV	maneuvreable re-entry vehicle
Max T.O. weight	maximum take off weight
MBT	main battle tank
mech	mechanised
MF	multi-fuel
MG	machine gun
MICV	mechanised infantry combat vehicle
MIRV	multiple independently targetable re-entry vehicle
mm	millimetre
MR	maritime reconnaissance
MSB	minesweeping boat
Mt	megaton (1 million tons TNT equivalent)
n.a.	not available
NATO	North Atlantic Treaty Organisation
NPT	non-proliferation treaty
para	parachute
P	petrol
PDM	point defence missile
PLO	Palestinian Liberation Organisation
RASD	Republique Arabe Sahrawi Democratique
RBU	anti-submarine rocket launcher (Soviet)
RCL	recoiless launcher
RL	rocket launcher
rpm	rounds per minute
RPV	remotely piloted vehicle (pilot in other aircraft or on ground)
SADARM-P	sense and destroy armour projectile
SAL-P	semi-active laser projectile
SAM	surface-to-air missile
SAR	search and rescue
sec	second
SLBM	submarine launched ballistic missile
SLCM	sea launched cruise missile

S.O.	of Soviet origin (or manufactured by one of the Warsaw Pact countries)
SP	self propelled
SSM	surface-to-surface missile
STOL	short take-off and landing
T	turbine
TV	television
UNO	United Nations Organisation
WAAM	wide area anti-armour ammmunition
W.O.	of Western origin

Bibliography

Arab Israeli Dispute and Great Powers Behaviour; Lawrence L. Whetten; Adelphi Papers no. 128, 1977, IISS London.

Arab Israeli Wars; Chaim Herzog; Arms and Armour Press, London, 1982.

Arms Control; Stockholm International Peace Research Institute, 1978.

Arms Control in the Middle East; Yair Evron; Adelphi Papers no. 138, 1977, IISS London.

America and the Third World; J.M.M. Mojdehi; *Survival,* March/April, 1982, IISS London.

Assault on the Liberty; James M. Ennis Jr.; Random House, New York, 1979.

AWACS; (Letter from President Reagan to Senator Baker); *Survival,* Jan/Feb 1982, IISS London.

AWACS Debate; Alexander Haig (documentation); *Survival,* Jan/Feb 1982, IISS London.

Brezhnev Plan (documentation); *Survival,* Nov/Dec 1982, IISS London.

Caveat; Alexander M. Haig Jr.; Macmillan, New York, 1984.

Constitution of the Arab Republic of Egypt; English and Arabic.

Crossing of the Suez; Lt. General Saad El Shazly; American Mideast Research, San Francisco, 1980; in Arabic & French by Societé Nationale d'Edition et de Diffusion Alger, Algeria, 1983; in Arabic also by Dar El Karmal, Damascus, Syria, 1984.

Detente after Helsinki; Speeches by President Giscard d'Estaing and President Brezhnev; 14.10.75 (documentation); *Survival,* Jan/Feb 1976, IISS, London.

Encyclopedia Britanica, London.

Energy (Security and Energy Crisis); Adelphi Papers no. 115, 1974, IISS London.

Fez Plan (documentation); *Survival,* Nov/Dec 1982, IISS London.

Four years in the Diplomatic Service; Lt. General Saad El Shazly; in Arabic and French by Societé Nationale d'Edition et de Diffusion Alger, Algeria, 1984.

Impact of the 1973 War; Adelphi Papers no. 114, 1974, IISS London.

In the Land of Israel; Amos Oz; Chatto & Windus, The Hogarth Press, London, 1983.

Islamic Constitution (a model of); English and Arabic; Islamic Council, 1983, London.

Israel's Defence Budget; Paul Rivlin; *Survival,* July/August 1978, IISS London.

Israel's Inquiry Report on the Sabra and Chatila Massacre; documentation; *Survival,* May/June 1983, IISS London.

Israel's Lebanon War; Ze'ev Shiff and Ehud Ya'ari; Simon and Schuster, New York, 1984.

Israel's Nuclear Policy; Lawrence Freedman; *Survival,* May/June 1975, IISS London.

Israel's Plan for the Occupied Territories; Statement by Prime Minister Begin, 28 December 1977 (documentation); *Survival,* March/April 1978, IISS London.

Israel's Role in a Changing Middle East; Yitzhak Shamir, *Foreign Affairs,* Spring 1982, New York.

Jane's All the World's Air Craft, 1983–84; London.

Jane's Armour and Artillery, 1981–82; London.

Jane's Fighting Ships, 1983–84; London.

Jane's Weapon Systems, 1983–84; London.

Joint Arab Economic Report; English, 1982, Tunis.

Joint Arab Economic Report; Arabic 1983, Tunis.

Joint Arab Economic Report; Arabic 1984, Tunis.

Judaism and the Vatican; Vicompte de Poncin; Britons Publishing, London, 1967.

Keeping Faith (Memoirs of a President); Jimmy Carter; Bantam Books, New York, 1982.

L'Affaire Israel; Roger Garudy; 1984, French.

Lectures on the Middle East Problem; Prof. Dwight James Simpson 1982, 1983, 1984; San Francisco, USA.

Military Balance, 1973–74; International Institute for Strategic Studies, London.

Military Balance, 1983–84; International Institute for Strategic Studies, London.

Military Balance, 1984–85; International Institute for Strategic Studies, London.

Military Balance, 1985–86; International Institute for Strategic Studies, London.

Newspapers and magazines;
   ALAHRAM; Egyptian, Cairo.
   Almustakbal; Lebanese, Paris.
   Alnahar; Lebanese, Beirut.
   Asharq Alawsat; Saudi, London.
   Herald Tribune; American, Paris.
   L'Expresse; French, Paris.
   Le Monde; French, Paris.
   Newsweek; American, The Washington Post Company, U.S.A.
   Sunday Times; British, London.

Nuclear Deterrence Policy; Statement by Caspar W. Weinberger (documentation); *Survival,* March/April 1983, IISS London.

Nuclear Deterrence Policy; Statement by General Secretary of the Soviet Communist Party Andropov (documentation); *Survival,* March/April 1983, IISS London.

Nuclear Deterrence Policy; US Statement on Soviet INF Position, (documentation); *Survival* March/April 1983, IISS London.

Nuclear Weapons and Soviet-American Relations; President Reagan's Speech to the Nation (documentation); *Survival,* March/April 1983, IISS London.

Palestinian National Council (Statement on 16th session) (documentation) *Survival* May/June 1983, IISS London.
Palestinian State; Avi Plascov; *Adelphi Papers* no. 163, 1981, IISS London.
Political Declaration of the Warsaw Treaty Members (Documentation); *Survival,* March/April 1983.
Price of Power; Seymour M. Hersh; Simon & Schuster, New York, 1983.

Qur'an (The meaning of the glorious Qur'an); Islamic Call Society, 1970, Arabic and English, Tripoli.

Reagan Administration Strategic Programme; Defence Secretary Weinberger; 5.10.1981 (documentation); *Survival,* Jan/Feb 1982, IISS, London.
Reagan Plan; (documentation); *Survival,* Nov/Dec 1982, IISS London.

SALT II Debate in Context; Collin S. Gray; *Survival,* Sept/Nov 1979, IISS London.
SALT II Treaty; (documentation); *Survival,* Sept/Nov 1979, IISS London.
Saudi Arabia and the United States Security and Interdependence; Jim Hoagland and J.P. Smith; *Survival,* March/April 1978, IISS London.
SIPRI Yearbook, Stockholm Peace Research Institute, Taylor & Francis, London.
Soviet Arms Transfer as an Instrument of Influence; Roger F. Pajak; *Survival,* July/August 1981, IISS London.
Soviet Decision to Upgrade Syrian Air Defences; Cynthia A. Roberts; *Survival,* July/August, 1983, IISS London.
Soviet Global Strategy; Curt Gasteyger; *Survival,* July/August, 1978, IISS London.
Soviet Influence in the Middle East; William E. Griffith; *Survival,* Jan/Feb 1976, IISS London.
Soviet Kuwaiti Communiqué; (documentation); *Survival* July/August 1981, IISS London.
Soviet Policy Towards Iran and the Gulf; Shahram Chubin; Adelphi Papers no. 157, 1980, IISS London.
Soviet-Syrian Treaty of Friendship and Co-operation (documentation); *Survival,* Jan/Feb 1981, IISS London.
Soviet Union and the PLO; Galia Golan; *Adelphi Papers,* 131, 1976, IISS London.
Story of My Life; Moshe Dayan; Weidenfeld & Nicolson, 1976, London.
Strategic Arms Limitation (documentation); *Survival,* Jan/Feb, 1975, IISS London.
Strategic Survey, 1973; IISS, London.
Strategic Survey, 1983–84; IISS, London.
Strategic Survey, 1984–85; IISS, London.
Study Based on Moshe Sharret's Personal Diary; AAUG, 1982, USA.
Super Power Relations; Address by US Secretary of State Alexander Haig, Aug 11, 1981 (documentation); article by Soviet Defence Minister Ustinov (documentation); *Survival,* Nov/December 1981, IISS London.

Taking Sides; Stephen Green; William Morrow & Co., New York, 1984.
Times Atlas of the World; Time Books, London.

United States Interests in the Persian Gulf; Speech by Defence Secretary Harold Brown, March 6, 1980 (documentation); *Survival,* July/August 1980, IISS London.
Universal Islamic Declaration of Human Rights; Islamic Council, 1981, London.

Vladivostock Accord; Michael Nacht; *Survival,* May/June 1975, IISS London.
Vladivostock Accord; Henry Kissinger; *Survival,* July/August 1975 IISS London.

White House Years; Henry Kissinger; Little Brown & Co., Boston, 1979.
World in Figures; The Economist, 1983, London.

Years of Upheaval; Henry Kissinger; Little Brown & Co., Boston, 1982.
Yom Kippur War; Sunday Times, 1974, London.

Index

DS
119.7
.S3819
1986

40.00